Ke
The Dream
Alive

RAYMOND
THOMPSON

CUMULUS PUBLISHING LIMITED

For all those who are special. You know who you are

For all the cast and crew of the programmes produced by
Cloud 9

For Bob the Dog (for being a friend)

For the fans around the world of The Tribe

But for Amanda Jack especially for suggesting this book
in the first place

Thank you to all for being there.

And

for

KEEPING THE DREAM ALIVE

SCREENPLAY OUT-TAKES

FADE IN

Imagine - the sounds of a pulsing, beating heart. And breathing. Becoming increasingly labored. The heartbeat matching the pace of the cuts, which speed up in the following montage, culminating in only split-second, fragmented images as if Mother Earth is breaking up, society dying ...

EXT. CEMETERY. DAY.

A coffin lowered into a grave. A MOTHER trying somehow to contain her emotion and comforting her distraught CHILDREN.

EXT. HIGHWAY. DAY.

BIRDS falling from the sky. DEAD BIRDS. Hundreds of them. Plummeting onto the highway. And vehicles. DRIVERS freaking out. What's going on?!

Not solely dead BIRDS but swirling feathers, smeared blood, obscuring views through windshields - some shattering from the impact, exploding shards of glass.

ONE LADY DRIVER AND HER KIDS

recoiling, screaming hysterically.

As the dead, panicked, WILD EYE of one BIRD stares through the windshield seemingly right at her. And us. In torment. Terror.

TRUCKS AND CARS

careening out of control, crashing, rolling, swerving to avoid a mammoth pile up.

INT. SEALED CHAMBER. DAY

SCIENTISTS, looking almost sinister, futuristic, not of this world in protective, hooded masks and decontamination suits examining test tubes.

INT. CORRIDORS OF POWER. DAY.

A government AIDE, carrying a file, his, footsteps echoing as he picks up pace, walking briskly with not only a sense of urgency - but absolute panic.

EXT. BEACH. DAY.

YOUNG LOVERS walking hand in hand. Barefoot through the water as the tide laps ashore. Romantic. The Sun sinking on the horizon. KIDS paddling, FAMILIES swimming, TEENS surfing.

Now though, some are SCREAMING. In horror! Oh, my God! Yuck. Dead FISH are surfacing, floating to/on the top of the water. Amongst the SWIMMERS. Surrounding everyone.

The YOUNG LOVERS gaze down, repulsed, cry out, gag. They are wading in a sea of death. Thousands and thousands of carcasses of dead FISH are being washed ashore.

INT. OVAL OFFICE. DAY.

The government AIDE bursting in, handing the file to the PRESIDENT.

> AIDE
> Mr. President! We've just received an updated report. The mutation has now been classified X18! Containment doesn't seem to be an option!

The PRESIDENT reads. His expression says it all.

SPACE

A SATELLITE circling our MOTHER EARTH with news 'CHATTER'.

A myriad of VOICES in various languages - through which we hear snippets of English. And although we have no idea of exactly what - clearly something ominous of a significant magnitude is happening globally.

> VOICES
> The security council is meeting again in closed emergency session. (overlap) Meanwhile segments of the population are being tested to identify those more likely to be at risk.

EXT. HOSPITAL. DAY

A mammoth QUEUE, pushing, shoving, glimpses of frightened faces not solely of being squashed, crushed. These are desperate PEOPLE in need of help.

INT. HOSPITAL. DAY.

Pandemonium, OVERCROWDING, panic, SECURITY and RECEPTIONISTS unable to cope with the volume and swell of PEOPLE. And we hear an assortment of fragmented VOICES, begging, pleading.

                    VOICES
                   (OVERLAP)
        Please, I've GOT to see a Doctor! We've been waiting for over three hours! Where else can we get vaccinated?! If all the Doctors and nurses are so busy, what about the vaccine? Can we get the vaccine and I'll vaccinate myself?! I've got a temperature! I need to see a Doctor - NOW!

INT. HOUSE. DAY.

A news ANCHOR on US television.

                    ANCHOR
        Authorities are appealing for calm throughout the evacuation process. Priority will be given to those aged under 18 years old with a certificate of being uncontaminated.

A FAMILY

clinging to each other, saying their heartbreaking goodbye, KIDS sobbing, PARENTS urging.

                    MOM
     It's too late now for me. Or
     your Dad. But you've got a chance
     to   save yourselves. And MUST take
     it!

A MONTAGE - WITHIN THE MONTAGE (SPLIT
SCREEN?)

Airports, train stations, chaos, PEOPLE
scrambling, fighting, to get on trains,
through the departure gates of airlines.

One MAN breaking the line to get even
a few feet ahead is shot - dead - by
a frustrated PASSENGER. And the fading
resemblance of any order is gone. SECURITY
GUARDS are unable to control the panicked
stampede.

FRAGMENTED NOW (LIKE THE SCREEN IS
SHATTERING - WITH A MYRIAD OF BROKEN
IMAGES)

A mass exodus. Leaving towns, cities.
Trails of REFUGEES on foot, traffic jams
on the freeway, panicked FACES, scared
CHILDREN, yelling, screaming, gridlock.

And by now the cuts are so fast and the
sounds of the heartbeat palpitating
seemingly out of control with the
breathing almost like hyperventilating,
panting, searching desperately for air,

as if fighting for not only even a fading gasp of breath - but life itself.

EXT. SUBURBIA. DAY.

Sinister-looking security VEHICLES with tinted glass (so that the occupants are obscured) patrolling deserted streets. An ominous voice blaring through a loudspeaker.

                    VOICE
                  (distort)
        Code one. Isolation now in effect.

Finally the heartbeat stops. And the breathing. Replaced with a sustained WHINE. Flat-line.

FADE OUT

INTRODUCTION

JOURNAL: FEBRUARY, 2011

It had always been a problem. From the very first time he started writing. No matter how much research, thought or days, weeks, months of planning, structuring, developing characters and an overall plot, deciding where and when to start a story always presented a seemingly insurmountable challenge.

And this screenplay was no different.

To make a career out of filling blank pages was a true love-hate relationship. In the beginning, hate mostly. Searching to find a way into any story was like trying to figure out how to enter a gigantic puzzle, a maze, so complex it would occupy his mind each and every day. And keep him awake most nights.

It was almost masochistic. Torture. Yet he couldn't help himself. It was something Ray always felt compelled to do. Like a calling he wished he never had.

He was sitting at his desk in the Florida room of his holiday home in Australia. On the Gold Coast, in Queensland, near the Warner Bros. theme park. Which also had an impressive studio facility, with several sound stages, a state of the art post production facility and a good range of available crews. Many Hollywood productions had been filmed there.

And it would be perfect for a production like The Tribe. Good weather. Important for any location footage. With mostly sunny, deep blue skies. Very similar to the weather in California. It was hardly surprising that the Warners Bros. lot was marketed as 'Hollywood on the Gold Coast'. The bonus was that it was only about a ten minute drive away. Offering a few valuable minutes to sleep in. Important when you have to get up so early when in production, with unit call often being as early as five am.

The television series of The Tribe, along with most of Ray's other productions, had been filmed in New Zealand. A country with such breathtaking scenery, diverse locations, facilities and such talented crews. Although Queensland, Australia was an option - along with other countries - it would be difficult to chose anywhere else better to shoot the motion picture version.

Especially since Ray also had an affinity with the Land of the Long White Cloud, considering himself to be an adopted Kiwi. New Zealand was his prime home base where he would spend as much time as he could on his vineyard. With the natural world of viticulture providing a welcome contrast to the motion picture and television industry.

But just as Mother Nature presented all manner of obstacles before any grape was harvested, bottled and enjoyed in a glass, there were probably more hurdles in bringing a television series or motion picture to fruition. The first one being to develop and deliver a screenplay. Which works. That was the blueprint for any successful production.

Ray had long discovered when he first started out in the industry that the old saying of 'If it ain't on the page, it ain't on the screen' to be very apt, though some considered it to be no more than a superficial adage concocted by a writer at some point. Writers would say that, wouldn't they?

He re-read the first three pages of the screenplay, wiped at small beads of perspiration from his forehead, wondering if it could actually be blood. At times it felt that way. As if he was spilling blood on every page. With each word not only ripping his heart out - but his very soul.

The Florida room was screened in to protect against any insects. A gentle breeze flowed through the wire mesh, ruffling paperwork on the desk, but the humidity was increasing - as it is prone to do in this sub-tropical region every February - and it felt like someone was standing nearby with a hairdryer blasting warm, sickly air. To make matters worse, from the weather forecast the temperature was due to increase even higher.

The constant sound of the crickets made it difficult to concentrate. They appeared to be desperate. As if they were complaining that it was too hot. Even the kookaburra perched nearby in a tree seemed to wail for some respite as it emitted its unique, repetitive call. But as it continued it sounded more like derisory manic laughter. Ray wondered if the bird had somehow read the first few pages of the screenplay.

Hardly surprising with writers' paranoia being what it is. Ray took a team of them once to a rugby match. When the players huddled in the scrum, he thought that the writers were probably convinced the players were discussing their scripts. And being overly critical. When the words don't flow, it's like the whole world knows and points a finger in contempt, drawing attention to signal absolute failure.

For all of the stifling heat, just the sheer thought brought an involuntary shiver down his spine. So Ray took some time out for a dip in the pool, deciding to come back to all the writing later.

The sun was so intense it was like a thermostat. Rather than being refreshed, Ray felt as if he was swimming in a bath of warm water. Which also seemed to be evaporating in the heat as fast as any words he could find to fill any blank page. The level of the pool was certainly so much lower than earlier in the morning.

Part of the routine after a swim was to do a gentle work out. Nothing too strenuous. It was too hot for that. And Ray was far from being the athletic kind. But he promised himself to try and stay in shape this year, aware that sitting at a desk for hours and hours seized up the body almost as much as choosing what words to type on a page played total havoc with the mind.

As he started to stretch he noticed out of the corner of his eye - a kangaroo approaching on the other side of the fence which separated the garden and landscaped grounds bordering the house, with the golf course extending to the distant horizon far beyond.

The view was spectacular. Like a natural wonderland. Acres and acres of greenery, with a huge lake carved out in the middle of the fairway, framed mostly by palm trees, though there were other species, like gum, which attracted the occasional koala bear.

The water features on the course were not only scenic but challenged even the best golfer and had also evolved to become a regular habitat for swans, pelicans, native birds. Others - like galas and multi-colored lorikeets - squawked in the foliage of an abundance of tropical plants, drawn to the exotic fragrances of the natural world.

The wildlife never ceased to amaze Ray. Particularly, that rather than the isolated outback, kangaroos could also be seen so regularly in suburbia. Let alone this popular golfing and sailing resort of Sanctuary Cove where his holiday home was located. He visited as often as he could as a retreat to escape the pressures that came along with being in the television and motion picture industry.

When the kangaroo finally arrived, it watched Ray intently over the fence, working out, absolutely fascinated, totally absorbed.

Then suddenly as Ray stretched to the left, the kangaroo did the same!

Ray cast a dumbfounded glance at the animal who eagerly returned his gaze. That's odd, he thought. Really odd. Then he stretched to the right.

The kangaroo repeated the move.

What's going on? Ray wondered if he was hallucinating. Or had the first aborted pages of the screenplay driven him totally insane.

He slowly crouched, circled one arm, then the other. Again the kangaroo mimicked each move, like a surreal mirror image.

'Marina! Come here!' Ray screamed to his Philippine house maid, who was dusting inside the house. 'Quick!'

She rushed through the patio doors and into the Florida room. 'What wrong, Mister Ray?' Marina enquired, sure that she would find her employer collapsed on the floor from dehydration.

'I don't know,' replied Ray, still staring at the kangaroo in pure disbelief. 'Check this out.'

He stretched to the left. But rather than copy, this time the animal just grazed at a strand of long grass protruding at the bottom of the fence where the gardener couldn't reach with the lawn mower. He would soon need to clear the area with a strimmer.

'No! Don't do this to me!' Ray sighed, in utter frustration.

'Do .... ah, what, Mister Ray?'

'I wasn't talking to you, Marina. 'I was talking to the kangaroo.'

'Huh?'

'The kangaroo, Marina.'

'Maybe he no answer cause he no speak the English,' Marina smiled, proud of her own wit. But then seeing Ray gazing intently at the animal, realized that he was actually serious.

'Come on! It's your turn. Show Marina what you can do,' Ray called out desperately, circling one arm, trying somehow to encourage the kangaroo to put on a display.

The kangaroo took another bite of grass, cast Marina and Ray an impassive, sneering glance as if to say humans are crazy, then leaped away, back across the golf course in search of somewhere more peaceful to graze.

'I swear, Marina. That kangaroo was copying my workout. Doing EXACTLY the same movements.'

'Kangaroos gotta stay healthy as well, Mister Ray. Just like you. Now maybe you been in sun too long and should have lie down.'

'You don't believe me?'

'You been working hard all day,' Marina said, sympathetically. 'Maybe too hard.'

'And only three pages to show for it. Even then, I don't know if 'they' work.'

'Why don't you give imagination a rest and I fix you up a long, cool drink of water?'

'Put some gin in it,' Ray sighed. 'I could do with it today.'

'So would I if I sit at a desk out here in this weather,' said Marina, already perspiring in the stifling heat. 'You could die of heat stroke. Might feel better if work in study with air conditioning.'

'Then I'd die of pneumonia. It's always so freezing in there.'

'Gotta die of something, someday,' the house maid reflected. 'Makes no difference if it pneumonia or heatstroke. Just make sure it not vivid imagination, eh?'

Marina, ever the philosopher, cast Ray a wise smile then retreated through the patio doors back into the house - and a welcome blast of arctic cold air from the conditioning vent.

Ray sat at his desk, rocked slowly back and forth on his high back swivel chair and thought about what Marina had said. How would he prefer to die? From the cold? Or heat? Or just slowly fading away due to a lack of water? What about starving to death? Better still, being attacked by a petulant kangaroo driven over the edge to strike fatal blows because it didn't like the workout Ray was doing?

That would be a dramatic way to go. Then at least Ray wouldn't have to write. The mere thought brought a huge smile. What was all that about? A fear of success maybe? Rather than just failure?

Whatever the reason, deep down he knew that it was always the same when he started on a story. Any story. A large part of the process was - avoidance. And here he was doing an outstanding job. Occupying his mind with killer kangaroos when he should be working out the beginning of the screenplay.

If only he had a so called normal job. Or had pursued a different career path. Then he could have just enjoyed a movie or television series like any other member of the public. But no. Rather than restrict himself to being a consumer, he had decided that he would write and produce. To do one was a challenge. To try both was synonymous to embarking upon a self inflicted nervous breakdown.

Yet once he made a start, those initial feelings of torture would also evolve into a rewarding and fulfilling experience. Like climbing a mountain and arriving at the peak, against all the odds, it all brought about such a feeling of triumph.

So the paradox was that as difficult as it was to start telling any story, by the time he reached the end, he almost found it even more difficult to stop. To tear himself away from whatever fictional world he had created. And above all, from the characters. Who had grown from biographical sketches to become real people. Friends. And he always missed them.

Missed spending every day with them, morning, noon and night.

The phone rang. 'How is the writing going?' It was Ray's assistant, calling from the New Zealand office.

'Great,' replied Ray enthusiastically. But he sounded more convinced than he looked.

'What page are you up to?'

'Well, I'm not exactly up to any page as such,' Ray sighed, trying to remain positive. 'I've just been sketching out some thoughts.'

'Like where to start?, his assistant probed. She had worked long enough with Ray to know the painful process and torment he always seemed to go through.

'Something like that.'

'Well, I hope I'm not disturbing you?'

Disturb all you like, Ray scoffed to himself, pleased to be distracted from the task at hand.

'It's just, I was wondering if you had given any more thought to doing the book?' his assistant continued, knowing that Ray had a memory like a gold fish.

Yet he also had an instant recall in most matters visual and could identify a stock shot and time code in no time at all. But would struggle to find where he left his car keys, even an hour before.

'What book?', Ray enquired warily.

'The behind the scenes - for The Tribe?'

Ray vaguely remembered answering an email from one of The Tribe fans about the possibility of recording an inside story of how the series came together.

'One day, I could always try and do one,' he replied. 'I'm just not sure if there would be a big enough of a demand and market for it.'

'According to the Facebook team, there is,' his assistant stated confidently. 'So many fans have been posting that they're not only interested in any novels - but would also love to read anything about the making of the actual series. And I keep getting requests from other fans about all the other shows as well.'

'Really?' Ray enquired, encouraged that his Cloud 9 portfolio of programming touched people in such a way.

The company had exported series which Ray had produced to over 130 countries through its distribution subsidiary, Cumulus. Although Ray knew that there was hardly an hour that passed when someone in the world would not be watching one of the episodes, it was still a little overwhelming and difficult to comprehend.

'Some of the fans are studying media or scriptwriting and thought a book might also give a few tips. It's amazing really - so many more are seemingly just as interested to have a behind the scenes insight into the industry. As well as your own life and career.'

Ray had been approached by a few publishers to do an autobiography but had declined. At least for the time being. He was an intensely private person. And decided never to expose his wife or children to what he had to experience being in the public eye and all that entails, preferring to keep details of his personal life separate to his professional one.

Besides, he was bound by so many confidentiality clauses in all the contracts he had signed throughout his career that he wouldn't be able to reveal all the details or he would be in breach until the clauses expired.

The biggest problem though, as always, was that with all going on in Ray's life he would be stretched to find the time to write a book at present. His assistant, more than anyone, was aware of that given that she looked after and organized Ray's hectic schedule and knew there would be little or no opportunity for a full autobiography for a long while yet.

But she thought that if he could combine even some of the elements into a diary of memoirs, he could satisfy at least some of what had been requested, rather than not doing anything at all. Even if it was just to let people know of the creative process, like a journal of a writer's mind.

'Don't think anyone would be interested in that. It'd be like a horror story. But you never know,' Ray pondered, as they discussed it further. 'Plus, if I did write one, I'd want to do it in the third person.'

When Ray finally got around to writing an autobiography, he explained that he would utilize the conventional first person. But for any other form of writing, such as even a non fiction journal or memoir, he would prefer to write it in the third person since he would not only be a participant, but still primarily an observer, as he had been in any story to date he had ever told.

'Should I take that as a yes, then?'

'A maybe. Let's see how the diary is looking in the next few months and if we can schedule it, well take it from there.'

Ray replaced the receiver and thought about all the fans of the Cloud 9 shows. The Tribe fans especially never ceased to amaze him with their loyalty and devotion.

The Facebook page was only a few weeks old and had already attracted many thousands who had discovered it through word of mouth and were now interacting with each other from every corner of the globe, united as only true Tribal brothers and sisters can.

And the Tribeworld website would soon be reactivated after being placed on hold, along with series six, when Ray decided to rest The Tribe. But he was really the one in need of a rest himself.

With the advent of so many different platforms coming on stream in the digital domain, at that time Ray felt that the fans would prefer to utilize outlets such as Wikia which they could revise and administer rather than rely on the confines of Tribeworld. But being a traditionalist - let alone sentimental - had left all the content up on the website for posterity so that fans could refer to it in perpetuity whenever they wished.

The world of The Tribe was certainly unique, special. For many it was more than just a television series. Almost a way of life. The underlying thematic of building a better new world order had taken on a life of its own. As had the aspiration for so many to keep the dream alive, in whatever form.

An inside story might work well, Ray reflected. And the more he thought about it, decided that if the fans were truly up for it, he would be, too. Then it dawned on him. Only one problem. An agonizing one. Where would he start?

Marina stepped through the patio doors and placed a long glass of water, with ice cubes floating on top, on the desk.

'There you go, maybe this make you feel better.' She watched him sip on the water and noticed that he seemed to be not only preoccupied - but despondent.

'What is it, Mr Ray? You look like you got weight of the world on your shoulder'.

'I've been struggling all day on the screenplay. Now it seems that I might have to do the same with a book.'

'You want me to get the blue socks?' Marina asked, aware that Ray was wearing dark socks - and of all his rituals and superstitions. Or so she thought.

'They only help when I'm in music mode.'

'Ah,' Marina replied, still confused that if wearing the blue socks seemed to inspire Ray to compose - why they wouldn't work writing.

'They just don't.'

Ray, tried to explain why, knowing that it all sounded more than a little weird.

Yes, he had a few obsessions. The blue sock music one he was able to chart back to the time when he was just a young boy of about six years old and wrote his first song about the death of his beloved dog, Shona. She liked to tug on his favorite blue socks and for some unexplained, irrational reasoning, Ray had always attributed being able to write the song to wearing the blue socks.

So all through his ensuing career, if he was ever struggling or blocked when composing music or a song, he would search through his wardrobe and sock collection for any colored blue (and there were many). And when he put them on, for some inexplicable reason - it seemed to help.

'All in the mind,' said Marina, sure giving birth to music couldn't just be down to the color of what socks anyone wore.

Ray agreed on one level but on another level he was faced with so many soundtrack deadlines that he wasn't taking any chances. A pair of blue socks was always at the top of his Christmas list every year. He was forever intent to ensure he had a good supply.

'I know!' Marina suddenly stated as she considered the problem further. 'If the socks no work with writing and you struggle to think of where to start, then no start - at the start. Why no start in the middle?'

A light suddenly went on in the darkest recesses of Ray's mind.

'But wouldn't the middle .... still be the start?' he asked, as he thought more about what Marina was suggesting. It certainly seemed logical. Though also illogical. But an interesting notion.

'No. Still middle,' Marina replied emphatically. 'Even if middle a start. So just like blue socks for music, if the brain think you not starting at start but starting in middle - then maybe you find it easier to start. Even if middle is start. Brain think it middle. So you don't have to worry about start. See? Simple.'

Ray exchanged a long glance with Marina. The way he was feeling today he would try anything.

'You know something, Marina?' he said, amidst a growing sense of relief and hope. 'Here am I thinking I hired a house keeper. But I might have actually hired a genius. That sounds B-R-I-L-L-I-A-N-T. Where have you been all my life?!'

CHAPTER ONE

JOURNAL: OCTOBER, 1998

British Airways flight 0342 from London Heathrow Airport banked steeply across the Mediterranean sea, then levelled for its approach to Nice airport. A flight attendant tapped Ray on the shoulder to waken him, requesting that he fasten his seatbelt. The aircraft would soon be coming in to land.

The journey had begun in Wellington, New Zealand almost thirty hours before. On a flight bound for Auckland. From there, Ray transferred from the domestic to the international terminal for his connecting flight to Los Angeles where he met up with William Shatner in the Air New Zealand first class lounge.

They were both due to attend the MIPCOM Television Festival in Cannes, in the south of France, for the launch of Cloud 9's latest production: William Shatner's A Twist in the Tale.

William had agreed to appear at a press conference which was scheduled for Tuesday, the third day into the festival. So he had some free time to allow for a short break in London with his wife. Ray had no option but to continue on to Cannes as he needed to brief his Cumulus distribution team before MIPCOM got fully underway.

It would be a very busy few days. His assistant had arranged appointments with buyers every thirty minutes on the distribution stand. In addition to breakfast meetings, luncheons and dinners with key broadcasters and press. There would be no room to go over the finer details with William when he was due to arrive so it made sense to utilize part of the twelve hour flight from Los Angeles to London.

After dinner, the lights in the cabin dimmed. Before long most of the passengers were asleep. But Ray's body clock was all over the place. He had managed to get a few hours rest over the Pacific on the initial leg of the journey but now felt totally alert and tried to work out what time it might be in New Zealand.

He thought it was about 2pm in the afternoon, but after a few glasses of fine red wine with his meal, along with a jet lagged haze, Ray was having difficulty in deciphering if it was 2pm tomorrow, today or yesterday? A price he had to pay being based in the Southern Hemisphere.

He smiled to himself at the irony that he was traveling with a companion from the Starship Enterprise, known to many millions around the world for exploring future undiscovered galaxies. Now Ray was also living in the future, though usually no more than thirteen hours ahead of Greenwich meantime.

Whatever time it was, Ray decided to try and maximize every spare hour available. So he switched on the seat light to illuminate a pad of paper while he made some notes to record thoughts and ideas he had on some possible story lines for his next project which was in production, an exciting concept of a world with no adults which he had tentatively given a working title, 'Keeping the Dream Alive'.

Filming had commenced six weeks earlier at the Cloud 9 production centre in New Zealand but the last block of scripts hadn't been written yet so it was still possible to alter direction if needs be. For whatever reason, be it logistical or fiscal restraints, as well as for any creative reasons. It was always an organic process. But the key was to ensure that there was enough lead in-time for any changes to be implemented.

There was a window to revise the scripts delivered to date and which hadn't been shot. So alterations could still be made to reflect and match the individual qualities of the actors and actresses he had cast. The written word was so different to the spoken word. Often dialogue which worked in a script didn't quite flow when spoken. And similarly, questionable lines in a script sometimes just came alive when played out in the scene.

From the initial read-throughs, rehearsals and first few episodes which had been filmed, Ray was becoming more in tune of what was working and what was not. It had nothing to do with the quality of any of the scripts which were all in very strong shape. Nor the talent of the cast. Ray was impressed by all the performances to date. It was more about comfort zones. Although the job of an actor or actress is to interpret a script, Ray was aware that the young cast were all of an age that it would never take long to identify if they struggled with anything which doesn't quite ring true when delivering the lines and formulating all the aspects of a character. The Tribe needed to have 'street cred' if it had any hope of resonating with its intended audience demographic.

Ray hoped all would go well back in the studio while he was away. Especially that everyone was continuing to settle in. It was a tough schedule - 52 episodes in six months. With a further six months of post production when all the music and sound effects would be added.

The young cast were not only around the same age as most of the characters but also of Ray when he first had the idea

23

for the series. Several years had passed since then - more than he would care to remember - but Ray was thankful that he could still identify with the spirit and unique sense of hope which seems to inhabit the young. When everything is still possible in life. Age might bring wisdom and experience but also a degree of cynicism on what might still be possible to be achieved, causing so many to give up on the pursuit of a dream.

Ray had long dreamed of bringing this series to fruition. In a surreal way, he felt that he was still about the same age, caught up by the sheer enthusiasm from all the young cast when he welcomed them and their families to the meet and greet party.

This was a regular event at Cloud 9 before filming began. An opportunity for everyone to get together socially. For the cast and crew to be introduced, to get to know each other and to have a tour of the studio facilities.

And there were always so many questions, an undercurrent of nervous energy, a collective consciousness of excited anticipation. It was always the same before starting any new production. Like the countdown to Christmas. Or starting a new school or a new job or preparing to go on holiday, wondering what adventures might lay in store along the way.

This time though, Ray had noticed an additional element. It was as if the theme of the series was transcending and the young cast were also about to embark upon a quest to build a better world - though the tenants of that ideal were in reality in the hands of all the young, being the true life force of shaping the future since time began.

Parents welcomed the open forum so that they would become familiar with all the surroundings and could meet the chaperones, house parents of the particular cast houses where their child would be staying, along with the applicable tutors of the Cloud 9 school. And in some ways it was as if the young cast were being sent away for six months to boarding school.

Now after all the anticipation, the reality would have set in. The production of any series involved such a grueling schedule. Ray hoped all were coping with the workload but perhaps was overly concerned due to the fact that he, himself, was struggling to keep on top of all the tasks he had in hand.

He would only be away for about ten days. But felt strangely anguished by the separation, almost as a mother might feel having given birth. And although bringing a new production to the screen was in no way as profound, it evoked a similar sense of protectiveness. After all, Ray had been carrying his creative baby for over twenty-five years, hoping but always wondering if it would ever be born!

As well as making notes on the new series, he also wanted to review territories which were open on past productions and which would be available to license at the festival. Also to ensure that key buyers were on the invitation list for the Twist in The Tale press conference.

He always found it difficult to keep all the plates of all the Cloud 9 titles in the portfolio spinning. More product brought more plates. In the past five years he had produced almost 140 episodes and 25 mini movie specials. Now he had just embarked upon another 52 episodes and was beginning to feel as if his head was spinning as well.

The series with William had completed filming and was in the closing stages of post production. All of Ray's team in New Zealand had more or less stamped the end on that title and were focusing on the new series which was being shot, as indeed was Ray.

But although A Twist in The Tale had come to the end in production terms, it was just the start of the distribution process. That in itself was a full time job and he knew he was pushing the boundaries overseeing both production and distribution, let alone an international company with all the myriad of tasks that involves.

'Do you think the 'Captain' would mind?', the flight attendant whispered excitedly a few hours later.

Ray glanced up from his note pad. The attendant could see that he was clearly confused and whispered again in an attempt to clarify.

'Do you think the Captain would mind if I ask for his autograph?'

'You want to ask the Captain ... for his autograph?' Ray enquired incredulously, unable to comprehend why the attendant would want this in the first place, never mind asking Ray for permission first.

'I've always been such a huge fan,' she continued to enthuse in an undertone. 'Captain James T. Kirk. He's such an icon.'

'He's also fast asleep. Why don't you check when he's awake?'

The flight attendant eventually obtained an autograph during breakfast. As did several other grateful fans who recognized William when he and Ray arrived at Heathrow. Ray noticed many others who just stole a few star-struck looks but were probably too embarrassed to ask, feeling it to be an invasion of privacy.

William never seemed to mind, was always friendly and tried to make time for his fans. Ray was impressed with such a generosity of spirit. William not only possessed unique gifts as an actor but also as a human being. He was a real gentleman.

One obtrusive fan caught the sharp end of Ray's tongue though when he crossed the line literally, pushing and shoving, snapping away with his camera as feverish as any paparazzi while Ray and William tried to retrieve their luggage from the encircling belt, causing both to lose out on the chance to grab the last remaining cases and they had to wait for what felt like an eternity for the belt to complete another cycle.

Which was frustrating. Ray could ill afford to lose any more time. The Los Angeles to London flight had arrived late due to head winds, exacerbated with passport control being particularly slow.

William wished Ray the best of luck for the start of the festival, they exchanged goodbyes, then went their separate ways.

Ray rushed flat out to the British Airways terminal, hoping he would still catch his connecting flight.

If only he could have been beamed up in true Star Trek mode from New Zealand to the South of France, it would make life so much easier, he thought, darting between the crowds of passengers. The journey was starting to feel as if it had taken forever, especially considering that he had just left Spring yesterday in the Southern Hemisphere, while today in the Northern hemisphere, Europe was heading into Autumn.

Ray finally arrived breathlessly at the gate and presented his boarding pass, which was zipped through the automatic machine. The ground staff member checked Ray's passport, then considered him in growing intrigue.

'Off to the television festival?'

'Yes', replied Ray, wondering how the member of staff knew.

'Don't I know you?'

'I don't think so,' Ray stated quickly. He had been interviewed on television on several occasions but being involved mostly on the other side of the camera, was far from having a famous, familiar face.

'I could have sworn I checked you in a few months ago. On a flight to New Zealand, was it?'

'That might explain it,' Ray replied. He lost count how many times he was traveling back and forth between London and New Zealand these days but thought it must be becoming a little too much for airport staff to notice. And it was starting to irritate Ray but he smiled politely, eager to obtain his passport back and board the aircraft, realizing that precious seconds were ticking away.

'Wish I could travel a bit more often,' the lady reflected, 'but they don't give any discounts for ground staff anymore.'

'Very interesting,' Ray said, not that interested, but then he felt guilty. He was not by nature intolerant. The lady was just being friendly.

'So me and the hubby have decided to rent a caravan on the south coast.'

'Really? That should be nice for you both.'

'Ever been to the south coast?'

Ray stared at the lady in mounting frustration but contained the need to scream at her and almost begged in a great effort of self restraint.

'Just give me my passport. PLEASE?'

'Oh, right. You can't stand around talking here all day or you'll miss the flight! Safe travels,' said the lady, handing Ray his passport back.

He faked a smile, then rushed down the boarding ramp, making a mental note to attempt suicide if he encountered the lady ever again in the future. There was something about her, the way she moved, even the way she spoke that was in direct contradiction to the world Ray inhabited. As if she lived her life in slow motion. But it felt strangely appealing. As did a week away on the south coast in a caravan. He could do with a break.

Ray's work load was increasing, bringing so many pressures and demands he wondered how long he could go on like this.

An overwhelming sense of fatigue set in as he buckled his seat belt for yet another flight, but was thankful that he had at least made the onwards connection. There were several flights throughout the day to Nice across all airlines, departing regularly - especially with the Festival occurring - but after such a long and arduous journey Ray was determined not to elongate the trip even a minute longer than he had to.

For a while as the aircraft left the gate and taxied to the runway, he became engulfed in a profound sadness. Was his life now reduced to trying to save a minute of time? But he lifted his spirits, reflecting that it all went along with the lifestyle and career path he had chosen. No point feeling sorry for himself. He needed to get a grip.

The aircraft wasn't even airborne before he had fallen into a deep sleep.

As busy as Heathrow Airport had been, it was total gridlock at Nice airport. Like the whole world had descended, which in a way it had. The world of broadcasting, that is. Delegates attended from every country. In the next few days decisions would be made for what television programs viewers would be watching in every far reaching corner of the globe.

There were actually two festivals held through the year. In addition to MIPCOM, convened every October, MIP was held each April, about a month before the Cannes Film Festival. In many ways the glittering motion picture forum was very similar to its television cousin, attracting the attention of the world wide press and general public, especially with so many stars of the small screen in attendance.

This year at MIPCOM a range of high profile names were scheduled to appear. Ray was sure he recognized the wrestling phenomenon, Hulk Hogan, ahead going through passport control and there was no mistake that he was now standing behind the Hoff in the long, slow-moving queue.

They exchanged a few jet-lagged pleasantries while inching closer and closer to the customs desk where an officious-looking and miserable officer seemed to be purposely pedantic, slowly examining travel documents, visas and passports.

Come on, Ray thought. Get a move on. And he could see the slow pace was infuriating many other delegates, desperate to get settled in their hotels, rest up and try somehow to adjust to a different time zone, let alone the busy week which lay ahead.

Ray wondered what David Hasselhoff would be promoting. A remake of 'Knight Rider' perhaps? Or another series of 'Baywatch', which had enjoyed much success? But he decided not to ask, sure the Hoff would not be in any frame of mind to discuss it. He would probably speak of nothing else in the ensuing few days. Ray was far from interested in pursuing it anyway, realizing that it might precipitate questions about A Twist In The Tale which he preferred at this point not to answer.

For all of the camaraderie which existed within the industry, everyone always liked to remain discreet at the festivals, aware that it was, after all, a business. Every delegate attending was a colleague, some were even friends. But they were also competitors. A launch of a new program was rather like the launch of a new model of a car. No-one ever wanted to dilute the impact of any press conference by leaking advanced detail.

What felt like an eternity was probably no more than an hour before Ray finally managed to get into the arrivals hall to collect his luggage. Then he was met by the Cloud 9 head of security and chauffeur who would transport Ray - and William when he arrived on Tuesday - between their hotel in Juan les Pins and the distribution stand in Cannes, where the Cumulus team were based.

'Good flight?' they asked wheeling the trolley laden with suitcases which were then loaded in the back of the limousine. Ray just groaned.

They knew their man well enough to know that he was not exactly in a mood to be overly social. So the journey from the airport to the hotel was mostly in silence, except for the occasional question, checking if Ray wanted the air conditioning on or for any music to be played.

Ray never considered himself to be anyone special. He always preferred to be treated just as any other member of the team. The reality was that he was different, being head of the company he had founded. But any success had not really changed him in any way and he was always amazed when people would comment when they met him that he was so down to earth. Which is what Ray perceived that he was.

He could see though how some might have felt that, because Ray had thought just exactly the same with William when they first met.

'Hi, I'm William Shatner,' he had said when he arrived in New Zealand.

It was endearing that William thought that he had to introduce himself as if Ray - or no-one else - would not know who he was. And it made Ray smile and warm to William immediately. He was a legend to many. Especially Star Trek fans. But was so unassuming, with no ego or pretense.

Most on the Cloud 9 team were dedicated trekkies. One waved and called out, 'Beam me up Scottie' as he passed Ray and William getting out of the car when it arrived at the studio.

'How many times have you been asked that?' Ray asked, leading William to the main administrative building.

'It's the first time this second,' William smiled. 'But that's part of the price for boldly going where no man has gone before.'

'Well, it's a great pleasure to welcome you to Cloud 9,' Ray said, as the automatic doors swung open and they walked into the main reception.

A lot of people thought Ray and his team were 'out there' and he was intrigued to see what the Captain of a Starship would think. Thankfully William seemed to enjoy his time filming the series. And all the team certainly enjoyed working with him. He was the consummate professional and just like

31

most - though sadly not all - of the people Ray had met in the public eye. Just a normal, everyday type of person.

One of the benefits of being a writer or producer was that Ray did not attract the same attention. He still had a profile though and for some reason any kind of celebrity made people think that someone with it was somehow different.

It might make some people change, of course. Especially those who started to believe their own publicity. But Ray hadn't changed and wondered if any success had made the people around him change. Maybe?

Ray was pleased to be surrounded by a team who were sympathetic to the burden of all the responsibilities he had to carry, knowing that it could be a heavy load to bear at times. Some, no doubt, may have considered him to be temperamental. But most made allowances, tried to adapt to his needs, and were in tune and considerate of his moods.

By nature he was usually laid back, easy going. Except when he was tired. Or frustrated by any creative matter. Then Ray could be irritable, liable to erupt without any warning. So those who worked for him closely grew to learn to identify all the signs. If he wanted to talk - they would talk. But if not, it was wise to let silence prevail.

'Bonjour, Monsieur Thompson,' the concierge said, opening the back door of the limousine. 'Good to have you back with us, sir.'

'It's good to be back, Savard,' replied Ray as he got out of the vehicle. It felt that no time had passed since he was last a guest, attending the MIP festival in April.

He always preferred to stay out of town rather than in Cannes. It was so much more relaxed and he had actually started to wind down the minute the limousine pulled into the impressive driveway of one of his favorite boutique hotels in the world. One which could rival the very best of what any hotel could offer anywhere in the world, in Ray's view - the five star, Hotel Juana.

There was no need to go through the formalities of checking in. Everything had been arranged well in advance by his assistant. And if by any chance she had missed anything - which was highly unlikely, efficiency was her middle name - Ray had been a regular client for years. All were well aware of his requirements, which had long since become a matter of routine.

An ice-cold bottle of aged champagne was waiting in his hotel suite, along with a selection of canapes stylishly laid out on an antique silver plate. Ray was not a great drinker of champagne. He enjoyed an occasional glass. But even the finest varieties never really endeared him. He preferred a quality red wine - but since the first time he had discovered the hotel, a bottle of champagne, glistening in an ice bucket, had always been made available upon arrival.

Now that had evolved into somewhat of a tradition. And Ray was never one to break with tradition. Trying to maintain it in whatever form had become habitual, an ongoing ritual that some observed could be down to more than being just a little eccentric. As if he could only find emotional stability through an almost obsessive search for continuity to satisfy a dysfunctional psychological need. Ray considered it to be no more than a harmless pursuit of routine. He just liked 'things' to be normal.

He took a shower to freshen up. That was normal after every flight. Then he sat in a chaise lounge on the balcony overlooking the Mediterranean and decided to take some time out to enjoy the picturesque view. The waves from the sea gently overlapped onto the hotel's private sandy beach, littered with palm trees, straw huts and sun beds. Most were unoccupied, being out of season. With the absence of many tourists, the resort felt even more appealing, tranquil.

This was another 'normal'. An attempt, or more of a need to be precise, to try and slow everything down now and then in moments of solitude in order for his mind to either wander or to process his thoughts so that Ray could organize them into some form of structure. Otherwise he would struggle.

The late afternoon Cote d'Azure sun was starting to sink slowly on the distant horizon, the sky becoming ablaze with a multitude of extraordinary, changing colors.

He sipped on his glass of champagne, welcoming the opportunity to just switch off for a few hours before dinner with the Cumulus team, and soak up the special ambience of the French Riviera which today felt so strangely peaceful.

But Ray knew it was the calm before the storm. In the next few days he would be caught up in a whirlwind of exhausting activity which would leave him feeling even more drained. And exhilarated if the launch of the new series went well. Or devastated if it did not live up to expectations.

This was the last hurdle in a long race to get product on the screen before the real consumers, members of the general public, who ultimately decided the fate of any series by the use of their remote control switch. They held the sole option of what they wanted to watch. But all the buyers at the festivals had the power to decide if the international viewers would ever be given the choice.

Fortunately Cloud 9 was evolving into a brand and enjoyed a growing reputation of delivering quality programming. So buyers were always keen to see new product. But it never paid to be overly confident and complacent in this industry. For all the courting and show biz bonhomie, Ray knew in reality that everyone was only as good as their last movie or show.

Beneath all the schmaltz and smiles, ratings and box office returns seemed to determine the speed at which telephone calls were returned and what the agenda for 'we must do lunch' could be. More often that not, Ray could suss out if any invitation was genuine within a matter of seconds but was pleased that overall he enjoyed a close and meaningful relationship with most in the business, which he valued.

But he had been around long enough to know that for some, an invitation to lunch could also be a superficial pleasantry to keep him sweet in case he might be needed and could deliver product of value. Otherwise, invitations strangely seemed to evaporate.

This was an industry of 'When you're hot, you're hot. And when you're not, you're not.' That's when you discover who the genuine people really are. Those supportive not only through the good times, but the bad. When it's good, success draws so many people like bees to honey. But if the fiscal returns fade, some of those who once championed all the creative efforts like a best buddy pal - seemed to mysteriously disappear.

CHAPTER TWO

JOURNAL: MAY 1981

Ray was first introduced to the community of Antibes as a young screenwriter when he had been commissioned by a producer - and wealthy Asian shipping magnate - to work on a film which was being launched at the Cannes Film Festival, way back in the early 80's.

It was his first real commission. And a daunting experience. He was to undertake a re-work of 'The Bengal Lancers' set on the North West frontier and wondered at one point if he would need to travel to the region for research. But that was all done at the local library.

Ray was more than naive on how the industry worked. Most of all, how he would work and measure up to the task at hand. Struggling to get established and writing on spec was one thing, but to actually have someone willing to pay him to write, quite another. He spent the first week just staring at the blank page, having no idea where to start. Followed by the next two weeks, going over and over the first page, sure that it was not good enough and that it would disappoint.

There were no word processors in those days. So any changes had to be made with tip-x, a white correction ink, which would erase a word. The smell of the white liquid was like glue. Ray had made so many changes over the first few weeks that most days he felt light-headed, wondering what time his small study at home might arrive at Heathrow, sure he would faint.

At the end of the third week, when the phone rang, he almost did pass out when he heard a very concerned voice on the other end of the line.

'What do you mean, you've just finished the first page?!' his agent asked, dumbfounded, checking in for an update.

'I've got page two, along with the rest of the story, all mapped out. I just wanted to make sure I started it all in the best possible way,' Ray replied, hoping to make the agent feel a little more reassured, but was secretly cringing, reading the growing panic that replaced the initial concern.

'The contract states six weeks for delivery of a first draft. The way you're going, you'll be lucky to finish in six years! You've got to speed it up - understand?!'

'Ok. I'll try. Promise.'

'I don't know if I can stall the producer. He's chasing to read what you've got so far. God knows what I'll tell him. But it sure as hell can't be to send a courier - for the first page?! I thought you'd be half way through by now.'

'So did I.' Ray cringed again, then added quickly, to avert any notion that he was finding it all so difficult, which in reality he was, 'But there's not a problem.'

'Long as that 'page' - and the next 120 - are good. If not, you will have a problem. Get your skates on. And I'll catch up with you later.'

Ray replaced the receiver and re-read the first page, wondering if it WAS good. It seemed to be the last time he had gone over it. But now there was only one way of describing it - distinctly bad. No, worse than bad. Awful. Which brought a feeling of nausea to the pit of his stomach.

He wearily ripped the page out of his old Underwood typewriter, scrunched it up into a ball, then tossed it despondently in the litter bin, already filled with paper from aborted past attempts to fill the first blank page which had failed. He resolved to start yet again. And this time, it would not only be good - but sensational.

But then he agonized - what happens if it wasn't? The pressure felt unbearable, as if his head would explode along with his career, seemingly destined to soon finish before it had even had a chance to get started.

The producer extended the deadline to twelve weeks for delivery of the first draft. The agent explained to Ray in no uncertain terms that this producer was not like a normal one. Being a multi-millionaire shipping magnate meant that he could afford to rework schedules. But if Ray wanted to make a go of writing for a living, he really had to learn to meet deadlines.

Fourteen weeks later Ray delivered the first draft, having stayed awake most nights to try and get it all finished in time. The producer seemed to be pleased with what he had read, at least enough to invite Ray to attend the Cannes Film Festival where discussions with potential distributors would be taking place.

Ray was to be on standby to go over script notes and thoughts the producer had, between meetings on his yacht, which was to be used to entertain - and no doubt impress - all those in attendance, and recommended a small family hotel where Ray could stay in Juan les Pins, a few kilometers outside of Cannes.

Intent on trying to stretch his screenplay fee for as long as possible in case no-one ever hired him again, Ray caught a ferry from Dover to Calais and drove all night to Cannes to save on costs.

When he arrived, unshaven and disheveled at the Hotel Juana, he felt more than a little out of place as the valet parked Ray's rusty old Fiat in a bay between a Porsche and a Ferrari belonging to some of the other guests.

It was true that the Juana was a small family hotel and had actually been owned by three generations of the same family, but it was in no way the modest bed and breakfast Ray had been expecting. On the contrary, he noted a plaque illustrating that the establishment was one of the leading boutique hotels in the world.

Ray filled in his name and address on a form in a leather-bound folder at the registration desk and noticed that the restaurant had also been awarded Michelin stars, along with a host of other accolades. And he could see why. Not only did the furnishings and design ooze luxury, sheer elegance and style, the service was exceptional. There seemed to be more staff than the amount of guests a small hotel of this size could hold.

The concierge snapped his fingers. Porters converged out of nowhere in long, white aprons, instructed to take Ray's luggage to his suite. Immediately.

Ray didn't trust the lift which looked to be ancient. Guests entered through a sliding wrought iron gate manned by a very smart, pinstripe-suited operator to be whisked up to the upper floors.

Instead, Ray passed maids in black uniforms and small white aprons, polishing antiques and brass railings bordering a magnificent twisting mahogany wood staircase, who nodded humbly in a subservient greeting, 'Bonjour, Mousier' as he ascended, his running shoes sinking into deep piled carpeting on each step.

His luggage had already been neatly stored on a side table by the time he arrived in his suite which, as expected, was tastefully furnished, littered with more expensive-looking antiques, original oil paintings and other objects of art.

He checked out the bathroom which was decorated in Italian marble and seemed to have gold taps on the sink and bath. He was puzzled when he examined the bidet, having never seen one before, and wondered what it was used for but was distracted by a door chime.

Ray crossed back into the main living area and opened the door, to be confronted by a room service steward in an immaculate white uniform with gold epaulettes on each shoulder, who indicated and displayed a bottle of champagne and silver plate of canapes which had for some reason arrived.

'There must be some kind of mistake. I didn't order anything.'

'No mistake, Monsieur,' the steward said, placing the bottle in an ice bucket, then the canapes on another side table which had already caught Ray's eye. 'It is with the owners' compliments. Shall I open the champagne and pour a glass?'

'Not right now, thanks,' Ray replied, and offered a five pound note as a tip which only seemed to offend the steward as much as it made Ray feel awkward.

'That will not be necessary, Monsieur. At Hotel Juana it is our duty, as well as my pleasure, to be of service.'

The steward smiled with more than a hint of haughty disdain, then left. Ray closed the door and sighed to himself, then checked out the bottle of champagne which looked to be expensive. If it was complimentary and they were to make a profit from his stay, he was now starting to worry, wondering just exactly how much this place would cost. Probably a small fortune from what Ray had seen of the glamorous and clearly expensive region so far.

Juan les Pins was conveniently located approximately half way between Nice and Cannes, each being about a 20 minute drive away. A small community, the historic town had distinguished itself over the years as a playground of the rich and famous international jet set attracted to the chic boutiques, award-winning restaurants, nightclubs and casinos, along with the elegant villas and stylish hotels dating back to the glorious days of France's indulgent and decadent Bel Age.

With the advent of the motion picture and television industry, Cannes had occupied the dazzling spotlight. But before long, many preferred the sanctuary of Juan les Pins, which was a little more understated, stylish - and discreet.

The silent screen heartthrob, with the melodramatic make-up around the eyes, Rudolph Valentino, owned a luxurious mansion in the surrounding area of Antibes in 1920 - now an exclusive, highly-rated resort hotel and once favorite destination of a range of celebrities through the ensuing years, from Josephine Baker to Pablo Picasso, Edith Piaf to even Princess Grace of the tiny nearby principality of Monaco.

Like Prince Rainier, many had become enamored with Grace Kelly. As was Ray as a young boy, when he saw her in the musical film 'High Society'. The camera also seemed to fall helplessly in love with such a captivatingly beautiful leading lady who starred opposite other legends Bing Crosby and Frank Sinatra in the motion picture. Rumor had it that she had affairs with both Hollywood icons.

But that might have just been the spin of a press agent. It couldn't have been that difficult to get coverage with readers and gossip magazines seemingly unable to satisfy an insatiable appetite for news of any screen god or goddess from the Hollywood silver screen.

'Excalibur', 'Heavens Gate', and 'Chariots of Fire' were in competition the first year Ray attended the Film Festival, along with some more esoteric, mostly European titles, for the prestigious Palme d' Or award.

More commercially-driven, mainstream vehicles were screened in all the luxurious hotels, with many more in development for future release being discussed. Hollywood had swallowed up what had once been a forum for art house innovative cinema. Now the Cannes Film Festival had become more of a place to network, wheel and deal, and hopefully sign and seal.

Gigantic billboards of so many so-called 'A' list stars of the day smiled down upon the crowds along the Croissette, made up of locals trying to go about their business, tourists eager for a glance of a famous face, a glamourous starlet hoping to be discovered - but mostly those involved in the motion picture industry trying to cram in as many meetings as their already overspilling appointment diaries would allow.

Ray heard two executives discussing a deal on the street as he got out of the taxi and paid the driver. One of the men sounded desperate, advising that he had about 80% of the finance in place for his latest production. The other man mentioned that he might be able to help with the deficit but wanted to recoup in first position, with a piece of the gross and not just the back end, suggesting to the other man, before rushing away, to send over the script to his hotel and he would have it assessed.

It all sounded like a different language. Ray had no idea what the men were talking about. But it must have been important as he noticed a huge sense of relief on the one who appeared to be desperate, now breaking into a sly, devious smile.

Ray wondered if he was the type who could be trusted. Whatever they were discussing, Ray hoped the other one who was going to have the script assessed had his wits about him. There seemed to be something a bit shady going on.

But he was more concerned by what lay in wait for him. Ray had been summoned by his producer to Queue 9 for a meeting about his own screenplay and recognized the Palais de Festival as he walked to the jetty.

He had often seen the building on some newsreels when stars attended the red carpet premiers and was sure he also passed Roger Moore, who had just disembarked from a yacht berthed nearby, surrounded by a huge entourage. This photogenic harbor looked like the kind of stylish location 007 would frequent.

And the towering body guard who stood at the entrance to the gangway of the luxurious yacht, Labor of Love, would have been perfectly cast as a menacing arch villain in any Bond movie but seemed more relaxed as the producer, sprawled on a sun bed on the deck sipping a cocktail, noticed Ray and called out, 'Ray, my friend. Welcome aboard.'

Ray liked the sound of that. He was now the friend of the producer who must have really been impressed with the first draft script.

The producer asked a member of the crew to arrange for the chef to prepare something to eat as he and Ray were going to have a working lunch in the main dining room going over the script - and Ray was in for a few more surprises.

By 'yacht' he had imagined a boat with sails, whereas this vessel was like a small luxurious cruise ship. He had never seen anything so opulent.

The wine over a lunch of pheasant was accompanied by an aged Bordeaux. Both of which he had also never experienced before.

'How is the pheasant, sir? The chef hopes it is to your liking,' the waiter enquired, as he eagerly watched Ray sample another delicious bite.

'Please tell the chef that the pheasant is very pleasant. And the wine is really divine,' Ray said suddenly, feeling a little awkward amidst all his nerves. 'That's odd. I seem to be speaking in rhyme.'

'Relax, my friend. That's hardly a crime,' the producer reassured Ray, reading his unease.

'Ah - you're a poet as well and you don't even know it,' Ray continued, wishing he could stop. 'Sorry. It must be the wine. Hope yours' tastes as good as mine.'

''63 Chateau Margaux', the producer said smoothly, as he sipped and swirled the wine around in his mouth, savoring the taste. 'It affects all the senses. The memory will remain forever.'

'That's a nice way of describing it. Very clever.'

As soon as he said it, Ray silently cringed, reminding himself again to try and stop the rhyming while he drank more of his wine.

He had never tasted anything so exquisite in all his life. The first sip went right to his head, but now the flattering comments the producer was starting to make were as equally intoxicating. He hadn't really known what to expect as he had never had any creative notes from anyone before.

'This script you have written - has anyone ever called you a genius?'

'No,' Ray shrugged modestly, enjoying his first trip to Cannes and story conference with a producer - now his friend - more and more.

'I tell you, it is special.'

'Glad you think so. I tried my best.'

Now Ray was wondering if maybe next year he and his friend would be accepting the Palme d'Or Award.

'All my people will find it truly inspired,' the producer enthused, flipping through the pages between bites of food as the steward topped up Ray's wine glass. Ray was more inspired and wondered if he and his friend might be up for even an Oscar!

'First though, we have to deal with Prince Khalil,' the producer continued. 'I was initially thinking of offering the role to Omar Sharif.'

'He'd be ideal.'

'Absolutely. But so would I.'

'I .... didn't know you ... ah, were an actor?'

'I'm not. But there can't be that much to it.'

Ray flinched and gazed open-mouthed as the producer suddenly stood, sweeping his arms in a grand theatrical gesture.

'Imagine Prince Khalil - me - riding towards us on a white stallion, with a bird of prey on his shoulder which he unleashes to rip out the eyes of Major Adams.'

There was a manic look in his eyes now. Ray was also aware of not only a simmering anger but the tone in the producer's voice was also laced with bitterness and venom.

'The British dog deserves to die! So we have to work out a scene to give him a long, lingering death. With no mercy, I tell you!'

'But he's the .... hero?'

'Not to me, he isn't,' the producer snapped angrily. 'It is Prince Khalil.'

Ray's heart sank. As well as his jaw. Prince Khalil was an evil force of darkness in the story. There was no way he could be made into a hero, without alienating and confusing the entire audience - except maybe in the producer's home country. Which also was part of the motive, it seemed.

'And all my people will love him for making sure the sun sets in the West - and rises in the East!', said the producer, in a surge of jingoistic pride.

'That means .... a .... total rewrite.'

'Think of it, my friend, as not just rewriting the screenplay - but history! I want this to be a story of not only victory. But total revenge!'

Over the next six months Ray struggled with eight drafts, incorporating more and more changes the producer wanted. The hero in the first draft had now been killed in the first page and the story bore no resemblance at all to anything Ray had ever imagined.

As well as the hero having his eyes ripped out and dying in the opening minutes of the first reel - Ray felt as if he was also blind. Word blind. Lost. Feeling more like a secretary taking dictation than a writer. Slavishly revising whatever he was asked, where nothing about the story or characters made any sense to him anymore.

Besides planning to star as the once villain but now new hero, Prince Khalil, the producer had decided that he was actually also going to direct, which further compounded problems.

The film was in pre production, already going way over budget before even a second of footage had been shot. With an army of stuntmen training hundreds of arabian stallions for a huge battle sequence where the army of Prince Khalil would slaughter the Bengal Lancers. And a huge team of location scouts were scouring the globe for the perfect location, while crews were building expensive studio sets.

Whatever locations were finally chosen could precipitate a logistical nightmare of scheduling to transport the cast and crew between the sets and locations. But it was what the producer, lead actor and director wanted. And being also the prime investor of the movie - meant that he got what he wanted, whatever the cost.

And Ray learned the first of many painful lessons. Not only was it important to try and protect any creative integrity in his work, but he needed to follow his instincts. He felt like not just walking away from it all but running as fast as he could on so many occasions. Which he probably should have done. Rather than soldier on.

If something is broken in the beginning, then it is rarely fixed in the end. Ignoring one's instinct was tantamount to switching off an in-built navigational system. When the first alarm bells start ringing, warning of heading to the rocks, one needed to take evasive and decisive action to avoid disaster. And in this industry - heartache.

Ray also was starting to realize that talent was not the only element which one needed to succeed in the industry. A lot came down to being in the right place at the right time with the right project and the right people. Luck also played a part. Certainly to help try and differentiate if one was with the wrong project at the wrong time with the wrong people.

The producer might have been endowed with hidden talents as an actor and director, may well have been the next Orson Welles, but his vast wealth had given him an accelerated back door entry into the industry where money didn't just talk - it screamed.

Those who either had it or could make it through the box office had all the power and were not only courted but totally indulged. The golden rule seemed to be that those with the gold, made the rules.

The biggest lesson was to identify who had the gold - which became evident in the form of a phone call from Ray's agent.

'I've got good news. And bad news. The good news is you can stop writing.'

'Really?' Ray replied, with an overwhelming sense of relief. 'Finally. The producer liked the latest draft?'

'I don't know. He's done a runner, leaving behind a mountain of debt. The bad news is the screenplay is now owned by the liquidators. So it looks like you can kiss goodbye to the last delivery fee. And I'll lose out on my ten percent as well!'

The norm in the industry is that when a writer is commissioned, he or she would obtain 25% of the initial fee on commencement of the screenplay, 25% on completion and delivery of the first draft, with the remaining 50% payable on acceptance of the final draft, which in this case seemed to have gone on forever.

Ray had been encouraged to try and deliver what the producer wanted as it could be an important credit, as well as being fiscally rewarding, with another vast payment due on the commencement of principal photography, basically when the film started production.

But he wondered if the agent was more interested in obtaining his commission from the overall fee, which might have explained why he didn't advise Ray to withdraw. Even being a novice in the business, Ray could see that the story was broken and would hardly launch his career.

'What about all the expenses? Will they be repaid?' Ray had incurred a lot of costs during the course of the writing, including all of the Cannes trip which had yet to be reimbursed, deciding to put one claim in to cover it all at the end of the assignment rather than do it piecemeal.

'Sorry,' the agent advised. 'Looks like you'll have to lose out on the expenses as well.'

Ray couldn't believe it, discovering later that the producer's entire empire had crumbled like a house of cards, bringing down a merchant bank; law suits were filed with other banks; assets were frozen and seized in a desperate attempt to minimize all the huge fiscal loss. There were even allegations of fraud at one point.

What had begun as a dream commission had ended in heartache and had become a total nightmare.

But it also gave Ray much needed closure. Without the delivery fee and the expenses he had incurred being reimbursed, for all that Ray would now be probably just as broke as, in reality, the producer, he was also relieved that he could at long last stamp the end on this frustrating saga.

It had been a very painful and expensive lesson, one he would never forget, which would prove to be a valuable experience.

Especially an awareness that he had chosen to pursue a career in an industry where nothing was ever quite what it seems.

CHAPTER THREE

JOURNAL: APRIL 5TH, 1949

Ray was born in a small, semi-detached house - 10 Salters Lane, in Redditch, Worcestershire, England - in the early hours of morning. And his father was thrilled. As well as being blessed with his first son, he would also receive a tax rebate!

The baby had come into a post-war world of new-found freedom and hope but also great austerity and hardship for many. And just in the nick of time. Meeting the deadline of the very last day to claim for an extra dependent meant that it was possible to obtain a refund of any tax paid. Ironic that both tax and deadlines would play such a vital part in Ray's adult life as a writer/producer and had actually even been so relevant when he had taken his first breath of air.

The rebate was desperately needed to help pay some long overdue bills and put food on the table. It was a real struggle for any family throughout the nation. Especially in this working class area in the heart of the Midlands where jobs and opportunities were scarce as Britain set about trying to rebuild itself after all the deprivation suffered after so many years of being at war.

Ray's father had been in the Navy. Any leave at home rarely provided any respite from active service, with his family being from Coventry, a city ravaged and almost destroyed by the Blitz. Toward the end of the war he spent as much time as he could across the border in Dundee, Scotland.

He had met and eventually married an attractive young Scots lass who was a cook in the ATS, based in an army camp in Stranraer, near the naval station where the mine sweepers he had served upon as a gunner were deployed on the North Atlantic convoys.

Though she hailed from Aberdeen, there was also Romany Gypsy blood in the family. Many thought that this might explain why she and her husband seemed to be constantly traveling back and forth between Scotland - where their first child, a daughter, had been born just after the war - and England, where she had given birth to Ray.

But the reality was that apart from visiting families on each side of the border, the main pursuit was not due to wander lust but a search for employment. And with a secure job, some stability and hope for the future.

Having no real formal education, Ray's dad worked in a factory in Fintry, near Dundee, where the young family lived on a rough council estate - more a tenement slum - and Ray's younger sister was born.

With another mouth to feed and constantly struggling to make ends meet, the family yet again traveled back across the border to England. But this time employment had been found with real prospects. If Ray's dad could find time to study and obtain some qualifications, he would be trained as an industrial engineer. A white collar position, which might even lead to a role in management.

The family lived in a small flat in Palmerston Road, East Sheen, a suburb of London where Ray's younger brother was born and the elder siblings started a new school.

Ray's classmates gave him the nickname of Jock, sure that with his accent he was as Scottish as William Wallace. He was certainly as wild. One poor boy - the school bully - made the unwise decision to pick on Ray and bestow upon him the nickname of Gypo, after discovering his Romany heritage. In return, the bully received a suspected broken nose and black eye.

'You stupid idiot boy,' said Ray's mother scolding him, with a clip around the ear. 'You've got to control that temper of yours', laddie, or you'll end up with the police after you. And where will that lead? Nowhere but Borstal.' Which was a custodial institution for juvenile delinquents.

'He said I was a Gypo tinker.'

'He what?!' Ray's mother said, with sudden fire in her eyes.

'And that I looked like a walking jumble sale.'

It was true enough though. Rather than a new uniform, Ray and his sisters wore mismatched clothes to school obtained from second hand shops, and mostly the wrong size, including even the shoes. But it was all that could be afforded.

'Well, if his mum and dad or that school want to make anything of it, they'll have me to answer to!' Ray's mother said, trying somehow to contain her own fury.

She was only a small, diminutive figure, but when riled could be a formidable adversary. A warm and true friend for life. But an enemy to the death.

'A Gypo tinker, eh? Always remember to treat people with respect. As long as they deserve it. But if not, don't let anyone push you around, laddie. Ever. You did the right thing standing up for yourself!'

There was no need to worry about that. Ray, like the rest of the family, had an almost Sicilian code of honor and justice. All at school quickly realized that this boy would never back down from any kind of scrap.

He wasn't the type to go looking for any trouble but he wouldn't run from it either. And was more than capable of taking care of himself from a very young age, having been brought up in the gutter of some very mean streets where fists would do the talking faster than words to settle any score.

Before long, the family moved to Deadworth, just outside Windsor, Berkshire where Ray started yet another new school. His father had received a promotion and was able to save the modest sum required for the deposit on a small, semi-detached house, 33 Green Acre Estate.

It was far from being an affluent suburb, still so-called working class, but compared to what the family had been used to, it was sheer luxury. For all that there was a huge mortgage on the property - and one the family could still ill afford - the notion of actually owning soil, bricks and mortar rather than renting, filled Ray's parents with a sense of hope. And pride.

All Ray had hoped for though was some furniture which could only be bought as funds permitted. And any spare funds were forever in short supply.

As the snow fell softly outside during the first Christmas in the new house, the family enjoyed their festive meal inside. The seasonal ambience was punctuated by the warmth of an open fire and lights twinkling on the tree. But the turkey dinner and all the trimmings were set out on a tea chest rather than a table. With no chairs either, they had to sit on the floor.

Although the house was devoid of much furniture, it was always filled with an abundance of love, laughter, and joy. The family played games and feasted on an array of food and treats they did not normally have. Ray and his elder sister were given a glass of babycham, even a sip of mulled wine. But there were shades of disappointment, too, when excited expectations during the lead-up to Christmas were not totally met.

'Just one thing I don't understand,' Ray's younger sister had said, when the family opened their presents earlier that morning. 'How come I didn't get a bike? And why does Father Christmas bring old toys? Some of my stuff looks like it's been used.'

Ray noticed a look of despair as his parents exchanged glances. As did he, himself, with his older sister. Both knew only too well the great effort and sacrifice their parents always made to spend as much as could be found to make every Christmas and birthday special.

'The elves always do their best to make sure Father Christmas brings what every child wants, but it's not always possible,' Ray's father said gently.

Before his mother cut in, not in the mood for any nonsense or for the day to be spoiled, determined to place it all in perspective.

'You got a doll and some books, which is what you wrote on your Christmas list, right? So just be thankful, my girl, for what you did get. Maybe next year you'll get a bike. Must be difficult for everyone at the North Pole to find enough toys to go round.'

'I suppose you're right,' Ray's little sister sighed.

'I AM right,' replied Ray's mother. 'Anyone would think we're all in the poor house. We've got food and shelter and each other. What more could you want?'

'A bike,' Ray's sister replied, with a glint of mischief in the eye, and it brought a smile to everyone else, including her mum.

'Well, you'd better write to the North Pole to complain. You'll get no sympathy from me, my girl. Now let's clear the ... ah ... 'table' ... Who's got room for some homemade Christmas pud? You might even find a sixpenny piece inside - so be careful before you swallow.'

Ray was the lucky one to find the sixpence which had been mixed in with the pudding and decided to give it back to his mother and father. But they insisted that he start saving so it could go toward two things he wanted most in life - an electric guitar and an amplifier.

He had discovered a real love of music several years before, having been taught by his father to play the guitar back in Scotland. An old, gut string acoustic guitar had somehow come into his dad's possession. And he had taught himself a few basic chords which he then passed along to Ray.

His parents were surprised that rather than just a hobby, music became a real passion for Ray, who spent many a long night in his bedroom going over and over scales, working out various chord structures.

Few could have foreseen, let alone Ray or anyone else in the family, that in later years some of this work would feature in soundtracks. And one piece was destined to form the base structure of a movement which would be performed by a full symphony orchestra.

At that time Ray reflected and was able to articulate when looking back, that music was almost as a portal which had taught him so much as a young boy. About life before he had lived it, evoking emotions so deep within before he had even been able to comprehend the complex depth and true meaning of what the feelings represented.

Musical structure was such that for him as a child, it had the capacity to communicate more profoundly than often any language. And as such was a temple so exalted that it could cleanse or stir or inspire the human condition by its purity and clarity in a way nothing else could, which was certainly majestic, but also as if it emanated from a different spiritual plain and level of consciousness.

Way back then, in the early sixties in Windsor, owning an electric guitar and amplifier seemed almost impossible, a million miles away, let alone any fanciful notion that music would play such a prominent part in Ray's life and career.

His parents were hopeful that he might get his long-awaited wish as his eleventh birthday approached. But Ray was doubtful. His mother was working part-time at a cafe in town. And with his dad carrying on with studies out of office hours, he didn't really have a chance to earn anything extra in his spare time simply because there was none.

With his parents' hard-earned money just about covering essential items, and any spare sums left over being set aside and saved for furniture, rather than drain the coffers further Ray set about getting some part-time work himself. It was either that or sending a begging letter to the elves himself. But Christmas was such a long way off.

He found a job at a fruit and vegetable stall every Saturday at the local market. Then another delivering grocery orders for a local shop, conveyed in a cardboard box in the rectangular front compartment of a bicycle, after school. And found yet another delivering newspapers early every morning before rushing off to school.

When he attended school, that is. He hated it, was bored more often than not and regularly played truant, much preferring to hang around music shops in the town, examining various instruments. Or spending time in the local library where he enjoyed reading all manner of books, almost as if he realized a need to self-educate himself. Schools never seemed to teach what he was interested in.

After his dad took him as a rare treat to the cinema to see 'Bridge on the River Kwai', Ray devoured anything and everything he could find to read about Japanese culture, Shintoism, the code of bushido, and was keen to learn all he could to do with the works of the great director of the film, David Lean.

This led to the discovery of a Japanese actor, Toshiro Mifune, and a director, Akira Kurosowa. Ray was desperate to see one film in particular he had read about that they both made and which invoked absolute intrigue: 'The Seven Samurai'.

'I know why it's not on at the pictures,' his mother said, 'because it's in Japanese. And no-one would go and see it. We live in England, remember? Not Japan. Now stop going on about it.'

'Can I go and see Elvis then?'

Elvis Presley was starring in a new film, 'Blue Hawaii'. Ray's mother shook her head and smiled, 'You're something else, laddie, you really are.'

'I can pay for it myself. Out of my wages.'

'I'm not talking about the cost of the ticket, you stupid idiot boy. You've been going on and on about this Japanese film for weeks and weeks, like nothing else mattered. And now - Elvis?'

'He's the king.'

'He is that. But I don't think he's Japanese. Unless I missed something?'

Ray's mother was a huge fan of Elvis, as was her eldest son. But she was also aware that there was something a little different about Ray that she couldn't quite put her finger on.

The latest obsession about all matters Japanese was a good example of his fascination with unusual 'things' and determination to learn all he could about whatever it was that interested him.

He seemed to enjoy so-called normal activities just like any other child. Such as being a fan of the 'Lone Ranger' television series, which was popular at the time. But as well as wanting an autograph of the hero, Ray was more fascinated in his sidekick, Tonto, which led him to research Native American culture.

This precipitated Ray getting into more trouble at school, which occurred on a regular basis. He hadn't completed his french homework as a result of his latest quest to discover more about the wild west. The teacher thought he was joking with his suggestion that rather than learning to speak French, perhaps he could take Apache, and he was given a detention.

This type of injustice stirred up his innate rebellious streak against authority, culminating in him kicking a teacher in the groin who caned him for no apparent reason. At least, in Ray's mind. It occurred during a history lesson when Ray asked why a particular Viscount of the English historical aristocracy was named after an aircraft when it hadn't been invented yet. Also, why an aircraft was named after Viscounts. Was it due to the fact that maybe some of them fled any war and an aircraft manufacturer made a mistake with the word thinking that they flew instead?

It was easy to see why the teacher thought Ray was being mischievous and playing the fool to obtain a laugh from his classmates. Something he was prone to do. He was always a popular boy. His friends enjoyed his whacky sense of humor and seemed to respond to his non-conforming, wild, rebellious attitudes.

But the teacher was unaware that Ray's house in Windsor was under the flight path approach to Heathrow Airport. And that he liked the shape of one particular aircraft he had noticed. Rather than wondering about which exotic destinations the flights traveled to, Ray was more intrigued by the shape and design of the aircraft. After researching all he could about it, he had yet to discover why the aircraft had been named as a Viscount.

He also couldn't understand why his parents were so furious that he defended himself when the teacher had attacked him.

'He didn't attack you, he was punishing you,' Ray's dad tried to explain.

'For what? All I did was ask the teacher a question and I got the cane. So I put the boot in. Right between the legs, in the goolies.'

Neither Ray's dad or mum could make him understand that this was not the way to behave. When Ray explained the whole background to the Viscount situation, they could see he had a point and perhaps felt aggrieved that he was treated unfairly because he was, after all, only telling the truth. And while it was right that he tried to defend himself - that didn't apply to a teacher.

'I don't get it. So if I'm bullied or attacked by someone my age, then that's alright to try and take care of myself. But if an adult tried to do it ... then I'm in the wrong?'

'No. But it would be unwise to get into any kind of scrap with an adult. If anyone ever tried to attack you, it would be best to run or phone the police. That would be a very serious crime'

'What - I should have phoned the police after I got caned?'

'To report that a teacher caned you? No!' Ray's father said, frustrated that his son could not comprehend. 'You'd only do that if a teacher tried to harm or hurt you.'

'But that cane did hurt. Look. It stung for hours,' Ray said, showing the palm of an outstretched hand.

Ray's parents exchanged exasperated glances. Their son was certainly different alright. He struggled with a lot of areas which didn't seem to make sense to him but could make a strong and stubborn case why, which further complicated matters, especially for anyone trying to help him understand.

They mentioned that they understood what he was getting at but would try and come back to it later as they were getting a bit confused themselves, agreeing with Ray that with all the different rules and regulations it was indeed a weird world, with often conflicting theories regarding what was right and what was wrong.

School didn't seem to teach it, along with anything else which Ray was interested in. So he played truant at any and every opportunity.

One day on the way back from the library to research more on the warrior code of bushido, he took a stroll along the bank of the River Thames to feed some bread to the ducks and noticed a motorcade making its way up the steep road toward Windsor Castle. And he ran up to the top of the hill to see what all the commotion was about.

In a gleaming black Bentley limousine Ray caught a fleeting glimpse of HM Queen Elizabeth. And no-one in the crowds lining the streets would have ever thought that the young boy standing by their side, casting an eager wave to her Majesty, would be destined thirty years later to receive notice from the monarch herself that he was to feature in her New Year's honors list for services to film and television. The odds were highly unlikely. Or more realistically, virtually impossible.

To his school, with his poor attendance, the odds were nil. He was the type of pupil destined to fail, although the headmaster recognized unusual traits, suspecting that there might be something there if only the school could tap into it.

But the lad also had a defiant streak. Along with a determination to do things his way. If he could only be taught to channel that, then it might lead to some positive results. If not, then it would herald problems. He was the type who could either end up a millionaire. Or in jail.

The new source of research and fascination over the ensuing days for Ray was predictably not the Queen - but her official car. He flipped through all the books he could find about Bentleys, wondering initially what was so special about that particular make of vehicle to be fit for - and chosen - to transport a Queen. And he soon began to realize why, as he stared in marvel at the photographs of all the elegant designs of other models available.

At that time in Britain the majority of the population did not own cars. Only a very elite few were privileged to drive a Bentley, so unique, with individual specifications built to order, distinguished by its sheer handmade craftsmanship, rather than a mass of vehicles emanating from an assembly line.

The frequent absences from attending classes were brought to the attention of Ray's father and mother by the school board who thought he must be ill. And his parents were furious. Not only at Ray. But at his sister, who knew all about his escapades but remained silent out of loyalty, not wishing to get him in trouble. Now both were in trouble.

'You should have known better and said,' his sister was reprimanded by her dad.

'And you, laddie, have to realize you have to go to school. Not when it suits you but every day. I'm warning you, if you don't, forget about the school board or headmaster punishing you because your father and I - we'll ring your neck!' Ray's mother threatened.

Ray and his sister were sentenced to go to bed early for a week. With Ray having to do extra chores around the house for the entire month. He could handle that. He was more concerned what the headmaster would say, having been summoned to his office, and begged his mother to accompany him.

'This school has rules and regulations and we expect all pupils to adhere to them,' the headmaster warned Ray the following day while his Mother sat in a chair beside him. 'Truancy is a very serious issue. You'll get nowhere by playing truant, boy. The only way to succeed is to attend school and study.'

'Sorry, Sir,' Ray replied sheepishly, as the headmaster glared, his steely eyes visible above his bifocal spectacles which seemed as if they were penetrating Ray's very soul.

'Well, what have you got to say for yourself?'

'I don't know. Except if you want to give me the cane, I might have to call the police.'

The headmaster missed Ray's mother casting a quick glance at heaven. He was considering Ray intently, who was trying to stop himself from breaking down in tears, his lip quivering as if he was about to sob any second. He knew he was in deep trouble and just hoped that if he was to be caned, it would be on his right hand. The left one might make it difficult to play his guitar for a few days.

'What do you want to achieve in life, boy? Any idea?'

'A Bentley. And a table. But not in that order.'

Ray's mother blurted out in uncontrollable laughter. She just couldn't help herself, though Ray couldn't see what was so funny - and he wasn't the only one.

'I hardly think your son's insolence is amusing,' the headmaster said angrily. Ray's mother immediately stopped laughing.

'Now just you hold on a minute,' she said, glaring at the headmaster, trying to contain her fury. 'I don't need any lecture from you on what I find amusing!'

'Yeah, right!' Ray said, sniffing back the tears that still wanted to flow but feeling a bit more brave now that his mother was on his case. The battle lines were being drawn. Or so he thought.

'Quiet!' his mother snapped angrily. And now Ray started to sob, confused and hurt that she reprimanded him when he was only trying to join forces to protect her. But then he watched proudly as his mother continued her tirade. She never needed protection and was capable of giving as good - if not more - than she would ever get.

'I would ask that you don't insult my son! Yes, you can scold him for playing truant. He knows what he did was wrong and he's apologized. But don't accuse him of being insulant when he was just answering a question honestly.'

'A Bentley and a table?'

'He saw the Queen arrive in a Bentley when she was in residence at Windsor Castle and has spoken of nothing much since. And as far as the table is concerned ... '

There was a posh, almost snobbish element in her tone now and she almost sounded like the Queen.

'My family and I have yet to find one to meet the level of our requirements. So, until we source a suitable one - we have been dining on a tea chest.'

'I see. Thank you for explaining,' the headmaster faked a smile to Ray's mother and she forced one back in return, continuing in a veiled threat. But the headmaster got the message - though Ray didn't. All he knew was the headmaster was looking a little more worried than he was when Ray and his mother arrived.

'Now I would suggest that while you investigate all the reasons why the poor laddie has been walking out of his classes so often - you might ask the teachers why my son seems to find lessons so boring. Enough for him to not even want to go to school, if you understand my point. Unless, of course, you want me to ask the school board for an explanation.'

'I don't think that will be necessary. I'll have a word with the teachers and let you know the outcome. I've always been of the view that your son has ... great potential.'

'Well, that makes two of us. Three, if you include my husband.'

'Four, if you include me,' Ray said. Which caused an astonished look to come from both his mother and the headmaster.

'That's good to hear, boy,' the headmaster said, as he stood to shake hands with Ray's mother.

'Thank you for taking the time to come in. I'll be in touch.'

'That would be very much appreciated. Good day,' replied Ray's mother. Then she fluffed her son's hair and took his hand, leading him out of the office with great dignity. 'Come on, you. Cheer up.'

She could see that Ray was deeply upset by the encounter. She knew he might not have been the brightest student in the class, but he wasn't stupid either. Nor lazy. He was keen to learn and there were bound to be reasons why he didn't want to go to school which she intended to get to the bottom of.

Ray was given an ice cream as a treat on the way home. But the greatest treat was knowing that he had his parents' support and that he had been under the 'protection' of his mother at the meeting with the headmaster.

It was a comfort to know that deep down she was a loyal ally and like any mother fiercely protective of her brood. She could dish out any punishment or insults and was the first to lash out with a clip around the ear if any of her children didn't toe the line. But if anyone else tried to harm or treat them unfairly, it brought only one thing - war.

Ray had been taught a lesson that day at school which he would never forget. And that was to stand up for what is right. And to protect his rights - or the rights of others - whatever the cost.

CHAPTER FOUR

JOURNAL: 1963

The teachers weren't to blame for the malaise in the classroom, however. Nor Ray. For all of his hunger for knowledge in often the obscure, he struggled with conventional learning, finding it difficult to concentrate, and much preferred to go at his own pace. Sitting in a classroom with so much information to try and assimilate was exhausting.

What no-one realized, least of all Ray until much later in life, was that his somewhat eccentric behavior and non conforming, often rebellious behavior was probably the result of Asperger's Syndrome, a condition out of the autistic spectrum.

He found it difficult to even tell the time, unsure if the hands pointing to 12.30 meant that it was 6 o'clock. It was always a chore to tie his shoelaces and he just couldn't seem to master the recorder in music lessons as a result of being seemingly uncoordinated, due to the complexities of inadequate fine motor skills. Yet he could easily master other instruments.

When he received a 'D' in music, his parents were confused as he seemed to possess a natural aptitude for it. As well as an obsessive interest in it.

If the music teacher had only known that he played the guitar, he might have received more encouragement, along with better marks. But he never told her he could play other instruments besides the recorder. Because she never asked. He had a knack of being able to pick up any instrument in the music shop and in no time at all was able to play a tune, which again he never told anyone, even his parents - simply because they never asked.

And he never explained the difficulties he had with the recorder to his parents either. So it made no sense for them to read on his report that he was bottom of the class in music and didn't seem to have much interest in it. The entire family knew he had little interest in anything else, obsessed with practicing for hours and hours till his fingers were sore.

'Don't you worry, laddie,' Ray's mother said, when he told her about the low grade and she tried to lift his spirits. 'No matter what that stupid music teacher said, I think you've got a real talent. So you keep the dream alive.'

Ray loved that saying. He didn't understand exactly what it fully meant but the words gave him comfort somehow and he resolved that whatever dream he had or set out to achieve, he would keep the dream alive for as long as it would take to succeed.

Before long, Ray had saved up enough to purchase his electric guitar and amplifier. The family even acquired a table, along with other furniture. And eventually a second hand television set on which Ray used to love watching 'Doctor Who', starring William Hartnell, which was transmitted in black and white every Saturday night just before 'Juke Box Jury'.

Ray was given the chair in front of the fire to enjoy his routine Saturday night viewing to help warm up during the winter after his job at the fruit and vegetable stall in the town's central square market place.

His duties initially were to cut cauliflowers, with freezing fingers which could barely hold a knife they were so numb, so the leaves of the white heads were visible and looked more presentable, along with unloading and polishing all the other produce, such as tomatoes and apples, so they could be stacked neatly on display.

He was thrilled to get a promotion after a month where he was able to sell, and enjoyed copying the pitch men, shouting out to any passer by that if they were after a bargain and the best produce available, then they should have a word and he would see them right. All the stall holders were from Petticoat Lane in Covent Garden but most originated from London's rough and ready East End.

Ray became adept at mimicking their cockney accent which fascinated him, regularly shouting out to any potential customer, 'Once a grape?' Translated, that meant to Ray, 'Who wants any grapes?'

'I'm not askin' half a crown a pound. Or even two bob. 'Ere you are then, my darlin's. It's yours' for a tanner.' Again, roughly translated, Ray was offering a pound of grapes for six pence, which was a great reduction on the advertised price.

He became a favorite with most of the customers, especially elderly ladies, who must have taken pity on the young soul looking like an orphan out of a Dickensian novel, out in the cold with his fingerless gloves and scarf, clearly trying to earn an a little bit extra to survive.

Ray's day started at 6 am. He walked the few miles into town rather than ride his bicycle. He had to help unload all the produce first thing in the frosty mornings but was able to take any leftovers home, which he used to carry in a crate on one shoulder. He couldn't have done it if he rode his bike.

And he loved showing all the family what he had been given, which meant they rarely had to purchase any fruit and vegetables. It was like Christmas every Saturday night as the family gathered around when he arrived to see what might lay in store this week. Everything from grapefruit to pomegranates, brussels sprouts to king edward potatoes.

On top of that he was paid a wage and even got some tips. So his reward for paying his own way and contributing to the household expenses was to be able to sit in the comfy chair by the fire and watch his favorite two shows on television. While his mother prepared a hot chocolate for him to sip on while he tried to thaw out after a long winter's day at the market, enjoying the shows.

In November, 1963, 'Doctor Who' and 'Juke Box Jury' were both interrupted with tragic and extended news coverage - President John F. Kennedy had been assassinated.

There was only one television channel in Britain in those days. And no commercial radio. No outlet as such to listen to popular music except for Radio Luxembourg and a few pirate stations, which introduced Ray to a range of artists from Gene Vincent to Eddie Cochrane, The Everley Brothers to Buddy Holly.

Every spare penny he earned was spent on vinyl, purchasing 45 rpm records or 33rpm LP'S. With most of his spare time spent going through albums at the local record shop in town in a search for different styles of music available, as an alternative to the mainstream favorites such as the Beverly Sisters, Cliff Richard, The Shadows, Helen Shapiro, and Bobby Vee.

Ray enjoyed them all well enough but became interested in some of the more obscure recording artists such as American blues singing legends Howling Wolf and Muddy Waters.

Another singer caught his eye in an article in the Melody Maker, which was a trade paper for the music industry and also hard core fans. Ray was disappointed to learn that the singer and his band were based in Bournemouth on the south west coast of the England rather than the cotton fields of the deep American south and were more into jazz, as well as soul, rather than just rhythm and blues.

But the name fascinated Ray. Zoot Money. And his big roll band. Ray didn't know why but just thought it sounded so amazing. With a name like Zoot Money, the singer just had to be destined to record something special.

Ray had a wide taste in music across the whole spectrum. From Elvis to Frank Sinatra. He even enjoyed many of the songs from the Fred Astaire and Ginger Rogers Hollywood musicals which were shown occasionally on television. But he had recently discovered the blues and was eager to learn more about it all.

When he saw a poster promoting that a little known group who played the blues would be appearing at a club overlooking the Star and Garter pub in Windsor, he persuaded his dad to take him to check it out.

The club was almost empty and Ray managed to have a chat with the band about music in their break. All had a similar interest in the blues and they suggested he listen to any album of Bo Diddley.

Ray excitedly relayed the news to members of his own group which he had formed at school. They were called The Avengers and got together as often as they could to practice in the hall of their local youth club.

'What was the name of that group again you were telling us about the other day, the one you saw at the Star and Garter?' one of his fellow group members asked, wanting to see them himself the next time they played a gig in the area.

'The Rolling Stones,' Ray replied. 'Not many people have heard of them. But I reckon they'll do well.'

And he was right. Before long, the Rolling Stones were appearing in other clubs, like the Crawdaddy in nearby

Richmond, and soon signed a recording contract, releasing their first single 'Come On' which Ray watched on 'Juke Box Jury'. Most of the judges gave it a score of five, voting it a hit. And it was, reaching #21 in the UK singles chart.

But it was a group from up north in Liverpool which captured Ray's total musical imagination and profoundly inspired him from the very first time he heard their first single 'Love Me Do' which charted at #17.

This was followed by a second single which reached #2, 'Please Please Me', and a third single 'From Me To You' which very quickly reached the top of the charts, heralding a phenomenon, the likes of which had never been seen before and will probably never ever be seen again.

The music industry and popular culture would soon be caught in an unprecedented revolution, becoming totally transformed as Beatlemania spread like wild fire right across Britain, and later, every far reaching corner of the globe.

Like so many teenagers throughout Britain, Ray read every magazine and trade paper he could find about the Mersey Beat, grew his hair long, dressed in a Beatle jacket and cuban heeled boots which he wore to local gigs where his group started to enjoy a growing and loyal following - especially from a few very attractive girls.

Some fans became his first ever girlfriends. But the relationships were never serious. Ray was more focused on his music.

When he left school, just turning fifteen years old, he considered pursuing music as a career. But his parents agreed with the teachers, thinking that he might be better off trying to obtain some vocational training and experience, given that he had no formal qualifications. He didn't even sit the 'O' or 'A' level exams. With his learning difficulties, he would have probably failed. And the statistics of so called 'making it' with his group were heavily not in his favor.

The career advisor thought that Ray might do well in retail as he seemed to possess excellent interpersonal skills which might help offset his lack of academic prowess. And an interview was arranged at Caley's department store in the town center.

Ray greased his hair back, put on a collar and tie and sat nervously in front of the personnel officer who scanned his application form.

'So tell me ... Zoot, is it?'

'Yes. Zoot Thompson, sir,' Ray replied, sure that the personnel manager was as impressed with the name as Ray was when he first heard it.

'Why do you think you would be best suited for the position?'

'Because it's important to dress smartly at a posh place like Caley's.'

The personnel manager deadpanned, and considered Ray, who smiled politely.

'Well, that's one way of looking at it, I suppose,' he said, glancing at other papers on his desk. 'Just one thing I would like to clarify. It says here on the reference from your headmaster that your name is .... Ray?'

'It is, sir. Well, Raymond actually, if you want to be precise.'

'Then why did you put the name of Zoot on the application form?'

'Because I thought it would be better than Grey Owl.'

'I beg your pardon?!'

'I didn't think you'd be very happy if a supervisor said to a customer, 'Sorry to keep you waiting. Grey Owl will be with you in a minute after he finishes serving his current customer.'

'Indeed. But I don't think you still quite understand. Because I certainly don't.'

'Grey Owl was entrenched in the Mohawk and Iroquois tribes,' Ray explained enthusiastically. 'You should read his book 'The Falls of Silence.' It's awesome.'

'And .... Zoot?'

'That's just another name I love as well. I was going to call myself Sun Tzu. You know, after the Chinese warrior philosopher who lived about 4,500 years ago? But I didn't think that would work either.'

'Yes, quite,' the personnel manager said, not really sure what to make of this candidate or what he was talking about.

'He had an amazing mind,' Ray continued, in full enthusiastic flow, 'but I don't think that anyone should promote deceit or betrayal in the code of bushido even if it's disguised as a form of pragmatic reform to justify victory. That should only come with honor. Wouldn't you agree, sir?'

'Oh ... er ... absolutely,' the personnel manager said weakly, staring at Ray as if he was from another planet.

He managed to decipher what Ray had in mind but tried to explain that just because Ray had left school, that didn't mean that he could - or even should - change his name. It was true that the career advisor might have stated that entering the job market was totally different from school, but having that new independence didn't require someone to change identity, as if they had become reborn.

Ray clarified that he wasn't trying to change his identity as such. He just liked the name Zoot. And thought he might refer to himself as it as a nickname. Viewing getting out of school as a fresh start and maybe the time to use a fresh name. But he was happy with his real name and could see that it might be a bit confusing for anyone. So he had no problem at all being known as Ray. He was sure he could always use the name of Zoot on another occasion if he ever wanted to.

The personnel manager must have either been impressed by Ray or had taken pity on him as Ray was offered a position in the menswear section. But in the interview Ray couldn't understand why he outlined the great pension opportunities he would receive when he retired. He never considered the position as nothing more than a stop gap.

He enjoyed the work initially - as with any novelty - but couldn't see himself doing it until he was 65. He thought he would be lucky to last the first month. There was a television series Ray noticed in later years - 'Are You Being Served' - which always reminded him of his brief time at Caley's.

The shop was very formal. Even if he had still used Zoot, no-one on the staff would have referred to him as that. Everyone used surnames. The men wore a red carnation in the lapel of their suits. The few ladies seemed to be ancient and reek of perfume, with blue rinses in their hair.

All were as snobbish as the customers and it was a real struggle to settle in - and so difficult to be addressed as anyone other than Ray.

'Would you take care of Madam and Sir, please, Mr Thompson?'

'Yes, of course, Mr Booth. It would be a pleasure.'

Ray faked a smile to his section manager who was with another customer but always seemed to be overly humble and grovel like a servant. Ray could understand the importance of giving good service but there was no way he would ever lick anyone's boots.

'Mr Thompson is a just a junior. So I trust Sir and Madam will bear with him during his training. If there is a problem, any problem at all, then perhaps you can ask Mrs Beech to assist, Mr Thompson?'

Ray detested being patronized. Just a junior? After working the Saturday markets, he was sure he could handle selling a shirt to the customers, no problem at all. So he decided to get his own back.

'And where would I find Mrs Beech, Mr Booth? If Sir and Madam 'run into any problems?' Ray asked, but in reality knew the answer to the question he was asking. He was just preparing Mr Booth for a set-up.

'Mrs Beech is deputy section manager of mens' suits.'

'Oh. I could have sworn I just saw her in mens' underwear.'

Mr Booth looked disgusted at the mere thought of it and almost blushed. The customers could hardly mask a hint of a smile as they exchanged a polite nod with Mr Booth, who almost bowed to them, then glared at Ray as he led Sir and Madam to the shirt section.

Soon Ray began to detest the routine and being subservient to officious, demanding customers. Every day felt like a year watching the clock inch slowly toward 5 pm when his day would be finished and he would be free.

But the feeling of freedom lasted only a few hours when he realized he would have to wake up and go through it all again. Each day was filled with counting down the days until Friday when he would enjoy the weekends playing at gigs, only to have a feeling of dread when Sunday came, knowing that the Monday morning blues were less than 24 hours away. It was worse than school, where at least he could escape by playing truant.

It came as no surprise to his parents when he told them he wanted to hand in his notice. They agreed that he could do his music and writing until he worked out an alternative career path.

Fortunately Ray was able to earn enough from the gigs and although not as much as a normal wage, had spending money, as well as a small sum he could put toward room and board, which Ray's mother and father thought was important. Increasing feelings of pride and self esteem, which come along with a work ethic and a capability to contribute and pay one's' own way.

Every Sunday afternoon Ray hung out at the Carlton ballroom in Slough, either performing, listening to or jamming with many groups who played there, including the M15. In addition to the Avengers, where Ray sang and played lead guitar, he joined another group as well - Malcolm James and the Callers - playing keyboards, having saved enough to purchase a small electric organ.

Then he started yet another, The Society, which were more blues driven, and was invited to perform with several other groups on occasion since he could turn his hand to drumming or even bass or rhythm guitar.

This eventually enabled him to earn more than he did in the menswear section at Caley's, and with gigs being held mostly at night he had more than enough time during the day to compose. And much to everyone's surprise in the family, including even Ray, he started to feel the need to write.

He always enjoyed poetry and lyrics of music, even sayings, and was an avid reader of books. He had written several songs but had never felt the compulsion to write stories until one day when he heard the lyrics of a song by a group who were making a name for themselves - The Who. They had just released a new single 'My Generation' which contained a line, 'Hope I die before I get old.' And this sparked Ray's imagination. A world with no adults. That was an interesting premise for a story.

'A writer, eh?' Ray's mother said, surprised when he told her that he might have an alternative career to music. 'Well, like I've always said, keep the dream alive in whatever it is you want to do and your dad and I will always support you. We just want you to be happy. But in your life you've got to earn a wage, laddie. So just bear that in mind. Besides, if you want to be a writer - you might also need to learn how to spell!'

It was true. Ray couldn't spell and always seemed to struggle with the English language as much as it fascinated him. To become a writer would be rather like someone with a fear of flying becoming an airline pilot.

Structures of words, lyrics of songs, poetry and stories were so seductive and inspiring - but were also frightening in many ways to Ray, finding it difficult to assimilate and process meanings and interpretations. The fear was almost phobic but the need to creatively experience more and more was like a hunger never to be satisfied.

Over the next week he tried to structure a narrative on how young people might exist in a world with no adults but never got beyond the basic premise, which brought no end of frustration - but also a sense of intrigue and great challenge as a platform to express himself and unharness all he wanted to creatively explore.

When the mods and rockers surfaced throughout Britain, it reminded Ray of two Tribes. Ray was a mod. Someone who followed the new wave music and fashion and traveled on motor scooters. Rockers remained rooted in conventional rock and roll, evolving out of the Teddy Boy, winkle picker shoe culture, but now dressed in leathers and traveling on motor bikes.

A rocker would never venture into mod territory and a mod would give any rocker hang-out a wide berth. Otherwise, both sides would clash, and fights between both sides became a regular occurrence.

Ray tried to write yet another story with a theme of two young Tribes battling each other and trying to dominate with their own particular ideology, but just couldn't map it out. So he decided to concentrate on his music for the time being and perhaps come back to trying to write another time. He certainly had enough to occupy his enquiring mind.

England was in the epi-centre of the swinging sixties, which was an exciting and vibrant time for anyone to come of age. But in addition, adults also became caught up in a whirlwind of music, fashion and changing attitudes associated with the revolution of a new age.

Tourists flocked to visit the boutiques in Carnaby Street - where radical new designers, such as Mary Quant, introduced the mini skirt, Vidal Sassoon avant guard hairstyles; the red London double decker bus and even the Union Jack became iconic symbols, placed on so much merchandise, branding an era which in itself had become a brand, precipitating a huge export boom for businesses in Britain.

Commercial enterprise was not alone to quickly note - and cash in on - the explosive new trend. Politicians, ever keen to tap into public opinion, were soon aware of the need to get in tune or they would be voted out of office. As the lyrics of a popular song of the day rightly stated - 'The time's they are a changing'. As indeed they were. Especially for Ray's family.

'You'll never guess', his father announced unexpectedly during dinner one evening. 'I've been offered a new job. In Canada!'

'Canada?' Ray's younger, four year old brother said. 'Where's that?'

MIP TELEVISION FESTIVAL

PROMO REEL

FADE IN

MIP TELEVISION FESTIVAL PROMO REEL

INT. STUDIO SET. DAY.

Crew are visible in the background. Cameras. Lighting. Sound. Others dressing the set.

And we pick up William with our promotional camera, eye-line right into the lens.

> WILLIAM
> Hello, I'm William Shatner. What a wonderful business this is. You can be an actor, a writer, or

                    WILLIAM
                  (Cont'd/...)
     director   or   producer. You   can
     be a captain of a starship or a
     cop on the beat.   But no matter
     what job I've taken or what part
     I've played, at the end of the
     day I'm a story teller. And now
     I'm part of an exciting new
     television production of quality
     children's programming and family
     entertainment. Fifteen one hour
     tales of imagination and wonder.
     'William Shatner's A   Twist in the
     Tale'... Come on, I'll show you...

We go with William as he crosses to a
leather chair in front of a roaring open
fire around which children are sitting.

Crew are lighting candles. A grandfather
clock ticks.   A huge black dog sits at
William's feet as he, too, sits.   Music
punctuates the evocative atmosphere.

                    WILLIAM
     For I am - the story teller. Magic.

The lights are now dimming and the children
gaze around, enthralled in wonder.   And
William now addresses the children, as
well as the camera.

WILLIAM

Do you remember the tale of the Emperor's new clothes? And who was the only person in the city who could see they weren't really there? A child. Well, I believe that children are given a simple gift ... a gift of sight. It's a gift we older people later lose along the way. You see, young people can see what's really there without a lifetime of superstitions or beliefs getting in the way. They can see things that are often not what they seem. And sometimes what children see will stagger your imaginations.

Feature the children. And it is clear that their imaginations are already being profoundly stimulated by what they are hearing.

WILLIAM

So I set about to collect a series of stories - stories of mystery, the supernatural, stories of ordinary people doing extraordinary things that happen to them along the way. Witnessed through the eyes of a child. Would you like to hear some? Okay, here goes. Close your eyes and imagine - this.

William closes his eyes, as do the children.

The camera moves in to whatever cast we are featuring in the promotional reel - as if they are whisked away to participate in the clip of the story William is telling...

CHAPTER FIVE

JOURNAL: OCTOBER 1998

The Cumulus distribution stand, D3,02. was located on the second level of the massive 21,000 m2 exhibition hall in the Palais de Festivals in Cannes, France. The event was not open to the general public. Only those in the broadcasting and media industry. Delegates attended from over 100 different countries.

Ray had arrived early with some executives from the Cloud 9 London office who had flown in on the morning flight. It was a matter of routine for them on the opening day of the festival to check out the stand.

As always, the Cumulus team had done a good job. Everything was in order. Pamphlets were displayed in all the racks, posters on the walls, the desks looked neat, enough chairs were available for buyers, and the bank of monitors all seemed to work when he tested the promo reels of all the trailers.

It seemed no time at all since Ray had written out the basic structure and footage had been shot for the 'A Twist In The Tale' promotional reel in excited anticipation as MIPCOM quickly approached, and he had worked with the post production team back in New Zealand choosing clips, editing, track laying music, then finally going into the mixing suite to bring it all together.

With a new series also in production, he didn't have a lot of time to spend on the trailer. He was keen to keep on top of the next series and ensure that it was bedding down, especially that the young cast were settling into their new roles and a new routine at the Cloud 9 studios.

The theme of a world with no adults provided for some really gritty story lines. And Ray also wanted to monitor how they were reacting to the material, and if they - as well as the entire team - could cope with the shooting schedule. 52 episodes had been planned over a six month production period and that was ambitious, to say the least.

The editing suite was located on the ground floor, at the back of the main Cloud 9 studio building. It was an alien environment and always reminded Ray of another world. The vast room was forever in semi darkness, slightly illuminated by an array of lights on the huge mixing desk which looked more like a high tech and overly complex control panel of a futuristic space craft.

Beyond the desk, a huge screen displayed all the assembled footage with a burnt in time code running at the bottom, outlining not only minutes but milliseconds to reference any changes which would have to be made.

Behind the desk the engineer and assistants sat in comfort in high back, deeply cushioned swivel chairs on small rollers for ease of movement along the desk, adjusting levels while they worked in a slow, methodical, pedantic manner going over all the elements to mix down and marry the sounds to the visuals.

The mixing team, along with editors and tracklayers - as well as Ray, when he was in post production mode - lived in a reclusive world of solitude within the post production rooms and suites. With no windows and isolated by thick walls so as not to be disturbed by any noise of everyday life, they were almost cut off from the outside world with no awareness of time.

Yet they were immersed with and constantly referring to the time-codes in all the raw material footage measured by 24 frames each passing second. Which meant that they were all working to the absolute minutia, dealing with milliseconds of time. Often deciding to start a music cue a few frames earlier or later, which was barely perceptual, being no more than a blink of an eye.

It was possible to insert a frame of footage in the television or motion picture world to penetrate the subconscious, known as subliminal advertising, which is illegal and had been banned from the very start of the industry, having been proven that although a frame inserted of someone drinking an ice cold beverage may not be seen at all on a conscious level - subliminally it was noted.

The same principals occurred in editing footage. With the only difference being that those who completed these tasks - and professionally did them for a living - were skilled enough to identify both on a conscious and subconscious level even if a 1/4 frame did not work due to a jump cut. So if one divided a second by the 24 frames and took a 1/4 of the net result - that would best illustrate the level of minute detail.

Tightening a shot by a few frames, or starting a sound effect or music cue or a dissolve a fraction of a second earlier or later could affect the overall flow of the material on which they were working. And ultimately affect the experience of the consumer.

As with subliminal advertising, a member of the general public might not be aware on a conscious level that something jarred in what they were watching or hearing - but subliminally would certainly note if an element just didn't seem quite right and it could abstractly influence a conscious level of enjoyment.

As always, the reel was finished with little or no time to spare so that the trailer could be shipped to Cannes to arrive in time for the television Festival.

So when Ray viewed it again on the stand, he knew every millisecond of it, having been immersed with the post production team in New Zealand.

It played all day continuously on a loop on the main screen on the MIPCOM stand. By the end of the festival, even the Cumulus distribution team began to feel as if they had been brainwashed by the footage and would have every second of it committed to memory.

Ray had briefed the team over dinner the pervious night at the Hotel Juana, in Juan les Pins, on the objectives of the week. The core focus would be on the launch of 'William Shatner's A Twist in the Tale'. But it was important as well to try and license any territories available regarding all the other titles in Cloud 9's catalogue which had been produced to date.

In addition, Ray wanted to let some of the key buyers know about the exciting new series which had commenced principal photography, just so that they were aware of what was coming down the line - but didn't want to provide too much detail and detract from the launch of William's series.

'Don't know if I like the title,' Cumulus's director of sales said. 'Keeping The Dream Alive sounds more of a theme.'

Ray agreed and explained where it originated from. And that it had actually served as a theme in many ways for his entire life.

'I thought of another title - Power and Chaos', Ray reflected.

The team laughed, thinking it was a humorous reference to the modus operandi of the fledgling company which was growing so fast that many in the industry tipped it as one to watch, feeling that it might well evolve to be a major entity in the industry. Some had even referred to it as being like a new Disney but Ray thought that was just due to the fact that Cloud 9 had produced mainly classic titles to date which targeted at a family audience with a child bias.

He wondered what the reference point would be after the new series was premiered at the following festival in April. He was really pushing the story line boundaries. And wouldn't be surprised if anyone suggested a change of company name, feeling that rather than Cloud 9, Anarchy might be more appropriate.

Ray could see what the Cumulus team meant about a title such as Power and Chaos. Although Cloud 9 was making its mark as a powerful new force in the industry - it left a degree of chaos in its wake.

The company was certainly prolific but perhaps lacked the infrastructure to accommodate all the activity. It wasn't the norm for a young upstart company like Cloud 9 to have its own distribution entity.

Cumulus was a wholly owned subsidiary and like its parent company, was punching way above its weight.

And it was highly unusual also to have a producer and writer sit on the stand to take meetings with buyers. But they found it refreshing to actually meet someone from the creative side.

They were normally used to dealing with distribution sales people. Ray was very hands on throughout the production process and knew the product inside out, so there was never any question asked that did not receive an answer.

The down side was that as much as the buyers enjoyed having the opportunity to meet and discuss creative matters with Ray, he was equally intrigued to meet buyers and gain an insight into that aspect of the industry. So his assistant was hard pressed to keep him on schedule to maintain all the meetings which had been planned.

Besides, Ray still struggled with any notion of time. And realized that he could bring about a fair amount of chaos himself with all his rituals and eccentricities.

He smiled at the thought of Power and Chaos paying homage to Cloud 9 but advised that he was actually being serious, only deciding to dismiss the title as it didn't really say what the series would be all about.

Thematically, although an element was indeed about Power and Chaos, the series was also positive and aspirational, about hope. So until he came up with anything better, he decided on using Keeping The Dream Alive as a working title.

Ray was proud of the Cumulus team. And held all of them in the highest regard. All were very bright and enthusiastic, with a passionate belief in the Cloud 9 product, convinced that all the shows in the portfolio were of a unique quality to appeal to their intended demographic target audience.

Like Ray, they all had busy MIPCOM schedules as well, with their diaries jammed packed with back to back meetings all week either on the stand or over breakfast, lunch and dinner with buyers from their particular territories.

One member of the team looked after South and Latin America, another the United States and Canada, yet another the Middle and Far East. Regions such as Australasia, Eastern and Western Europe, Japan, China, Asia had been divided amongst other members of the team to ensure adequate coverage.

All had great hopes that 'William Shatner's A Twist in the Tale' would follow the success of the previous five series produced to date. From the reactions of the buyers on the opening day of the festival, it was certainly shaping up that way.

The bank of monitors on the stand continually displayed all the trailers of all the Cloud 9 series available. And there were private screening rooms if any client or member of the press from any country wished to view any particular material.

The main official press conference had been scheduled for the following evening at the 5 star Carlton Hotel, which William Shatner would attend to take questions, along with Ray after the trailer was shown, with clips from some of the episodes.

And it was a great success. Cloud 9's press agent advised that she envisioned the series would receive prime coverage around the world and that she would circulate all the clippings post the festival.

'William Shatner's A Twist in the Tale' featured on the front page of the MIPCOM Daily News the following morning. It was an important industry publication. And to obtain such prime coverage was a real achievement given all the product which was available.

Also considering all the 'A' list marquee names in attendance over the course of the week. And especially the fact that Cloud 9 was only a small independent production company, like a David competing with Goliath - being all the iconic household brand names from Disney to Fox, Warner Bros. to Paramount.

'I think some of the majors will be starting to feel a little threatened,' the Cumulus team smiled, reflecting on all the coverage.

'Competition is good. For them. And us. It makes everyone try just that little bit harder,' Ray replied, aware that complacency was the kiss of commercial death. Not wishing to put a hex on any good fortune by being overly confident, he cautioned, 'But let's not get too carried away. It's early days and we've still got a long way to go.'

That was not to say that he wasn't encouraged that the series was being so well received. Because he was. But Ray had long since learned that in this business one should never count on anything and was keen for all the team - as well as himself - to remain focussed on doing the best they could do, rather than starting to believe their own press.

But the significance of press coverage and the growing profile of the company had not gone unnoticed either. With over 12,000 delegates representing all the major broadcasters and distributors, Cloud 9 was competing with not only the best in Hollywood but the best in the entire world, and was pleased with the progress.

No doubt William Shatner had made a difference to help the spotlight shine on Cloud 9. His name attracted, as with any marquee cast, a great interest. But Ray instinctively knew that the company he had founded was also very quickly evolving into a brand which brought about a great feeling of pride in all of his team and what they were achieving.

The next morning, Ray had breakfast with William and his wife Nerine, who had starred in one of the Twist in the Tale episodes, A Ghost Of Our Own, under her stage name Nerine Kidd. She was excellent in the role and popular with the cast and crew, as indeed was William.

Ray thanked them both for attending the Festival to launch the series. As they all said their goodbyes and agreed to keep in touch, Ray felt a wave of sadness when William and Nerine left for the airport. He had bonded with them both during the production and would miss spending time with them. And he hoped he would have the pleasure of working with William again at some point in the future.

William was a charismatic actor of depth. But Ray considered him also to be an absolutely fascinating and compassionate human being, with a mischievous sense of humor, a substantial intellect, and range of interests from writing himself, to breeding quarter horses at his ranch in Arizona, which William was particularly passionate about.

He and Nerine had an affinity with all animals and the natural world. And like Ray, also a great respect for our Mother Earth and were concerned about environmental issues. They seemed to really enjoy their time in New Zealand, a nuclear-free country, also aspiring to protect the planet with an enviable reputation of being clean and green.

With limited time and a hectic production schedule, Ray tried to arrange some sightseeing whenever there was a gap, including chartering an aircraft to visit Kaikoura in the South Island, where they all embarked upon a boat to observe marine life, which was a memorable and special event for all concerned.

In addition to seals, penguins and dolphins, they encountered Albatross and Petrels, but were overwhelmed seeing a magnificent sperm whale surfacing, its huge dorsal fin arcing as if in slow motion as the mammal dove down spectacularly back into the depths of the ocean.

Ray would never forget the look of sheer wonder and joy in their eyes. And often recalls that day when he thinks of William and especially Nerine, who drowned in a tragic accident in her swimming pool at home less than three years later.

The following days at MIPCOM sped past in a blur of back to back meetings morning, noon and night, just as they had at previous festivals. With several hundred other distributors also playing their promotional reels on their own stands and the throngs of crowds constantly flowing through all the floors in the vast building, there was a cacophony of noise which coalesced into one continual wall of sustained sound, like the buzzing of a billion bees.

Like someone afflicted with tinitus, Ray was sure he could even hear it in the recesses of his inner ear when he was not in the main exhibition hall and the sound still remained well into late evening back at the hotel.

Along with suffering jet lag, he found it difficult to enjoy any semblance of a peaceful sleep.

The days at MIPCOM felt long but the nights seemed to be even longer. After discussing the Cloud 9 portfolio of product over dinner, entertaining key account buyers or broadcasters, and with New Zealand being 12 hours ahead, Ray contacted the production team by phone to check in on the progress of the day's filming schedule.

'We got the day,' his executive in charge of production advised. This was the term used when the amount of footage planned to be shot had been achieved.

'How many minutes?' Ray asked, wanting to clarify. And was told that the studio unit had obtained just over twelve, with the parallel unit on location doing eight, which was really something.

In motion pictures three minutes of material would have been thought to be moving fast. In television, with a multi camera set up covering all the angles in a studio, eight minutes was a high target. So combining the two units meant that the team had shot about twenty minutes of material and must have been moving like greased lightning.

'How are all the cast?'

'We're keeping an eye on the young lad, Paul. His performance is great but he seems to be a bit homesick. Other than that, everyone's doing just fine.'

Ray was relieved. It was normal for some of the younger cast to miss their families, being away from home. But once they got settled into a new routine, they usually got over the initial feelings of homesickness. So Ray wasn't overly concerned. He relayed news on how the festival was going and promised to check in again the following day. Or in Ray's case, his night.

The problem was that he felt even more alert after the phone calls. So rather than lay in bed with all he had swirling around in his mind, he would usually get up, spend an hour or two sketching out ideas, any creative or logistical thoughts, which made him feel even more awake.

In no time at all his wake up call came and he had to rush to prepare for a breakfast meeting, feeling exhausted, resolving never again to stay up until the early hours. But that rarely happened throughout any festivals he attended. And this MIPCOM was no exception.

Ray welcomed the chance to take meetings outside of the main exhibition hall. It was also known in the industry as the bunker, due to the frenzy of noise and activity, and he spent most of the week rushing between his appointments on the Cumulus stand and in the nearby hotels. Or on the decks of the yachts. But preferred to have key business discussions over lunch at one of the many fine dining establishments in the picturesque old town of Cannes.

He also managed to walk around the exhibition hall to see what other product was on offer in order to do market research. His assistant had always been instructed to leave some space open on the very last day so that Ray could have time to process the events of the week, which he liked to do over a stroll by himself around the harbor. It was part of the tradition. A chance to slow down to reflect and try somehow to recharge.

And it always made Ray smile as he nostalgically walked along the jetty where the producer's yacht had been moored at the Film Festival and he affectionally recalled his first visit to Cannes.

CHAPTER SIX

JOURNAL: 1982

After the aborted Bengal Lancer film, Ray's agent submitted the first draft of the screenplay as an example of Ray's work to several producers, resulting in a commission to write a motion picture adaptation of a novel, 'The Uninvited' - about alien abductions.

Ray was relieved that no-one had read the last draft of the screenplay he had just written, sure they would have thought he was from another galaxy himself, killing off the hero in the first reel.

Sitting in his study, Ray became aware that although on one hand he was staring at a blank page and four walls, working as a writer meant that he could be anywhere in the world - or universe - that he wanted to be. Sharing his time with all manner of characters. From terrorists to hero Sheriffs, as in his first novel. Then he was transported back to the turn of the century in the North West frontier on 'The Bengal Lancers'. Now he was immersed with aliens and extra terrestrial themes, which gave him goose bumps at times. Even if it had all evolved from his own mind.

The story was chilling and the characters so real that Ray cast a suspicious glance out of the window at the gardener trimming the hedges, wondering if he was human. Or in reality from another world, soon to beam Ray up into a spaceship and whisk him away to another galaxy to experiment upon.

He found the entire writing process to be so difficult but yet so intriguing. And the experiences he encountered and 'people' he lived with every day and night was solely limited by the scope of his imagination.

After 'The Uninvited' Ray worked on another screenplay, 'The Last Samurai'. Then he was invited to meet Tony Adams, the producing partner of Blake Edwards, who was married to Julie Andrews. They were all in the UK shooting 'Victor Victoria' at Pinewood, in Iver Heath, Buckinghamshire which had become an institution in British cinema with so many classics filmed at the legendary studio.

Coming off the successful motion picture production of '10', starring Dudley Moore and Bo Derek, Tony was interested in an original story Ray was also working on called 'Hot Shot' and commissioned a screenplay which was well received. But Ray was disappointed that it got lost in what is known as development hell. A state of limbo where a project is put on hold. Seemingly indefinitely.

Ray later discovered that all in the industry suffer from it at one time or another. Some continually. Even if anyone is 90% sure that a project will happen, in reality it is still 100% unsure. And a project could collapse at any time due to a myriad of complex reasons.

For all that a producer might have an adequate track record and be committed to the project, he or she may be unable to bring all the elements together to green-light production due to recoupment structures, for instance.

Motion pictures and even television are considered to be very high risk for investors. The return can be substantial but the general rule of thumb in the industry is that an investor should never consider investing any more than what he could comfortably afford to lose.

So all manoeuvre themselves in a preferential recoupment position to mitigate any risks and maximize potential returns. Often seeking a percentage of the gross rather than the net, referred to in the industry as the back end, when prints, advertising, distribution and other expenses are taken into account, as well as the actual production costs and then profit participation kick-in.

If all the business and fiscal elements came together - sometimes schedules might place a project on hold if a director was not available until a certain time, which might then conflict with the availabilities of the cast.

And then if the schedules worked with the preferred cast or director having a window to do the project, elements of finance might unexpectedly drop out. When that was fixed, the cast or director may not be available again due to the delay so a producer might seek alternative names in the marketplace able to commit to a revised production start date.

Only to discover that they might not be on the so called 'wish list' and suitable to an investor.

When that was rectified and an alternate name was found, there could be a problem with the fiscal again which had fallen due to the delay.

Many producers continually live in an elongated series of frustrating, ever decreasing circles resolving one problem only to discover another had surfaced.

And writers suffered as a result in development hell. Hardly surprising that patience and persistence - and hope - are the operative words for all in the industry.

Although some projects in development hell never see the light of day, others resurrect and go into production. Eventually. But it might take several years, as occurred with Alistair Maclean's 'Unaco Files' which Ray had been commissioned to adapt following 'Hot Shot'.

After being lost and Ray thought probably buried forever, never to be seen or heard of again, the producer was successful in realizing production many years later. But in another incarnation. The project evolved into something entirely different to the one originally envisaged - 'Death Train' starring Pierce Brosnan.

Even 'The Last Samurai' was destined to come to the silver screen much later in a vehicle ironically shot in New Zealand starring Tom Cruise. But only the title remained the same. Ray's version was written for his favorite actor, Toshiro Mifune, who had inspired him so when he was a boy, after seeing the Japanese classic 'The Seven Samurai'.

With Ray's reputation starting to spread, in addition to receiving commissions to write screenplays, he was also offered the role as a script doctor on many projects, where he was hired to rewrite screenplays. He received good fees. But hated it.

Not so much as a result of a screenplay being dead upon arrival, with no hope of being resuscitated, but more that Ray felt for the original writers, knowing all about the painful process of putting one's heart on a page and he had difficulty reconciling this sentiment with whatever the reason or need for the rewrite.

He was going to get involved with 'Free Willie', the story of a whale being set free, but asked his agent not to pursue it as he read the screenplay and did not think he could bring anything better to the piece.

Besides, in his view, the title gave the story away. He knew exactly what was going to happen. Hollywood never wanted unhappy endings or for heroes to fail. Perhaps there is merit in that, with a mainstream audience probably feeling the same way. It wasn't exactly a matter of writing to a recipe. But Ray discovered that there was a required formula. In motion pictures, if a producer or studio sets out to make apple pie, they will expect that a writer will never try and make it with cherries. Until another recipe became 'in fashion'. Only then, different or new ingredients could be introduced.

Being a sought after script doctor may have coveted Ray's bank account - but there was no sum of money in existence which could save his undernourished creative soul. So he decided to check out what opportunities might exist in television.

His track record to date at least attracted some initial interest but no offers were forthcoming. Ray wondered if it might be down to his lack of education and qualifications. The BBC's definition of equal opportunities seemed to be to recruit half from Oxford and half from Cambridge.

There were a lot of other graduates in the marketplace with first class degrees knocking on the doors of ITV and Channel 4, as well as at the BBC. With the old boy network still rampant in Britain and also playing a part, it seemed virtually impossible to get even a foot in the door, let alone a discussion with any producer who might give Ray a start.

Feeling more and more disillusioned, Ray thought his agent had given up. But undeterred, he wrote to all the producers and script editors time and time again himself, enclosing copies of his screenplays as examples of his work.

And one day he received an unexpected call from a script editor at the BBC inviting him in for a chat.

'It's a different discipline,' the editor explained, trying to get Ray to understand why his screenplay credits to date elicited a seemingly uninterested response.

'It might be - but it's still writing,' Ray replied, still not grasping what the editor meant.

'That doesn't mean to say that being able to write in one medium necessarily means that it's possible to write in another. So many novelists are unable to adapt their work for film.'

'Well, I can understand that,' Ray reflected. 'I found it really difficult to get a screenplay in the right shape on 'The Number To Call Is .. ' and 'The Uninvited' was a real struggle.'

'It's unusual that you managed it. Believe me. Playwrights often can't adapt to television. A successful writer in television might not take to working on a book or doing something for the stage. And a journalist might not have a clue about how to structure a screenplay. Yes, it's all writing but it requires a different focus. And skill. Some can do it but not many, I can tell you. For anyone that can turn their hands to a different medium .... it's the exception rather than the rule.'

That made sense to Ray the more he thought about it. And besides, the script editor was experienced enough in the industry to know. He was highly respected for his editing work at the BBC but also an acclaimed writer on his own account and Ray was somewhat in awe.

The script editor was none other than Mervyn Haisman. He was currently working on 'The Enigma Files'. And had been the writer or script editor of some of Ray's favorite series that he watched on the BBC growing up. Such as 'Emergency Ward 10', 'Dixon of Dock Green' and 'Doctor Finlay's Casebook'.

But it was another Doctor which elevated Merv into the level of almost hero worship in Ray's eyes.

Mervin, along with his collaborator, Henry Lincoln, had written for 'Doctor Who' during the Patrick Troughton years of playing the role, including the creation of 'The Abominable Snowman', 'The Web of Fear' and 'The Dominators'. The episodes featured two enduring monsters, the Yeti and the Quarks, which Ray found to be as gripping as the ominous Daleks who intimidated him when he watched the series as a young boy, stealing wide eyed looks behind the couch.

Little did Ray know at the time that the writer would become a mentor, as well as a dear and valued friend. In later years Ray commissioned Merv to write many episodes in Cloud 9's portfolio.

Back then at the BBC he was script editing a series called 'Squadron' and took a huge gamble deciding to give Ray his start in television.

'Squadron' was about a rapid deployment RAF special forces unit. The BBC had been able to secure the full backing of the Ministry of Defense for location filming at various air force bases, with the balance being shot in standing studio sets.

All the so-called hardware was also to be made available and Ray set out to RAF Odium in Hampshire to research his episode which concerned a story of chopper pilots. It was a thrill, to say the least, but also nerve wracking to fly with the military in Puma and Chinook helicopters. But more frightening to be faced with the challenges of writing his very first television script.

Merv and the producer were pleased with the end result, enough to commission another episode. And at long last Ray would see his creative work being filmed rather than going through the endless development process which he experienced working on the motion picture side of the industry.

It certainly seemed a lot faster and easier to get into production in television, with fewer complications, Ray thought, compared to film.

Wrong!

The Argentinians invaded the Falkland Islands and Britain went to war. Which meant that the RAF had more pressing matters to attend to, urgently deploying most of their resources to the Falklands theatre rather than making it all available for a BBC television series.

So as with motion pictures, Ray became aware that television also had in reality a myriad of unknown hurdles which could surface at any time. The unexpected situation with 'Squadron' required drastic rewrites. Nevertheless, the series completed production and was well received by the audience and critics alike when it was transmitted.

This led to another commission at the BBC for a new project in development, 'The Boatbuilders'. Ray was commissioned to write an episode and during the process met another young aspiring writer, Harry Duffin, who was assistant script editor on the series.

Ray warmed to Harry's easy going personality and sense of humor, as well as respecting his creative abilities, integrity and great passion he had for the craft. Both men were almost kindred spirits and would become great friends, destined to work together on several occasions in the future, culminating in Ray recruiting Harry in the future as Head of Development of Cloud 9.

After delivering his Boatbuilders script, Ray was, as always, unsure of what the reaction would be but was relieved to discover that the producer was impressed enough to commission another episode. Then another. And yet another. Ray seemed to have grasped the tone and flavor of what was required to such an extent that he became lead writer on the family saga, which also changed its name during the course of post production.

'Howard's Way' was first broadcast on BBC1 in September 1985 and very quickly took Britain by storm, achieving high ratings in the coveted prime time Sunday evening slot.

Over the ensuing seasons, as well as lead writer, Ray was offered the role of story and script consultant, which meant that he worked closely with the producer, shaping the series, and now had script editors working to him. He also gained valuable experience across the entire logistical and production process.

The series sold well overseas and was a significant breakthrough in Ray's career in television. 'Howard's Way' emotionally connected with its audience in a very special way, to such an extent that it is still affectionally referred to by many as one of the BBC's best loved drama series even to this day, enjoying a resurgence through an international release of all six seasons of DVD.

But not all memories are happy. The nature of what the biggest problem Ray had encountered during filming or getting established in the industry was always a favorite of journalists and asked in press conferences.

It was a question Ray found difficult to answer. Like what is a favorite piece of music? He would need volumes of books to record the diverse range of problems he had experienced throughout his career to date. So it was impossible to choose just one. And certainly how to obtain his first break was also a major hurdle.

If he was pressed, the time with the most heartache was when the lead actor on 'Howard's Way' suffered an unexpected heart attack and died. Ray had become a close friend with the actor and was both saddened and shocked by his passing. He really felt for the actor's family who struggled and just could not come to terms with it.

The entire cast were devastated as well but through their grief had to continue filming as the tragic event occurred half way through production. And Ray had to place his own sense of loss to one side to re-write all the scripts to explain the sudden disappearance.

The problem was compounded by the fact that episodes are produced out of sequence and in an entirely different way than when they are screened at home and enjoyed by a viewer.

Most of the location footage had been completed by the time the lead actor had passed away but very few interior studio scenes had been shot. So the stories would make no sense with the gaps in continuity as nothing would match and cut together at all.

So Ray had to use what existing footage had been completed and come up with an entirely different story line and series of scripts to fuel the balance of production. The only possible way to resolve what happened was to imply that the character had also died, being lost at sea.

Story wise, it all worked out well. But Ray found the pressure of delivering the revised material difficult to bear on a professional level.

On a personal level he had no option but to try and compartmentalize the loss of his friend and the concern and sympathy he had for the actor's family.

It was difficult to reconcile all the emotions. He had experienced a role as a script doctor but felt almost like a creative mortician and found the entire event to be not only distressing but slightly surreal and macabre in many ways.

After 78 episodes of 'Howard's Way', Ray oversaw yet another popular drama series, 'Trainer', which ran for two years. In parallel to that assignment, he was approached to consult to the Head of Drama Series.

This led him to later become Head of Development, where Ray read and commented on new formats, along with a range of scripts for new projects being developed at the time, such as 'Eastenders' and 'Casualty', as well as existing favorites, from 'Bergerac' to 'All Creatures Great And Small'.

He enjoyed and was especially proud to see the BBC targeting a family audience with classic titles, such as the acclaimed production of Arthur Ransom's 'Swallows and Amazons', along with Gerald Durrell's 'My Family and Other Animals'.

When his contract expired in 1991, Ray decided not to renew it, preferring to go freelance and return to his original writing and new producing aspirations.

Over the following two years he developed a new series, 'Starting Over', for the talented and popular actress, Maureen Lipton, along with another long form drama, 'Winners and Losers', for Yorkshire Television, which was thought to be an ideal vehicle for Nick Berry and was in the franchise document for the commercial Network, ITV.

But just as Ray thought he had learned all about the vagaries in the industry, he was still in for a few more surprises. And disappointments.

He had come to realize that all it would take was for one person to say yes to green light a new project, even if one thousand said no.

Which was an important aspect to remember in order to maintain the motivation when trying to launch a new title, especially if no-one was remotely interested.

After a marathon to get all at Yorkshire Television to enthusiastically say yes to 'Winners and Losers', Ray was thrilled by all the support and that so many really believed in the project.

But he ended up devastated when, with the finishing line so close and in sight, he was to discover that one person said no at the ITV Network Centre. That was the last hurdle. And 'Winners and Losers' fell.

In later years Yorkshire Television would find great success with another vehicle starring Nick Berry - 'Heartbeat'. Easy to see why many in the industry consider it similar to playing a torturous game of musical chairs. Or snakes and ladders. Just as one might feel they are up, they can very quickly slide down. And when down, a meeting or even a phone call can herald something exciting and before long one can be up again.

Ray wanted to have more control of that game. Rather than have any third party decide his fate, he had become intrigued with the notion of starting his own independent production company. With the advent of deregulation in Great Britain, which was introduced to provide a so-called level playing field for all in the industry, the time felt right.

Deregulation would give the independent sector an opportunity of retaining a share in intellectual property, being the copyright of creative work, along with more editorial control, with broadcasters being required to operate in a free market commissioning from the independent sector rather than themselves, which spawned a monopolistic and tired approach to the industry.

So Ray set about developing a business plan.

But he lacked enough working capital and decided to test the reaction of various banks, starting at the very top with Coutts, a prestigious private bank patronized by several high net worth individuals, including the Royal family and even HM the Queen.

After researching, Ray liked the tradition and continuity of the bank which was steeped in history, having been established in the Strand in 1692. A gleaming brass plaque proudly stated that fact outside the listed character building.

Ray thought it felt more like a gentleman's club than a bank when he arrived, with all the employees wearing morning suits, complete with pin-striped trousers and tails.

'We would be delighted to advise on all fiscal matters,' the Head of Finance said humbly, as Ray sat in front of the desk.

'That's a relief,' replied Ray, concerned that the bank might not wish to be involved with television and motion pictures. 'The industry is notorious for being high risk.'

'But the returns can be significant,' replied the Head of Finance. 'We bank many in the world of media. And you can be assured that we will remain .... discreet.'

'Thank you. That's encouraging. So what kind of services do you provide?' Ray probed carefully.

'That all depends on the sums one has on deposit. You are interested primarily in investment, I gather.'

'Yes,' said Ray, feeling a little uneasy now. 'But I don't think it's the type of investment you mean.'

'What sums are we talking about? How much would you like to deposit? A million? Two million?'

'I wasn't interested in depositing anything actually. I was hoping more that I could borrow ten million.'

The Head of Finance almost fell off his chair and from his sick expression Ray could see that what he originally had in mind seemed like a good idea at the time.

But now he would have to rethink and come up with another plan.

CHAPTER SEVEN

JOURNAL: NOVEMBER, 1966

Ray sat gripping the sides of the seat. He couldn't understand the aerodynamics and how an aircraft could actually climb to an altitude of 30,000 feet when they had taken off from London Heathrow, let alone how on earth a piece of machinery this weight and size was able to stay airborne for so many hours.

He glanced nervously out of the window. All he could see were a few stars twinkling in the darkness. Surely they must be over the Atlantic by now and nearing Toronto's Malton Airport.

But how would the pilots know? How would anyone know where they were going? And above all, how to get there?

It wasn't as if a pilot would be told to head north for a few hours, look for the 15,000th star, turn right for another few hours till the 150th set of clouds, take the next left and Canada would be found about three miles below.

What happens if they were lost and ran out of fuel and the aircraft plunged out of control into the endless depths of the ocean? They would have no chance of survival. And be sure to drown. Maybe if it occurred over land? But not if a distress call couldn't give some indication of where all the poor souls on board might be trapped in the entangled wreckage.

What if they had to resort to cannibalism? To stay alive until rescue came. If it came.

He glanced at his family in the front rows. They would have nothing to worry about. He could never think of them as a snack. But what if they or any other passenger thought Ray whetted the appetite. And might be tasty?

Ray stole an uneasy glance out of the corner of his eye at the man sitting next to him. He looked to be the type who could be a cannibal. The man noticed Ray having a sneaky glance, and nodded with a faint trace of a smile. But it seemed more like a manic and sinister grimace.

With his bulging eyes and aquiline bony face, the man looked like a cross between a mad axe murderer who might even nibble on himself in order to survive and a Zombie from a horror movie who had already died. Years ago.

Just hope the man can't read peoples' minds, Ray thought. Then he would be in trouble. He had avoided eye contact and getting into any kind of conversation for the entire flight. Sure that if he looked up the meaning of the word weirdo in a dictionary - Ray would find a photograph of the man there.

In an emergency he would probably plunge a knife into Ray's back to get to the door first.

Ray tried to dismiss it all from his mind. But he couldn't. His imagination continued to outline a range of tragic scenarios which made him feel nauseous.

He just hoped the pilots knew where they were heading and that they would arrive soon so he could get his feet on solid ground.

Ray recalled seeing newsreel footage of the Pope visiting a country once and kissing the ground when he disembarked from the aircraft. Perhaps he felt the same way about flying. If Ray ever got off this plane alive, he resolved that he would kiss the pilot. Well, maybe not. But certainly the ground.

The flight was the first time the family had ever been on board an aircraft. Ray didn't enjoy the sensation at all. The aged Boeing 707 jet didn't seem to handle turbulence well. Ray sat, white-knuckled, watching the flight attendants most of the time, trying to read expressions. If they looked calm, then he felt a little more reassured.

But one in particular appeared to be very worried now as they hit yet another patch of turbulence and the aircraft lurched to one side and started to descend, as if it was falling right out of the sky.

Ray leapt out of his seat and followed the flight attendant to the galley. 'What's going on?!'

'Sit down and fasten your seat belt!,' she replied in equal panic.

'Why?! Are we crashing or something?!'

'Crashing?!'

'I saw you back there. You looked really worried. What is it? The plane seems to be losing height! Are we going down?!'

'I hope so. And you'd be worried with all I have to do when we start the final descent.'

'The final descent! Oh my God! I knew it!!!'

'Good. So please sit down and fasten your seat belt. We don't have much time. We'll soon be coming in to land.'

Ray returned to his seat, re-buckled his belt and took a few deep breaths trying to control his fear.

Now he was concerned and tried to work out how this huge hulk of machinery would ever be able to touch down safely without skidding off the runway, bringing certain death to all, when the pilot announced that it was snowing heavily at their destination.

As with most lessons at school, Ray was not that strong on geography. He knew where Canada was in the world, of course, but little else about the country and had visions of living with wolves and bears and moose. His father scoffed and tried to explain that there might be wildlife in the outskirts of Ontario but Toronto was a city.

Even still, it came as a bit of a surprise for Ray when he noticed out of the cabin window the twinkling lights of the vast metropolis of Toronto and surrounding suburbs sprawled out below as the aircraft banked for its final approach. And landed safely.

Ray and his family had never felt so cold in their life as they walked carefully down the icy steps from the aircraft. Rather than a new country, it was as if they had set foot in a gigantic freezer compartment.

Crouching to kiss the ground, Ray noticed his fellow passenger, the axe killer, looking at him strangely.

But Ray's mother was more than likely the one to strangle him if he didn't get a move on. The family just wanted to get into the warmth of the terminal. The snow was more like a blizzard now.

His parents fully realized that the move to Canada could provide a wonderful opportunity for the entire family, a real step up with a chance for a better lifestyle. But his mother had reservations about emigrating, having become settled in Windsor. In the end, the job offer was just too tempting to refuse. So she agreed to go, just as long as they would return to their homeland someday. Ray's father thought that could happen within about five years.

The new company, where his dad would work as an industrial engineer, arranged rental accommodation.

And it was fascinating for Ray and his family to experience a new culture, especially during the lead-up to December 25th, with houses decorated with bright, festive lights outside, as well as inside, the homes. With so much snow, the ambience was really festive. Bing would never have to dream of a White Christmas.

Ray's job was to stand in a trench, banked by huge levels of packed snow either side, and shovel sand on the path leading to the driveway to chart a safe passage to the car so the family could leave the house to go Christmas shopping and explore their new and exciting environment.

The tires on the car had to be bound by snow chains to provide grip and any hope of maintaining traction on roads the snow ploughs had not yet cleared.

Ray's younger brother and sister were always uneasy by the huge clouds of what looked to be steam billowing around all the vehicles. Ray told the young ones that it might be dragons keeping a watch out for Santa Claus, to check which child was good or bad. But in reality it was the air emanating from the exhaust pipes and being exposed to sub zero temperatures. Which affected even the breathing of anyone walking outside, with streams of vapor pouring from their mouths.

The family had never experienced Sunday trading in England, with it being disallowed at that time and most shops closing every Wednesday afternoon. It had become a retail tradition for some reason. So in Canada it was a great novelty to be introduced to even late night shopping in mammoth plazas where trade occurred seven days a week.

There were just so many consumer outlets and services compared to England. From fast food takeaways to drive-in movies. And with all the televisions channels, commercial radio stations, multi lane highways, huge left-hand drive cars with sleek fins on the body work, Canada was reminiscent in many ways to the neighboring United States. Offering a totally different lifestyle to anything they had ever envisioned.

It took a little time to get used to it all, let alone become familiar with a new currency, political system, national anthem, flag, dual English and French language, and the Canadian accent.

With the school leaving age being around eighteen when students reached a stage known as grade thirteen, which was the required entry for university, Ray's parents tried to encourage him to consider furthering his education. But he wasn't too keen on the idea, though he was intrigued by his notion of what going to a high school might entail, perceiving it to be full of attractive cheerleading girls in search of someone to accompany them to a prom or dance.

So he decided to take a few months out before making any final decision, until the family moved into their new home, 3557 Golden Orchard Drive, which his parents bought in Applewood Hills.

The house was located in an affluent suburb within the commuter belt, being about a one hour drive to Toronto where Ray's father worked.

Ray's days were spent either practicing his guitar or reading books about the history and geography of the country which really interested him. After discovering the Canadian poet, Robert Service, along with the writer, Pierre Berton, Ray was especially keen to find out more about the gold rush which had occurred in British Columbia and in the Yukon at the turn of the century.

It was difficult to comprehend that these provinces were almost as far away as England. Between Ontario and out West stood Manitoba, Saskatchewan, Alberta and British Columbia. And then East, yet other provinces in the Maritimes which embodied a totally different culture and economic base. The country was certainly vast, with a range of valuable natural resources.

One would need to drive for days before leaving Ontario and Ray was determined to discover all that he could about Canada, especially as he knew that Grey Owl, whom he had read about as a child, had lived in a remote region of the province with the Mohawk Indians.

Ray also found another series about Indian tribal folklore in syndication which he watched on television every morning, featuring Hawkeye, a fur trader who encountered all manner of adventures with his faithful Indian companion, Chingachgook, the last of the Mohican Tribe.

The series was all based upon a historical novel by James Fenimore Cooper, first published in 1826, when France and Great Britain battled for control of the new colonies. During the war the French called upon allied Native American tribes to fight against the British colonial forces. Ray found it so intriguing that he set about researching the period further and tried to devise a story about a conflict between the tribes, but couldn't get beyond the first page.

As summer approached, Ray's parents were concerned to discover another interest which fascinated their son - sunbathing. He loved getting a tan and they were never sure if he was trying to make his olive skin become darker to emulate the indigenous race which seemed to intrigue him so. Or Elvis, believing that a deep sun tan might assist in attracting girls, which Ray was forever seeking out in the local shopping plazas.

He promised his mother and father that he would start looking for a job but just wanted to settle in a bit first and enjoy an impending summer holiday which had been planned.

As well as being freezing cold in winter, with sub zero temperatures, the climate in summer was so opposite to what the family had been used to in Britain. Sweltering hot and humid - so they decided to explore the area known as cottage country, staying at a log cabin in the lakes where it was a little cooler, though still very warm. In the scenic and unspoiled region of Muskoka, inhabited with chipmunks, raccoons and even bears, as well as tourists.

Ray spent most days swimming in the lake and reading music papers, counting down the new release of the Sgt Pepper Album. His obsession with the Beatles and their music was still as strong as ever. The four mop tops were as popular in Canada and America as they were in Britain or anywhere else in the world for that matter.

And their song 'All You Need Is Love' had become an anthem as the hippie movement also began to surface and spread throughout the globe following in the wake of Beatlemania.

A new generation was now placing flowers in their hair, as well as the barrels of guns, believing that to be better than bullets. Particularly in North America, when young people marched in protest against the Vietnam War. Others dodged the draft in the United States by heading across the border to take refuge in Canada.

Ray met many as he grew his hair even longer and hung out in Yorkville, a section in downtown Toronto, reminiscent to Greenwich village in New York City. Inhabited by a bohemian, avant guard community of painters, artists and musicians, along with hippies extolling that war could be over if people really wanted it. After all, it was the people who voted politicians into power.

Much to the relief of his parents, Ray was able to at least earn something reminiscent to a wage when he obtained a few gigs, performing in coffee clubs and bars.

Living in a small, rented room over one venue in Yorkville, The Night Owl, he encountered another struggling singer songwriter who was destined to make a huge name for himself in the music industry in later years. Neil Young.

To help subsidize the meagre income from performing on the Yorkville circuit, Ray obtained a job at CARA flight kitchens, but his parents were worried what the future might have in store if he did not embark upon a more defined and secure career path.

But he seemed to be occupied and was gaining life skills and experience, as well as being happy, which was all important for them. As far as an occupation was concerned, they were sure that an opportunity might manifest somewhere along the way.

One day Ray was more than happy, thrilled actually, to catch a glimpse of John Lennon who had arrived in Canada for the Toronto peace festival with Yoko Ono.

Loading and unloading food from the galleys of all the aircraft which arrived or departed, Ray thought he would faint when he saw his musical hero in the flesh. He was not only inspired by the Beatles' music but the poetic and profound lyrics of John Lennon, along with his radical stance on a range of political matters which had become at the forefront of his activities.

Like so many, Ray considered John Lennon to be more of a guru and applauded his mantra for the politicians of the world to give peace a chance, which seemed to reflect the aspiration of a new generation around the globe to build a better future and world.

Having a father who had experienced active service in the Second World War, Ray respected all the brave men and women in the forces who had placed themselves in harm's way for the freedom of their country - but found it difficult to reconcile at times the entire political system and why young men and women had been sent to fight in Vietnam in the first place.

One political party advocated one view, yet another spouted a totally different rhetoric, with both sounding equally convincing but each capable of doing a total about-turn when and if it suited them. The ensuing spin often obscured all the facts, as well as the very mandate which they had been elected to carry out.

Ray became aware that politicians appeared to be very adept at avoiding any question which they did not want to answer and he just wished they would say what they mean and mean what they say, rather than confuse people with such a contradiction of terms.

So many in power seemed to bring about total chaos as well as confusion, as to what was fact and what was fiction, designed to sway public opinion.

Power and Chaos. An interesting ideology - and theme for a story which Ray decided to try and write, but again he struggled to find a narrative and character framework on which to hang it. So he placed the thought on a shelf but was determined to come back to it one day.

Over the ensuing year he did manage however to write a few scripts based upon an idea he had for a television series set against the Klondike. But as with the majority of the miners seeking their fortune, did not strike gold. Ray received either no response or rejection letters from all the submissions he made to broadcasters.

A workmate at CARA, knowing of Ray's love of music, told him about a report he noticed on the television news. It concerned a company from Hollywood who were traveling through the entire United States of America and Canada, visiting all the major cities to audition for five unknowns for a new group which was being formed, 'The Organic Vegetables'.

Ray found out more information and decided to have a go, wondering if he should dress as a carrot to gain attention but dismissed the notion, thinking it would be tacky and uncool.

And he didn't rate his chances at all when he arrived at the television station to be confronted by a queue which seemed to stretch for miles around several blocks.

If it was like this in other cities, then the producers would be auditioning tens of thousands, so the statistics of him even being auditioned would be slim, let alone being short listed as a possible candidate for the group.

Several hours later Ray was paraded before the panel of casting agents to display what he could do and sang an original song which he had composed the previous night, accompanying himself on guitar.

He didn't think the song was particularly good and hadn't sang or played well due to nerves, but now, for some unexplained reason, had a strong sense that not only would he be shortlisted but he would actually be offered the opportunity to join the group - which was statistically impossible, like winning the lottery.

It was an odd feeling and one he could never really understand. The casting agents had been retained by one of the producers of 'The Monkeys', who were putting together a new group for a pilot for a similar series. So music was only one part, with acting being the other.

Ray was no actor, so he could offer no skill at all in that area which held no interest to him whatsoever. And he didn't really think of the Monkeys as a real group. They were more manufactured, so on a musical level it all had no real appeal either.

But the strangest thing was that as soon as he felt that he didn't really care if he would get the part or not, at the same time he just knew that it was destined to happen.

'That's a real credit to get through the first round, but don't hold your breath if you don't get any further,' his parents said proudly, viewing it all as a fantastic achievement but also trying to prepare their son, not wishing for him to raise his hopes only to be disappointed.

They thought he certainly had talent in music but with the amount of people who had been auditioning in all the cities across Canada and the United States, he wouldn't in reality stand that much of a chance, especially if music was only an element and acting skills were also required.

It came as no surprise to Ray though to receive a call advising that he was through to the next round and that he would be required to have a screen test.

Following this, he didn't hear any more, and thought maybe his instinct had been wrong. And was really not that bothered as it didn't appeal to him anyway.

So having forgotten all about it, he was surprised when he returned from his stint on the night shift at the airport to discover his mother sitting in shock almost six weeks later.

'I've just had a call from the office of that producer. In Hollywood. They want you to phone them urgently. And I don't want you to get any fancy ideas like I've been having, laddie ... but I don't think they would bother wanting to speak with you to tell you that you haven't got the part.'

Ray exchanged dumbfounded glances with his mother for what seemed to be an eternity before she smiled excitedly, urging him to get on the phone to see what it was all about. She couldn't stand the suspense for a second longer.

And when he phoned, Ray was advised that he was to be offered the role just as he had predicted, before putting it all out of his mind.

His father's solicitor glanced over the contracts. Everything seemed to be not only in order, but if it all worked out Ray could become a multi-millionaire. Celebrations were in order. Ray's parents held a party for their son.

After waiting forever to hear back, it was now all moving so quickly. Ray didn't even have time to work his notice at CARA. They were understanding, really pleased for him.

Ray was astonished when he said goodbye to some of his workmates that they even asked for his autograph, which he found to be embarrassing.

He was no-one and hadn't achieved anything to warrant such special attention. But the Canadian press had picked up on the story and overnight he had become a bit of a celebrity.

He was no longer the English emigrant but perceived to be the local boy made good, picked out of so many thousands and now due to travel to Hollywood, about to become a star.

CHAPTER EIGHT

JOURNAL: 1972

Fame and fortune didn't exactly await Ray's arrival, but the longest stretch chauffeur-driven limousine he had ever seen whisked him from Los Angeles Airport to the luxurious Sunset Marquis Hotel on Alta Loma, near Sunset Boulevard. Which was a popular and discreet favorite for many in the industry, including bands touring America.

After checking into his suite, Ray was a little taken aback to recognize so many familiar faces relaxing around the pool.

The following day he rubbed shoulders with more stars. Such as Cher, who was shopping in the same exclusive Beverly Hills boutique where representatives of the production company had taken Ray and the cast to purchase the wardrobe they would wear for a press photo shoot, prior to starting filming the show.

Like Ray, all the cast were awestruck. And they got a taste of what might lay in store when they all attended a Bee Gee sell out concert at the Santa Monica auditorium.

As the limousine pulled up to the backstage area, throngs of screaming fans swarmed around the vehicle, mistakenly thinking that it had transported the Gibb Brothers.

When they discovered who was inside the limousine, no-one seemed disappointed. For all that they had never heard of Ray and his fellow cast members or recognized them, they had heard about the new series which was to be made by the same people who produced The Monkeys, America's answer to the Beatles. And just the association was enough to endow celebrity status. All of the cast signed autographs and posed with fans for photographs for seemingly forever. It was a strange experience and unnerving.

Ray was also uneasy to discover that besides himself, only one other member of the group could actually play an instrument. Session musicians had been hired to lay down tracks in the recording studio. Ray was concerned how this would be received. Not all members of The Monkeys could play instruments either and it was starting to damage their credibility, being perceived as a manufactured brand, as indeed in many ways they were.

Likewise with this new group, all of whom had been chosen and matched for a specific look or talent. Ray was the dark-haired, rebellious one, brooding and serious about music. Another male member had lighter hair and was more laid back, easy going and also a musician. Yet another was comical and fun loving, always ready to joke and mess about. He was a trained actor, as were the two female members who could also dance and sing. And were gorgeous. One blonde and blue-eyed. The other brunette, with brown eyes.

The premise was that the group hung out at a type of coffee house run by a Mother Earth, Mamma Cass-type of figure, who was to be played by Kay Ballard, a popular comedienne and television personality of the day.

Besides producing The Monkeys, Ward Sylvester managed the career of the teen heartthrob, Bobby Sherman, who wanted to pursue his aspiration to work on the other side of the camera and was set to direct the pilot episode.

But the Writers' Guild of America went on strike, causing filming to be put on hold. So Ray chose to rent a car and drive back across America rather than confront his phobia of flying. The journey to Canada took about 10 days but at least he didn't have to suffer sitting in an aircraft and could do some sightseeing.

Months later the Guild resolved their dispute but by then the window of filming the pilot in enough time to show the networks and subsequently be broadcast had apparently closed. So production was canceled.

The entire adventure just seemed to evaporate. Ray was paid a modest sum for the duration of his contract. His father's solicitor, who had gone over all the contracts, was more experienced in general practice, such as conveyancing house purchases, and was in no way an expert in entertainment law.

But re-reading the small print, he could see that any significant sums were only to be paid in the event the producer or the production company exercised options if and when the series went into production.

This hadn't happened. So once again Ray would need to find a job. Which he did, performing at a resort in Muskoka for the summer season. He would then have the remaining part of the year clear to work on his writing and music endeavors.

Ray discovered years later that a member of the cast of the aborted show, Wesley Ure, eventually did well, becoming especially known for his role in the cult television series 'Land Of The Lost'. But he lost contact with the other hopefuls. With the exception of his fellow musician, with whom Ray would become a life long friend.

Ray spent a few more summer seasons performing in Muskoka, which was also to serve as the training ground of another singer and songwriter struggling to become established, Shania Twain.

In the winters, Ray traveled to New York, Nashville and Los Angeles peddling songs to music publishers, enjoying a modicum of success over the next few years. But fell victim to an unscrupulous manager with questionable ethics who maneuvered himself into a position whereby he would fiscally benefit from the ownership of any of Ray's songs.

Feeling more and more disillusioned, Ray started up a duo with his friend from the television series, performing as 'Stillwater' back in Canada on a circuit of universities and clubs.

At the Firehall Theatre in Toronto they played downstairs in a mammoth bar. Upstairs, an improvisational troupe entertained in cabaret. This was a sister company of the soon to be iconic Second City in Chicago and Ray hung out with more of the stars of tomorrow who would become household names on Saturday Night Live, including John Candy, Gilda Radner and Eugene Levy.

And they were not the only ones who were destined to find fame. Back In Britain, some members of the MI5, such as the vocalist, Rod Evans, became the core founders of Deep Purple. The Avengers evolved into Edison Lighthouse, who enjoyed a number one world wide hit with 'Love Goes Where My Rosemary Goes'. And a member of Malcolm James and the Callers had started up another group who were soon catapulted into glam rock stardom, 'The Sweet'.

Ray considered getting back together with his old friends in the music industry but dismissed the notion, having become more and more disenchanted.

He still loved music, probably more than ever, but since being let down by his manager was finding that it was a ruthless, hard-nosed business and he nestled in bed with heartache more often than not, unaware of who he could really trust on the business affairs side of the industry.

So he decided to focus on his writing again, encouraged by the positive reaction of a producer who had shown an interest in a screenplay Ray had submitted and was developing. About the hijack of a television studio.

But then, after reading the latest draft, the producer thought it would be difficult to contain as a motion picture and to do justice to the scope of the story suggested it might be better served as a novel.

With some money saved, Ray followed his family who had recently moved back to England and he purchased a house in Sussex to base himself, deciding still to place his musical endeavors on hold while he set about trying to embark upon a career as a writer. From the results so far, the notion seemed impossible to achieve.

As it happened, the family had stayed in Canada for just over nine years, rather than the five years his father had originally envisioned - all becoming torn, really enjoying the country and all that Canada had to offer while at the same time nostalgically always missing the old world and feeling drawn by a need to return.

Ray also thought he might have more opportunity with the publishing and film world in the UK being a little more vibrant than in Canada at that time. And it was true. There were more outlets to explore but more in the market place trying to explore them and it didn't take long for doors to slam shut faster than Ray could find new ones to open.

When he finally sent out the first draft of the story, now in novel format rather than as a film, just as the producer had suggested, he was only to be told that it felt more a film rather than a novel.

Others thought it simply had no potential whatsoever and hinted that perhaps Ray would be better off forgetting pursuing a writing career.

But he kept his dream alive, persistently sending out the manuscript with renewed hope over and over again. Only to have that shattered with letter after letter of rejection from other publishers.

Ray wrote several other stories, scripts, formats, and ideas for television series - all of which were also still met with no interest at all. With a dwindling bank balance he considered trying to find a so called normal job. But had no idea what he would do as an alternative career. Music, although still a passion, had been replaced by an even bigger passion. All Ray wanted to do now was write.

But he needed also to pay the mortgage and put food on the table. So he obtained work as an extra in television and film, immortalized years later by the Ricky Gervais television series 'The Extras', which Ray thought was so well observed. And even found a role at Pinewood Studios as a stand-in for Christopher Reeve, on the production of the motion picture 'Superman'.

Returning home one evening after a long day at the studio, Ray was surprised when he played a message on his telephone answering machine from an agent who wanted to speak to him about his manuscript.

He eagerly returned the call the following day.

'Sorry it's taken so long to get back but we're swamped with submissions,' the agent said.

Ray tried to recall when he had sent the manuscript, sure it must have been months ago. Then he wasn't sure if he was hearing correctly, as the agent continued, 'But I've now had a chance to read it - and I think you've got something there. I'd like to send it to a publisher.'

Finally Ray received some interest. Then all of a sudden the hope quickly faded. He feared that it might be a waste of time for the agent to approach any publisher, sure he had tried most of them at least twice over. An entire forest must have been used to manufacture the amount of paper in his file of rejection letters. But the agent was undeterred.

Within a few days Ray received another call from him, advising that the publisher really loved the novel and would like to discuss releasing it in both hardback and paperback.

Several months later, Ray reflected on the irony that the publishing house who eventually purchased the paperback rights through a sub-license from the original publisher, who was to retain the hardback rights - had turned down the submission when Ray had approached them just over a year before.

And no doubt someone at a higher level would be asking questions why the novel had been rejected, which may have been a missed commercial opportunity.

It was such a thrill for Ray to have his novel published and be in all the leading stores he visited - and to watch people flipping through pages and actually buying copies.

'That's my story,' he said proudly to one purchaser. 'That book .... I wrote it.'

'Yeah, right,' the purchaser replied, stealing uneasy looks at Ray, thinking he was a real odd ball, before rushing to the sales counter to pay.

'The Number to Call Is ...' was eventually translated into several languages, with a lucrative option on the film rights being taken by Nems Enterprises.

And Ray learned that even if one thousand people said no, all it takes is for one person to say yes, and the pursuit of a creative dream can be fulfilled.

He would also discover later in his career however, that even if 99.9% people said yes, there could still be one waiting in the wings who could still say no. So nothing was ever sure till it was sure. And even then it could be unsure, as had happened with his experience in Hollywood.

But now he was encouraged, convinced that it was possible to overcome any setbacks. Against all the odds, his novel had been published and was selling well.

Nems Enterprises was once owned by Brian Epstein, manager of the Beatles, but had diversified into other areas of the media. Ray couldn't believe that he was indirectly associated with the fab four who had inspired him so.

Even though the link was somewhat tenuous and confined to only the name of the company he had read about in all the music trade papers so many years before, when he was first introduced to the Mersey sounds as a young boy. Nevertheless, he was still involved with Nems Enterprises. And that was good enough for Ray.

The novel in the end was never made into a film but it, along with his screenplay, served as a good example of Ray's work for his agent to send out to other interested parties. And he had taken a giant step forward in his endeavors to try and make a full time career out of being a professional writer.

'What do you know about the Bengal Lancers?' his agent asked, when he phoned unexpectedly one day. 'It's just, I met a producer who really enjoyed the adaptation of your novel. He's an asian shipping magnate - and interested to meet to discuss a film he'd like you to write.'

Ray replaced the receiver, hardly able to contain his excitement. His first novel had been published and now a real producer was actually thinking of hiring him to write a screenplay.

What a great year it was turning out to be. Or so he thought...

MORE BEGINNING OUT-TAKES

FADE IN

EXT. DESERTED CITY. DAY.

The OS sounds of distant chanting, 'Zoot, Zoot, Zoot.'   And a deep rumbling of something - reminiscent of very heavy duty machinery - approaching.

Graffiti on the walls, tagging, stylized street art portraying - 'Locos Rule'.

Smoldering vehicles. Looted buildings. A newspaper (like tumbleweed) blowing.

The fading, charred headline announcing that the Pandemic was reaching unprecedented proportions.

A cow ambling around, looking for a place amidst all the concrete to graze. Hints that nature is reclaiming the city, with stems and veins of plants climbing walls, roots of trees cracking foundations.

PICK UP A FILTHY URCHIN OF A YOUNG CHILD

running through the empty, ghostly streets. Flat out. Whimpering. Absolutely terror-stricken. Stealing petrified looks behind. As the distant chanting and rumbling reverberates around and around.

He is a STRAY. The term used for those not members - or under the protection - of a Tribe. Dangerous. Banishment from a Tribe is like a death sentence. So hard to fend for oneself in these, the cities of children, let alone in the suburbs or surrounding countryside now inhabited by only the young.

Now though, the STRAY is being chased by a wild, threatening looking Loco security PATROL, who speed after him on roller blades. They finally catch him, hurl him spread-eagled against a wall - and search him.

A RECONNAISSANCE MALL RAT PATROL

Suddenly appearing out of an alley way, ambushing the LOCOS.

They are led by the leader, AMBER. She looks like a very funky chick with an attitude as attractive and unique as the tight Zulu knots in her hair, her expressive make-up and grungy sense of individualist fashion punctuating that she rarely follows a trend - but sets it.

Another MALL RAT in this patrol is the sensuous and spiritual Tribe philosopher, TAI SAN. And like AMBER, also a capable warrior. But they have no need to use their weapons, clubs. Though there are only a few MALL RATS present, the LOCO patrol are outnumbered and scatter.

> AMBER
> You okay? (the STRAY nods) What's your name?

> STRAY
> Sammy.

> TAI SAN
> What are you doing? In the Loco sector?!

> SAMMY
> Looking for something to eat.

> AMBER
> Oh, and they figured you were an assassin trying to 'take out' Zoot, I suppose!

SAMMY is not smiling.

> AMBER
> Have you always been a stray? (he
> nods) Never been a member of any
> Tribe -
> TAI SAN
> (knowing where this is leading)
> Amber!

> AMBER
> We can't just leave him. Look at
> him. He has no hope of surviving
> on the streets. No way. Not with
> Zoot making an appearance. Spells
> nothing but danger. Or death, more
> like.

> SAMMY
> Can't spell, Miss. Was too young to
> go to school. In the old world.

That's got to AMBER. And TAI SAN.

> AMBER
> Well, Sammy, right now, I guess it
> looks like you're coming with us.
> (to the others) Better make a move.
> While we can!

ON THE ROOFTOP OF A SKYSCRAPER

BRAY crosses stealthily to the edge,
gazes down at the city square below.

Once a gamer, into Manga, all things Japanese (Shinto, the code of bushido which inspired so many of the online games he once played). BRAY is VERY 'Zen', enigmatic, accomplished in martial arts, exudes a quiet confidence, relates to the elemental rather than the material, considering himself an eco warrior. And has also clearly been influenced by nature. With braided, flaxen plants intertwined with feathers as hair extensions.

IN THE MAIN CITY SQUARE

A crack of deafening, almost unbearable noise, the rumbling and screech of metal, of something huge, powerful, approaching ... closer ... CLOSER.

The LOCO TRIBE are assembled, lining the streets. War paint streaking their faces, wild dreadlocks, scavenged clothes. They almost look feral. All now ululating in a frenzied shrieking.

And the legendary warrior, ZOOT - protruding from a decaying and mammoth graffiti-covered tank, accompanied by his second in command, EBONY, along with the MILITIA of the Loco republican guard, arrives.

This is still a world of no Internet, no power, and VERY primitive in many ways. But some - the powerful - such as ZOOT - with this tank, have traded to obtain gas to fuel the very few vehicles commandeered or scavenged.

FEATURING BRAY

furtively watching, listening to ZOOT addressing the assembly, with more than hints of a manic, zealot conviction.

> ZOOT
> Loco brothers and sisters. I stand before you with important news. We have intelligence that the god, Flame, and the Privileged are gathering support. And could be assembling an army. So the Locos must take this warning seriously. And be prepared. To protect against any invasion. Loco brothers and sisters, if the Privileged, or anyone else, ever want a war - what are they going to get? Let me hear the word of Zoot now!

He thrusts his arms aloft, crosses his wrists to cue his 'word' and motto. All respond in unison, chanting, whipped into a frenzy.

> THE LOCO TRIBE
> Power and Chaos! Power and Chaos!! Power and Chaos!!!

CHAPTER NINE

JOURNAL: OCTOBER 1998

On the return flight from Nice to London, Ray re-read some thoughts he had sketched out long before the development phase of his latest production had ever started.

He wanted to double check if there was anything he had missed that might work so he could alert Harry, who was busy overseeing the next block of scripts which were being written. Ray had been considering introducing a Tribe known as the Privileged. But decided against it, feeling that what he had in mind would be far too edgy and raw. So, no point. He could always feature them later. The Locos were enough of a threat.

Ray was relieved that that he had also dismissed one of his earlier thoughts to have the leader of the Locos, Zoot, travel around in a tank which could have been problematic logistically, along with being expensive.

Arriving at Heathrow, he caught a cab into London for a board meeting which had been scheduled at head office and ran into Bruce Dickinson in the washroom where they exchanged their latest news, standing side by side at the urinal.

'How's it going, Bruce?' Ray, asked making a conscious decision not to glance down.

'Good, man. What about you?' Bruce replied, probably just as uneasy not to avert his gaze, with male etiquette being what it is during such an encounter. A wandering eye could be misconstrued.

'Just in from Mipcom. In Cannes.'

'The launch of another series, eh?'

'William Shatner's A Twist In The Tale.'

'All go well?'

'Really well,' Ray said, crossing to the sink to wash his hands while Bruce remained at the urinal. And he wondered how many Iron Maiden fans would enjoy having a chat with their favorite lead singer in such an informal - and personal - way.

'You guys touring - or are you around for a while?'

'Should be around, if you want to catch up,' replied Bruce.

'I'd love to. But I'll be heading back to New Zealand in a few days. Can't stay in London for long. We've just started another production. Another time, eh?'

'You got it. Don't know when we'll next be on the road down under but I'm sure we'll get together. Somewhere.'

As well as being an icon of heavy metal, Bruce was an accomplished opera singer, a skilled fencer and qualified pilot, who really enjoyed flying and taking the controls himself. He had a variety of other interests including film and television and he and Ray had often discussed the possibility of doing something together.

Ray had resolved though that it would never include Bruce flying him anywhere on the Iron Maiden private jet. He had enough unease as it was traveling on a commercial carrier without a long haired headbanger as the pilot.

Flying around the world was a necessity to conduct business and still not something Ray would ever do by choice. But he had learned to cope with his unease. Though each time he arrived anywhere, he was always consumed with an overwhelming sense of relief, considering flights and safe landings tantamount to almost a failed suicide attempt.

Ray's joint venture partner in The Cloud 9 Screen Entertainment Group was a successful multi media company with offices all over the world, which facilitated a diverse range of activities. Primarily in the music industry across several divisions, including record labels, publishing, agencies, merchandising.

But their core expertise and business resolved around being a highly efficient and respected management organization, involved with several of the 'A' list and elite in the industry in one way or another, from Elton John to Beyonce, Led Zeppelin to Robbie Williams. It was not unusual to see many of the artists on the roster if they visited the head office for meetings, as had occurred with Bruce Dickinson.

Cloud 9 was founded in 1994. Shortly after Ray had been introduced to the Chairman of his future joint venture partner by a merchant bank, which had in turn been recommended by the head of media finance at Coutts. And Ray was immediately impressed with the range of unique skills, ethos and ethics of the company and the professional way in which they operated.

He had opportunities to go into business with other third parties in the industry but the chemistry never felt quite right as it did when the Chairman introduced Ray to the core executive team. And he knew immediately that this was the place he really wanted to be.

The company was keen to get into television. Ray was flattered that they had shown an interest in him and seemed to believe in what he was trying to set out to achieve in establishing an independent production company.

They agreed for Ray to have the majority shareholding, which was important to him. Not so much due to matters fiscal but more about artistic control. As with all the other artists with whom they were involved, the company never interfered in any creative areas, confining their involvement to protecting the commercial interests.

'Think of us as defense,' the Chairman said, when he first met Ray. He was a fanatical soccer fan and often used the game as an analogy. 'We view all our artists as strikers. And we back them in whatever then want to do. But if they can't score on occasion creatively, we'll be around commercially to make sure no-one puts the ball in the back of our - your - net. So the worst that can happen is a nil - nil draw.'

That sounded good enough for Ray. But he wondered if he should let the Chairman know that maybe he was a strong candidate for being unable to score at all if his continual struggle with filling the blank pages and deciding on how to start a story was anything to go by. Then it wouldn't even be a case of even hitting the post but striking the ball way off target. He was sure he had a capacity to miss the net, not only entirely - but by miles.

'Have you decided on a name for the company?' his family asked, when he told them of his ambitious plan to set up in business on his own account.

'Not yet,' replied Ray. 'I'll have to give it all some thought. Right now there just seems to be so many other things to do to get it all set up. But I'm determined to try and make a go of it. And if I can - I'd be on Cloud 9.'

There was a profound - and very special - moment for Ray as he and his family exchanged a long and silent glance. No words were needed. They could see from his expression that without even searching or thinking about it any further, he had found the perfect name.

Most of 1994 was spent developing possible titles for production, during the course of which Ray met Gillian Baverstock. One of Enid Blyton's daughters and a trustee of the vast literary estate. Gillian seemed to warm to Ray as much as he did to her from the very first time they first met.

Though elderly, she reminded him in many ways of a heroine in one her mother's stories, exuding the quiet confidence and eternal qualities of a head girl at a boarding school who would always do what is right in whatever event. And be certain to lead the hockey team to victory, overcoming any obstacle which Enid's wonderful writing imagination could concoct in every page right up until the end.

Ray wondered what it must have been like for her to have grown up as a child and be read bed time stories by the legendary doyen of children's literature.

Gillian was rightly proud of the substantial achievements of her mother. Ray noticed a glint of excitement in her eyes as he explained that he would like to secure the rights to the Adventure and Secret series, pledging to respect the creative integrity in the source material in any adaptation which he wanted to update, convinced that it could satisfy the existing fan base, as well as introduce the works to a brand new contemporary television audience.

'That would be so lovely,' Gillian said. 'Jolly good then. Leave it with me. I'll discuss your proposition with my colleagues and get back to you.'

Ray would have felt more hopeful if he was representing a company like Disney, which was on a par with the equally global brand of Enid Blyton, and knew that there was no way he could ever hope to match or even come remotely close to the type of fiscal offers the estate must continually receive.

But Gillian knew of Ray's body of work at the BBC and seemed to be impressed with it. Also with his assurances about doing an adaptation which would be faithful to the original works. He was banking on that to be a vital deciding factor. The estate would not be dealing with a faceless corporate entity who was solely interested in the fiscal bottom line. But someone who cared enormously and was committed to producing product of quality.

Being a writer himself, Ray genuinely held all within the profession in the highest of regard, being fully aware of the care they all had for their work and all they went through to give birth to it. But nevertheless, it was still a big ask to expect Gillian and the estate to grant a license to a new company like Cloud 9, which had only recently come into existence and had no trading track record.

Ray thought there was a chance or he wouldn't have attempted to secure the rights in the first place but was still slightly surprised to hear a few days later that his proposition had been accepted. He felt overwhelmed that so much faith had been placed in him and set about embarking upon what would evolve into a long and arduous journey bringing the titles to the small screen.

For all the supposed new level playing field which had been introduced in British television in the aftermath of deregulation, rather than a proliferation of independent companies being commissioned by broadcasters - there was a proliferation of subsidiary independent production companies coming into existence owned by broadcasters which many felt betrayed the spirit of the new legislation. Broadcasters were, in effect, still commissioning themselves.

Ray decided that strategically he needed to operate in a totally different way. So he traveled to Germany to discuss the projects with potential end users, such as the state broadcaster ZDF.

This was followed by more meetings at the MIP television festival, the first time Ray had been back to Cannes since the aborted 'Bengal Lancer' film saga, where he met a media conglomerate based out of Luxembourg who had television interests throughout Europe.

More discussions occurred in London and Luxembourg over the ensuing months between senior executives of both companies to assess in greater detail the feasibility of what Ray had in mind. Which was basically a joint venture between the conglomerate and Cloud 9 whereby Ray would create, develop and produce a catalogue of programming targeting an international prime time family audience, branded as the Classic Collection.

Rather than attempt to obtain a commission from a broadcaster to underwrite production costs, the portfolio would require some risk investment from the conglomerate as well as Cloud 9, possibly even from Ray, who offered to waive fees in return for a larger equity share.

He was just so eager to get into production and had a passionate belief that there was a huge gap in the marketplace for quality family entertainment which could be offered through an innovative fiscal model.

Normally broadcasters owned the underlying rights to any product they commissioned. Which was fair, due to the fact that they would be fiscally exposed covering the enormous production costs.

Now though, if they wanted to transmit any of the Classic Collection titles, they could acquire the titles at a substantially lower price through a simple license fee for so many showings over so many years. At the conclusion of which the rights would revert, having been reserved by Cloud 9 and the conglomerate, leaving them free to license again.

The fiscal risk would no longer be placed on the broadcaster but the investors. Ray wouldn't have to go through the long process of trying to obtain a commission. He could operate as a true independent with a higher degree of autonomy and editorial control, which was important to him creatively.

As far as commercial matters were concerned, the upside of the proposal meant that if it all worked out the conglomerate, as well as Cloud 9, would benefit under an almost venture capital methodology of high risk to high return through the ongoing ownership of a catalog of intellectual property which could be exploited in perpetuity

The issue of distribution was also discussed. Cloud 9 and the conglomerate decided to divide key territories. As a result, Cumulus was born. The company would trade as a distributing subsidiary of Cloud 9, which meant that Ray would also have a say in the marketing of all the product he wanted to produce.

Furthermore, Cumulus would participate in all ancillary rights, from music publishing to merchandising. Overall, it was an unprecedented and innovative aspiration for a small independent production company. The module was usually confined to the method of operation of a major studio.

When the contracts were signed, Ray did not know whether he should celebrate. Or run and hide. Due to the complex and exceptionally bold, ambitious task which lay ahead.

If it worked out as he hoped and envisaged, it could provide a valuable asset and return. But if not, and he failed, he would not only lose his house but the shirt off of his back. Everything was on the line, including his reputation. Failure would also place his joint venture partners in a commercially vulnerable position, with such a large amount of risk investment which would need to be made.

As Ray reflected upon all the challenges, part of him wished his proposal had been rejected. He felt a sudden surge - and burden - of unbearable responsibility. The pressure was immense. And he hadn't even started. He had certainly delivered as a striker, bringing the deal together. But Ray privately anguished, wondering if in reality he had scored a spectacular own goal, heralding absolute disaster.

He contracted Harry as lead writer and head of development, feeling there was no-one better to oversee the writing department. Harry and Ray set about assembling a team of writers they respected and Ray was especially pleased that his mentor, Mervyn Haisman, who had given Ray his start at the BBC, agreed to work on a few scripts.

The next task was to check out a potential production base. The Enid Blyton stories required a range of various backdrops, from forests to mountains, lakes to quaint fishing villages, even an area which could serve as a desert.

This could not be achieved easily in England due to having to move a unit continually to the various locations. It was always so much easier to operate within a radius of a studio base. So Ray considered Wales, even regions throughout Germany.

By the time the MIPCOM Festival was being held in Cannes, Ray knew he had a great brand in Enid Blyton, as well as first class scripts which were being written, all of which were like mini James Bond action adventures. But he still hadn't been able to identify a production plan on how it could all work logistically.

Cumulus had not started to trade at that point, with no footage being shot to show any outlet in the marketplace. The objective at MIPCOM was to announce that the Series was in development and to meet potential broadcasters who might wish to acquire the project early through a pre-sale.

His assistant had arranged other meetings, as well. Mostly with third parties, such as publishers, distributors and merchandisers who were keen to meet Ray, having read about his new enterprise. But also representatives of various television and film commissions marketing their particular countries as potential locations, were eager to make presentations of what they had to offer.

Many think of television and film as being of cultural and artistic significance. Which on one hand indeed it is - but it also brings employment across all trades, from carpenters to electricians, and stimulates the economy of a country in several vital areas. Consequently, many governments have official film and television bodies attending festivals, seeking to attract productions to the countries they represent - and investment across a wide spectrum.

Equipment might need to be shipped, crews and cast housed in hotels. They have to be fed, so it can be a boost for those offering catering services. Likewise, transport or location facilities. Raw materials are required for building sets, and overall with the trickle down economy, a factor of ten might easily apply.

So on a 10 million dollar production, 100 million of extra revenue might perpetually self generate to further filter down and swirl around, stimulating employment, bringing extra taxes, which are then reinvested back into the economy, nourishing it with further growth, like a financial snowball,

The film and television sector is also an important incubator for small businesses brought into existence to service the industry through an infrastructure across a diverse range of activity, from animal trainers to post production equipment and facilities.

And the icing on the cake is that with the reach and footprint of an international audience through the medium of television and motion pictures, the global coverage assists in showcasing and raising the profile of any country. Even if it is from a tourist simply deciding to visit, having been impressed by the locations which they saw on the large or small screen.

Certainly at the peak of 'Howard's Way', the huge ratings success was shared with all in the Solent, the region where it had been filmed, precipitating a substantial boost to tourism with visitors flooding into the area.

Export sales increased for the boating industry as a result of the exposure in the show as well. The influence of highly rated series on television or successful motion picture is wide ranging and immense.

'When are you thinking of going into production,' Ray was asked, by a member of a team from New Zealand.

'Next Spring hopefully,' replied Ray.

'Around September or October then?'

'No, April.'

'Autumn?'

'Spring.'

Ray and the team smiled at the confusion. It might be Autumn down under in New Zealand but it would be Spring in the Northern hemisphere. He really liked the team and all they presented, attending MIPCOM to market their studio facilities in Lower Hutt, a thriving suburb outside of Wellington.

Ray was impressed with their professionalism and style, believing that they were not only excellent advocates for their company but good ambassadors for their country. But he was especially taken by their enthusiasm. They were flexible, with an open mind. And their doors were very much open to do business.

Cloud 9 dispatched two members of its newly appointed production team to travel to New Zealand for a recce.

When they returned and reported back, Ray decided that he would be hard pressed to find a better alternative. It was always a risk filming overseas, rather than a home base, but New Zealand seemed to offer the range of locations required, as well as a good pool of crew and cast, in addition to all the facilities and infrastructure required to bring the Series to fruition.

Pre-production was set for January 1995, though in reality a lot of planning had already started between MIPCOM and the Christmas break, with Ray almost living on the phone discussing matters with the New Zealand facilities team at night. With the day spent working out production schedules, budgets and going over all the scripts with Harry, which were being delivered.

Before long, Ray needed to travel to the country known as the Land Of The Long White Cloud to oversee preparations. The flight from London through Los Angeles to Auckland felt like it would take forever. Ray transferred to the domestic terminal for the connecting onward journey to Wellington.

Although he didn't see much of the country beyond traveling between his hotel, the studio facility, and the locations which were to be used in the ensuing weeks, he was impressed. It was all, if not more, than what he had hoped.

He worked most weekends but managed to find a few spare hours to stroll around the capital city of New Zealand overlooking the harbor and bay. Wellington was just so scenic. Clean, safe, multi cultural, with good theatre, concert halls, fine restaurants, apparently more coffee shops per capita than anywhere in the world, some even alfresco, where people could meet and chat all year round, enjoying the warmth of the Winter sun.

The architecture reminded Ray of Scandinavian cities. And yet, with all the houses dotted up and around in the hills which surrounded the bay, it was also reminiscent in many ways to San Francisco. Very picturesque. As Ray would later discover, most of New Zealand was more like 'a world' in a country.

With stunning fjords, mountains, lakes and miles of uninhabited countryside in the South Island. The North Island also offered desolate rolling hills, rain forests, yet more mountainous regions and lakes, sandy white beaches bordering the Pacific Ocean on one side of the country and the Tasman Sea on the other.

Ray was especially taken with the indigenous Maori population and how all traditions - including most from all the neighboring Pacific Islands - had been integrated and respected within society, rather than ignored. With Ray's Romany Gypsy heritage, he found he had an affinity with the culture.

But what struck Ray the most was the space. With a population of only four million, and the density mostly located in the major cities of Auckland, Wellington and Christchurch, it was possible to drive for miles without even seeing a car in some areas.

And even the traffic congestion at rush hour in the city was nothing compared to what Ray had been used to in London, where it could take hours to drive even a few miles.

Wellingtonians, like most New Zealanders, were also very laid back, friendly. For all that they lived or worked in and around a city, there seemed to be a great sense of community. Ray thought of Wellington almost as 'a village with skyscrapers'.

A range of different locations were available within a radius of the studio base, which was about a half hour drive north of the city. And as crews were recruited, he was once again struck by the enthusiasm which was not confined to the representatives he had met in the South of France at the television festival. It extended across all departments. All the team exuded a positive, can do attitude.

Anything could be achieved with Kiwi number eight wire. A term which probably came into existence when immigrant farmers fixed fences - and everything else - with a simple piece of wire. And which had now evolved to have become a metaphor in the nation's psyche, representing 'ingenuity'.

If anyone encounters a problem, they look to Kiwi number eight wire to fix it. Number eight wire will always see anyone right. Basically a way, even if unconventional, to provide an innovative solution. And with this attitude and intent, it invariably does.

Calls went out to agents for casting. Open auditions were also held, drawing a huge response, with mammoth crowds lining up around blocks as parents accompanied their children hoping to be offered a part.

It reminded Ray, on a smaller scale, of what he had experienced himself as a teenager with the aborted American television series.

Against all the odds, one of the leading roles, Dinah, was shortlisted and eventually cast as a result of the open audition. Ray was pleased as it seemed to be only fair. He was grateful - though slightly amazed - by the sheer volume of people who had turned up on the day, many traveling from the length and breadth of the country, all corners of New Zealand.

The characters of Philip, Lucy and Jack were all cast through agents. Ray contracted Malcolm Jameson to play the part of the father, having worked with him at the BBC on 'Howard's Way', and the talented British actress, Kirstin Hughes, was cast as the mother.

Principal photography commenced in April, 1995.

Ray flew to Cannes to attend the MIP festival for a few days as he wanted to preview some earlier footage which had been shot for promotional purposes, some of which he was considering using for the title sequences. It was an exciting time. To showcase the very first title from Cloud 9, now officially in production on the company's very own distribution stand, Cumulus.

The distribution team had not been recruited as yet. So Ray and his assistant, along with a few of the London administrative staff, dealt with enquiries.

All the major studios had tens of thousands of episodes in their catalogue. Cloud 9 had just one title. With no other footage available other than the few minutes which existed on the promotional reel. But Ray and his team displayed it with pride.

With no experienced distribution team and limited knowledge of tariffs and terms and conditions, Ray and his staff had to learn more about these vital aspects of the business as they went along. But the reaction at MIP was very encouraging.

Broadcasters were interested in seeing episodes when they came off the line and Ray felt a sense of relief. Perhaps any notion of scoring an own goal had been totally ill founded.

Wrong.

Within two months he was commuting between London and Wellington on a regular basis, trying desperately to contain a serious problem, and would have felt relieved with even scoring only one own goal.

He was struggling to ensure that millions did not go into the back of the net.

CHAPTER TEN

JOURNAL: APRIL, 1995

The first Cloud 9 series seemed as if it would end in disaster. Although production was going well and the footage looked great - it was also tracking to go way over budget.

It all started with problems surrounding a gigantic water tank which was to be housed in one of the studios and used over several episodes. Structural engineers had been retained to calculate the weight so that builders could erect adequate support structures for the many thousands of gallons of water the tank would hold.

When the thick glass casing was lowered into the frame, much to all the production team's surprise and horror - it didn't fit. It was out by a few centimeters, representing the thickness of an extra layer added to the safety glass for extra cover. But no-one had taken that into account in the calculations.

The cost to remedy matters came out of a small contingency fund which had been set aside, but before long that was used up.

And as the series continued to limp along, it was evident that the production was really struggling, with further unexpected costs manifesting week after week, and would go over budget. It was a question of just by how much and where those funds would be found.

'It's so different from when I was at the BBC,' Ray explained to his board. 'At least there I had an infrastructure already in place. Systems and procedures. We've had to start totally from scratch and introduce it all. Even identifying where to source and how to cost a paperclip has posed a problem.'

Shooting in the winter on location, with unusually adverse weather conditions, was also playing havoc with the schedule. The production team were losing light by late afternoon and the minutage required each day to remain on schedule was slipping. Any extension of the proposed 26 weeks it would take to complete filming the series would result in more cost.

Ray had rewritten each script to see if it might speed up the process by bringing some scenes inside. It was always much easier to control production in a studio rather than on location. And being exposed to the outside elements was posing a real problem.

Not so much because of the cold. But the rain. The crew were struggling, having been bogged down in mud for weeks, and it was difficult trying to manoeuvre equipment and vehicles around all the locations.

The cast and crew continued shooting through light rain, which is customary in motion pictures and television. Rain rarely shows up on the screen. For an actual scene in a story that called for rain would mean that the set would have to be drenched by huge hoses spraying water, to have any hope at all for it to show.

But the production had experienced heavy rain most days on location so far, resulting in the cast and crew being absolutely soaked through to the bone, and on wrap they all left the location to race home and dry out, feeling frozen and weary.

Due mostly to the fact that the team were running out of adverse weather cover. If it was forecast to snow or howl a gale or bucket down with torrential rain, studio based scenes would normally be filmed.

They were getting used up a little too quickly for comfort. So Ray had been trying to rework the scripts. But there was only so much space available inside the studio, with new sets having to be built for future episodes. And some scenes just had to be filmed outside. There was no option. With stories featuring the cast pony trekking through mountains, for instance.

Ray had already revised some elements in the scripts, wondering if the creative aspirations were a little too extravagant with what had been budgeted in the first place. But he didn't want to trim back much more, fearing that it might negatively affect the production values.

He suspected that eventually he might have no other choice if the production continued in its tailspin. And he couldn't believe that he was entangled in such a mess. Perhaps the schedule was slightly flawed. Or maybe there were just too many variables outside the original set of assumptions.

Whatever the reason, Ray felt as if he was trapped in the Bermuda triangle, not exactly sure where he was or where he was going, with the compass readings mismatching the coordinates on the map. And at times he felt totally lost.

As if the logistics were not enough to contend with, the sterling to dollar exchange rates were fluctuating more than had been anticipated. Sums had been purchased well in advance to lock in and allow for any difference and there was a proportion left open to make provision if the rates had risen.

But now they were falling. So a 10% differential on even 10 million dollars of production expenditure would amount to 1 million overage - without even taking into account the additional cost of the production problems. Then to service the overage if a further 10% was added for interest, that could add another significant sum. Costs could compound and spiral out of control.

'Apart from all that - everything else is going really well,' Ray added, at the conclusion of his report, which drew inadvertent and despondent smiles.

Ray wasn't trying to soften the impact of the severity of the problem with ironic humor, he genuinely meant it. He felt that for all of the difficulty, the production values, along with the performances, were tremendous and was impressed with the quality of the footage the crew was regularly achieving as it came off the line. He was sure there would be a huge market for the series.

The board supported Ray when he requested formal sign off for the fiscal overage which he was determined to contain, rather than spiral upwards out of control. Cloud 9's Luxembourg partner confirmed their backing as well.

And although the first title in the Classic Collection portfolio did go over budget, as had been envisioned, after a seemingly impossible task 'The Enid Blyton Adventure Series' concluded principal photography and was committed to post production.

Fortunately it was well received when it was launched at MIPCOM, acquired by broadcasters all over the world, which helped mitigate the overages, though not entirely eliminating them, due to ongoing interest accumulating on any amounts still outstanding.

But with the investors taking a long term view on achieving fiscal returns and in line with a portfolio approach, 'The Enid Blyton Secret Series', which had been in development in parallel to the production of the first title, was green-lit and principal photography commenced in February 1996.

The New Zealand production team moved into their own facilities, having reference points from any problematic areas which had occurred on the first production. And with an infrastructure having also been put in place, along with essential systems and procedures now introduced, Ray was confident that any flawed assumptions or mistakes which had been made would not be replicated.

It had been a high price to pay. But that was the cost of invaluable experience.

The team were also able to draw upon some of the props and sets used in the previous production, so those costs were amortized across the second series. And with a clearer methodology of operation, 'The Enid Blyton Secret Series ran smoothly, eventually delivered on budget and schedule, making way for the next production, 'The Adventures of Swiss Family Robinson'.

With Ray now spending so much time out of Britain due to filming in New Zealand, accountants and lawyers of his joint venture partner recommended that when he was in the Northern hemisphere, he base himself in Guernsey in the Channel Islands.

It was all a little complex for Ray to fully comprehend, but many of the artists they represented, as well as sportsmen or anyone else who spends a protracted period of time out of their home country due to traveling extensively overseas, very often benefited from a different tax base.

In Ray's case, the benefits would not only assist him in the long term personally but in the short term corporately. Given that he was the majority shareholder and wished to maximize any and all available funds for further investment into Cloud 9's ongoing production portfolio, he was willing to do whatever was required.

'Can you book me into the St Pierre Park Hotel in Guernsey,' Ray asked his assistant, who was unaware of what was being planned.

'Guernsey? I thought after the MIPCOM festival you were going back to New Zealand.'

'I am.' replied Ray, trying to work out his diary. 'Why don't you book me in from next Friday?'

'For how long? Just the weekend?'

'No. Better make it three years. But I won't be staying there the whole time. I just need the room booked. In case I stay anytime,' Ray said, and his assistant could see that he was being serious.

Ray had a reputation for being more than a little eccentric but booking a hotel suite for three years and having it empty probably most of the time seemed to be really 'out there'. Even for Ray.

He explained what he was required to do and although it still didn't quite make total sense, his assistant had more of an understanding. But she was still embarrassed to make the booking, believing that the reservation centre would be sure it was some kind of a joke. And she was right.

When she confirmed all the arrangements and paid a deposit, the hotel realized that it was actually all for real and that they would be required to have Ray's suite available at all times, even when he was not there, for the entire three year period.

The rules and regulations stated that to be Guernsey-based, Ray could not stay in a house or he would be considered a tax resident of the Channel Islands. So the hotel suite was the only option. To qualify for what the accountants and lawyers had structured, Ray must be in transit. And for the specific three year period, the equivalent of a tax resident of nowhere.

He was allowed to stay in the UK for up to three months in any year and could visit the country outside of that time, just as long as he left before midnight. Otherwise, he would have broken the exile laws.

Ray felt more like Cinderella, with the Cloud 9 administrative team keeping a close eye on his diary and the days he was in Britain. And when he had used up his allocation, to ensure he returned to Guernsey by midnight.

The time spent in New Zealand had to be monitored closely as well. Ray was able to spend more time there, which was essential due to the country being the production base, but on occasion would need to travel to Australia to maintain the in transit, non residency code. Which was not a problem since he was constantly visiting different countries anyway.

The staff at the St Pierre Park Hotel made it a home from home and got to know Ray. Though not that well. He was rarely there. Even when he was there.

'We missed you at lunch today,' a waiter said, one evening serving Ray dinner. He had also seen Ray at breakfast earlier in the morning.

'I had a business lunch.'

'Anywhere nice?' the waiter enquired. There were plenty of wonderful restaurants on the island to choose from.

'Believe it or not,' replied Ray, a little uneasy. 'The meeting was over … an Italian.'

'Ah, that would be Da Nello's. In St Peter Port.'

Ray just nodded, not wishing to go into it, aware that he was a bit of an enigma in the hotel and he did not want to fuel speculation further. Besides, it was all far too complicated to try and explain.

It was true he had Italian. But not in the town centre. He had caught the early flight from Guernsey to London, connected to another flight to Rome, had spaghetti Bolognese with executives from the Rai Italian State broadcaster, then flew back to London for a connecting return flight to Guernsey, and had only arrived back at the hotel in the past hour.

The staff at the 5 star hotel were discreet and knew Ray was in the television and film industry. But some were confused why he would spend a month in the hotel, disappear for a few months with his suite still booked, and then out of the blue show up again.

Rai were interested in some Cloud 9 titles Ray was developing but he was worried that if he tried to shed light on where he was that day, the waiter might have suspected that rather than an aspiration to deliver a 'hit' television series to Italy - a 'hit' was in reality something else entirely. With Ray's unusual and mysterious lifestyle, was he staying at the hotel to lay low? Was he really on the run? Rather than in the television industry, could he even be - in the Mafia?

On one occasion Ray had flown from Guernsey to London to connect with another flight to Luxembourg for a meeting with the principals of the Classic Collection partner.

Arriving back in London, he was informed that all flights to Guernsey were on hold, due to being fogged in. It was about 8pm and he was tired. So he phoned his manager to check if he had any days left in the allocation so that he could stay in England overnight and return to Guernsey the following day.

'I'll have a word with the lawyers and get back to you' his manager said.

Ray bought a coffee, which he had to pay for with a credit card since he had no petty cash with him as he rarely needed it. Drivers met him at airports to transport him to hotels or to offices for meetings which were normally over a working lunch, as had occurred earlier in Luxembourg.

When his manger called back ten minutes later, Ray was informed, 'Sorry - but you have no spare days. So the lawyers would prefer you don't stay overnight. Why don't you see if the fog clears and the Guernsey flight operates? If not, try and get booked on a flight to Dublin or anywhere else close. If not,

I'll get a driver to take you to Dover and you'll have to get on a ferry to get out of English waters.'

Ray didn't like the sound of that. His cell phone battery was running low, so he kept it brief, promising he would phone his manager back after determining what was available.

He checked with the Guernsey carrier to see if there was any news on the flight, asking if the fog had cleared. They reassured him that the airline would transport him to a hotel, cover all the cost and he would be able to fly out to Guernsey first thing in the morning. He didn't need to hang around the airport.

Ray appreciated the offer but sensed that the staff seemed a bit concerned - at Ray's concern - particularly when he advised that it could pose a real problem for him. Leaving in the morning wasn't really an option. He had to leave England. By midnight.

He enquired what other flights were available and was told that he could be wait listed on one to Dublin. He held the reservation in case it came through and asked the airline staff to page him as soon as they knew. Then he strolled through the terminal to check what departures were scheduled with other airlines.

'What time is the last flight tonight'?

'To where'?

'Anywhere. I just need to know if you have availability'

The staff stole a wary glance at Ray. He was in shorts and a t-shirt, always preferring to dress casually, and never wore suits or a collar and tie to any meetings, unless it was absolutely necessary.

'There's one at 11-clock. To Singapore.'

'That would be too far. Anything closer?'

'How long are you planning on being away?'

'Just overnight. What about anything earlier?' he said, glancing at the display panels. 'Like that one to Riyadh.'

'Yes, we seem to have availability.'

'I might just take that then. It's just, I'm wait-listed to Dublin and also have a flight to Guernsey. But if they don't come through, then it might have to be Riyadh - where is Riyadh anyway'?

'Saudi Arabia', said the member of staff, staring at Ray incredulously.

'Maybe you can hold that, too,' Ray requested. 'It's a little further than I wanted. But I'll be checking with my people to see if I should maybe just try and get to New Zealand, in which case Singapore might be better. So you'd better hold that one as well'.

'Do you have any .... luggage?' the staff member asked, in mounting suspicion.

'No. I've just arrived from Luxembourg. I connected from Guernsey earlier this morning but only needed to be in Luxembourg for a few hours - so there was no need for any luggage,' Ray tried to explain, realizing that the member of staff was now becoming very uneasy.

'So where do you live - Guernsey?'

'Yes. And no,' replied Ray, trying to keep it all simple. But the harder he tried, the more complicated - and odd - it all sounded.

'It's a bit difficult to explain really. I live there on one hand, but on the other hand technically I don't live there. I just stay there. On occasion. As well as New Zealand. Sometimes Australia. I used to live in England and still do in some ways. But only during the day. Because ... well .... if you want to know the truth, in law I don't actually live - anywhere.'

The member of staff pressed a call button, Security converged and Ray was invited to answer questions in a private room.

They didn't quite know what to make of this strange person who claimed to be exiled in Guernsey, as if he was some multi millionaire. But he had no cash on him, or luggage, was dressed casually in shorts and t-shirt, said he was the main shareholder of his own business. But he certainly didn't look like a business man. Then he revealed that he was not, per se. But was more a producer and writer, and above all didn't seem to know where he was traveling to and was holding seats on flights all over the world.

Ray's manager was called and arrived at Heathrow to clarify matters. At the eleventh hour, the fog cleared. Ray was able to leave for the return leg to Guernsey just before midnight, feeling exhausted and drained by the day's events.

As the aircraft hurled down the runway and took off into the night sky, Ray smiled, thinking that Big Ben would have struck twelve-o-clock. And he wondered what would have happened if he was still being interrogated by Security - and had turned into a pumpkin.

Not all of the time when Ray was in Guernsey was spent rushing to catch flights. Often he was able to be based at the hotel for a few weeks without traveling anywhere. He could conduct business by phone or email and found the island to be a very peaceful refuge. A perfect place to write.

Located 26 nautical miles off the north-west coast of France and with a strong Normandy influence, Guernsey is the second largest of the Channel Islands but paradoxically only eight miles long by five miles wide.

Encompassed by beautiful sandy beaches and a rugged cliff coastline, the island is a popular destination for yachtsmen and women, as well as tourists drawn to the picturesque charm, temperate climate and range of elegant boutiques, restaurants and cafes which line the twisting pebbled streets in the historic town centre of St Peter Port, overlooking the harbor.

Guernsey is also a leading offshore banking centre. Many of the world's financial services companies have branches registered on the Island which is outside of the jurisdiction of Britain and the European Union.

The Channel Islands also offered a much needed sanctuary when Ray discovered, during the filming of the 'Secret Series', that his mother in England had unexpectedly died. He found it difficult to reconcile having to maintain overseeing the production, while at the same time trying to take some time out to grieve and cope with the loss.

Ray's mother's passing occurred when he was at Disneyland Paris preparing to film a promotional segment for a member of the cast who was due to arrive in Europe.

During the afternoon he experienced a strange sensation, as if something unseen was gripping his hand, and thought that it might have been due to the gloves he was wearing as the January temperature had dropped. Then all of a sudden, the feeling subsided. It was around 2:20 pm.

When he arrived back at the hotel Ray was presented with an urgent message to telephone his sister. And she broke the heartbreaking news that their mother had passed away. At around 1:20 pm that afternoon - 2:20 pm in Paris.

Ray was informed by his managers that bereavement was not recognized as a reason to break the in transit structure which had been set up. He had no days left for an overnight stay in England and there were no compassionate grounds which would allow him to do so.

He could visit England. But would have to leave by midnight. Breaking the arrangement before the three year period expired would entail a substantial tax penalty for him personally. And corporately.

Ray did not care about the fiscal implications. He just wanted to be with his father, brother and two sisters. But there were no flights to England that evening and the soonest he could fly over to share his grief with his family would be the following morning.

At Charles De Gaulle Airport, while waiting in the terminal to board the aircraft, Ray noticed a sparrow flying wild and free. Which astounded all within the terminal. But none more than Ray when the bird landed and perched near his seat.

His mother always loved to feed sparrows, saying that if anything ever happened to her, she would still be around. All Ray or his family had to do was to look for any bird. And they would know that she was there watching over them.

Ray was overcome him emotion. His eyes filled with tears as he watched the bird. Watching him. Was it just a coincidence? Or something more profound? It certainly brought about a feeling of peace amidst all the pain.

The staff at the airport tried to shoo the bird away, having no idea how it had gotten into the building. It hadn't happened before. But each time the little sparrow was chased, it returned time and time again to perch next to Ray. It could have chosen anywhere in the vast terminal.

And only left, casting a final glance at Ray, when he receded through the gate to board the flight to London. It remains a source of unexplained mystery for Ray to this very day.

The family persuaded Ray not to break the arrangement. His mother would never have wanted that. So he commuted between Guernsey and England each day so that he could spend time with his siblings and his father.

All found it difficult to come to terms with their loss but insisted that Ray return to complete the filming at Disneyland Paris, which was important given that the Disney Channels had purchased the Enid Blyton titles.

So Ray found himself directing the footage at the theme park where, less than a week earlier, he had found out about his mother's passing. And he dedicated the series to her memory.

It was a tribute to her and all the profound influence she had on him. Which enabled him to realize that he just had to do - what he had to do. So many people were dependent upon him.

His mother, of all people, had taught him never to turn his back on his responsibilities, no matter what the challenge. His family all agreed that she would be the first to say that Ray should continue chasing his dream and to achieve whatever he wanted in his life. His mother would expect nothing less and would have been disappointed otherwise.

She was a strong, spirited lady with a mantra to face up to whatever obstacle life might present. To meet it head on. Never run from it. But to dig deep, grit the teeth and just get on with it. Which is exactly what Ray tried to do.

But at times he wished that he could run and take much needed time out to try and come to terms with it all. He was struggling.

With the unrelenting schedule and work load, Ray found that an hour's stroll in solitude along the beach in Guernsey helped to nourish the soul, as he reflected that one can never ignore the whisper of mortality that inhabits every fading sunset. He knew that in his heart of hearts, although time might heal, the awful sense of loss would prevail. And last forever.

A vital element of his life was missing and could never be replaced. Which was testament to the huge capacity his mother had to provide love and nurture, wisdom and care. She was always there. An emotional anchor for all in the family who found, along with Ray, in future years that she was still there in many ways. Through all the memories. Her very essence, great spirit and influence continuing to shine down proudly on all her beloved brood. Like the brightest star.

In 1997 Ray was introduced to another island, but this time in Fiji, which served as the paradise base of Cloud 9's production of 'The Adventures of Swiss Family Robinson'.

'Return to Treasure Island' was shot at the same time to amortize cost. It was an ambitious task to attempt to film two productions in parallel, especially costume drama on location, with some footage at sea.

This was exacerbated by the fact that although Ray had found the perfect white sand, palm tree island, which was almost deserted, the problem of securing the ideal location might have been solved, but it caused other logistical difficulties. There were no hotels.

While on location the crew and some of the cast were delighted to be accommodated on two cruise ships which Ray had to charter and which remained at anchor just off the island, serving as their home base for the duration of the shoot.

But it wasn't all glamorous. They were also filming at sea in schooners and sailing ships, in shark-infested waters. And with the hurricane season fast approaching, the safety of the cast and crew was paramount in Ray's mind, to such an extent that he had to retain helicopters in case he ever needed to deploy an emergency evacuation plan.

The desert Island was an idyllic tropical paradise. Isolated, it had no infrastructure or facilities whatsoever which meant that supplies had to be either shipped in by sea from the nearest mainland port. Or serviced through the self contained facilities of the two cruise ships constantly moored and on standby to provide support.

Other location filming occurred back in New Zealand, where the sets were built. And if anyone ever encounters a trivial pursuit question, it might be worth bearing in mind that in addition to the Swiss Family treehouse displayed in the Disneyland resorts - there was another exotic one also built, just outside of Wellington, about a twenty minute drive from Cloud 9's studio base.

Ray cast Richard Thomas in the key leading role of the father. Richard, best known and loved for his portrayal of John Boy in the perennial family favorite, 'The Waltons', gave a powerful performance and helped punctuate the brand and tone of the series.

'The Adventures of Swiss Family Robinson' reminded Ray in many ways of the Waltons on a desert island. Richard was a real joy to work with and traveled to MIP for the launch and to promote the title.

It quickly distinguished itself with not only broadcasters but viewers around the world, who responded favorably to all the adventures encountered in the stories.

But the underlying thematic was a celebration of family values. With the morality, strength and ideals paying homage in some way to what Ray was fortunate to have experienced, having been raised within the loving support structure of his own family.

'Return To Treasure Island' also proved to be a success, which paved the way for the next Cloud 9 production and Classic tale.

In 1998 'The Legend of William Tell' commenced principal photography. Ray cast the same actor in the leading role who played Ernst in Swiss Family Robertson, having been impressed with his talent and screen presence.

Ray often wondered if he should have changed the title when he created the adaptation since it bore little resemblance to the Swiss national folk hero. The series was more like Star Wars on the planet earth. With mythology and fantasy, wizards and elves, swords and sorcery. But any concern was unfounded.

The series became a cult title, connecting with international audiences in a very profound way. But Ray still believes that the title does not fully illustrate what the imaginative series is really all about.

With 'William Shatner's A Twist In The Tale' nearing completion and being successfully launched at the MIPCOM festival in Cannes, the Cloud 9 board congratulated Ray and his team on the supreme achievements which had occurred since the company was founded.

In five short years, almost one hundred and forty episodes of programming had been produced. Comprising of five series and 20 mini movie specials, which was a prolific and some say, totally unprecedented output for an independent production company, let alone one with its own distribution subsidiary, Cumulus, exploiting the underlying rights.

'A Twist In The Tale' also concluded the joint venture with the Luxembourg conglomerate who would now go on to sharing in the catalogue of Classic titles, which all felt would entertain a prime time family audience in perpetuity.

The next project which had recently gone into production utilized an internal revolving production fund capability. So once again, apart from Channel 5 in the UK who championed Cloud 9, committing to its portfolio of projects as a catalyst broadcaster, the company was planning to underwrite production costs in an innovative way, resulting in the retention of rights. But as a trade off, it still carried a high degree of risk with the substantial investment which would be required.

With no pilot episode ever screened, Ray was intent on producing 52 episodes. And fortunately obtained the sanction of his board.

'Keeping The Dream Alive', they reflected. 'Sounds like a good title.'

'But all at Cumulus feel it's more of a theme,' Ray replied. 'And I agree with them. So it's just a working title. I've been trying to come up with an alternative. Such as 'Power and Chaos'. Or 'Cities of Children'. But they don't work for me either.'

'Well, good luck. Let us know what you eventually decide and we'll arrange a press release.'

'What it needs is something simple. To illustrate what it's all about - a Tribe.'

Ray exchanged glances with his board. What had tortured him over the past few months, even all the years since having the idea, now seemed to be so obvious.

Within a second of saying it, he knew 'The Tribe' was perfect.

CHAPTER ELEVEN

JOURNAL: OCTOBER, 1998

When Ray arrived back at the Cloud 9 studios production base from the MIPCOM television festival in Cannes, he felt as if he had been away forever rather than just ten days.

The team were surprised that he went straight to his office from the airport but Ray discovered that the shorter trips overseas really helped with jet lag. His body clock had less of a struggle to adapt to a new time zone.

Being unable to obtain much sleep in the south of France - let alone cope with the hectic schedule of the week - meant that as exhausting as it all was, he had remained on New Zealand time and now felt refreshed when he sat down in his office to get caught up on all the rushes which had been shot while he was away.

'I don't know how you do it,' his assistant said. She had also been at the festival and could hardly stay awake.

'I've just gotten used to it, I guess,' Ray replied.

And it was true. Over the past few years Ray travelled between the offices in New Zealand and London on average every six to eight weeks.

Now he was thankful that there was not another trip planned for about five months. He wanted to keep the diary clear to focus on the production of 'The Tribe' with no overseas visits scheduled until the MIP festival in late March, when the series would be officially launched to the global television market.

The initial episodes were also due to start transmitting in April in Britain so the pressure was on to keep ahead of the episodic flow chart. Otherwise, Channel 5 might run out of programming, which was an alarming - and commercially disastrous - notion.

The last block of episodes filmed would conclude not long before the first episodes were due to be broadcast, which meant that it would be very tight to remain on track to meet the transmission dates. A key element was to keep post production fed so that episodes could be delivered in time.

The scripts for Series One of 'The Tribe' were commissioned in early 1998. And although official pre production commenced in June of the same year, the actual planning had occurred in parallel with the production and post production of 'William Shatner's A Twist in the Tale'.

Principal photography of 'The Tribe' began in late August and would continue for another six months. With yet another six months of post production when the episodes are edited, sound and music effects added and mixed, and all the footage graded - at which time the episodes would be locked off and the masters shipped, ready for transmission.

There was a critical timeline path pinned to the boards on the wall of Ray's office above his desk but he didn't need reminding. As always, his life resolved around meeting deadlines.

Before even arriving back at the office, Ray decided that it would be prudent to maximize time and go over the footage which had been filmed while he was overseas. There was no room in the schedule for jet lag. An occupational hazard for a writer/Executive Producer.

'Why don't you get yourself home?' Ray said, trying to urge his assistant to unpack and rest up. 'If I need anything, there's enough people to call on.'

He didn't mean just within the production team. Ray's assistant had two assistants, who in turn had secretaries working to them. And with a runner, chauffeur, and security also on standby, there was always more than enough coverage.

If they were not available, then there was also a large administrative team supporting the entire Cloud 9 production cast and crew whom Ray could access outside of what some referred to as the 'inner circle' - the staff recruited to provide an adequate infrastructure to accommodate all the vast range of daily duties and tasks revolving around the executive offices.

Ray was Executive Producer on all of the titles the company produced. Corporately, he was also the captain of the Cloud 9 ship, and principal shareholder of all subsidiary companies within the group. But he was not like a so-called normal Chief Executive.

Although he had several hundred people working for him throughout the world, either in New Zealand, London or satellite representative offices in key cities such as New York, Ray never stood on ceremony. He considered himself to be one of the workers and tried to meet as many of the team as possible, whenever he could, wherever he could, knowing even the night cleaner by name.

His executive office was more like a large hotel suite. With tables and side lamps either side of three large couches and an easy chair, placed in front of a mammoth television set where he watched rushes or cuts of episodes. Which also served as a monitor screen, as it had a direct live feed into the sound stage studio, so Ray was able to see material in real time as it was being filmed.

On the opposite side of the office suite, in line with Ray's eccentricities and rituals, his desk had tape marks on the floor to ensure it was facing south and the piano in the corner was facing north. For some inexplicable reason, he perceived he could not create otherwise.

During the filming of 'The Legend of William Tell, the music suite in the post production department was moved to an impressive, more luxuriously furnished area. Ray was unimpressed. He simply could not function in the new surroundings. Runners were sent out to purchase all manner of shades of socks.

Ray liked to wear blue socks when he was composing, recording or spotting music but the ritual of wearing them did not achieve the desired effect. It was a serious problem and Ray felt panicked. The socks had never failed before. He sat blocked for hours. Unable to spot music cues and identify where music should be placed and edited to match and punctuate the footage on the screen. Nothing would flow. It was as if his creative lifeblood had been cut off, strangulated by an unknown force.

At first the shade of color of the socks was to blame. Then it occurred to Ray that it might be down to being in the new music room. He missed the smell, the lighting, the old furniture, the decoration and furnishing of the previous area he used to inhabit. The new suite just didn't quite feel right. Normal. As if it had no heart or soul.

Within hours of relocating back to the old music room, it was like Ray had been reunited and embraced by a familiar, trusted old friend. All of a sudden he relaxed and his usual creative energy was soon reignited. He was no longer blocked.

And at long last was able to identify what music cues were required.

Being also in tune with the natural world, Ray's executive offices had many water features and fountains to provide a peaceful ambience. It was derived from Ray's interest in Shintoism, but there were also aspects of feng shui in the way in which the office had been designed, decorated and laid out.

At the conclusion of Swiss Family Robinson, Ray used many of the palm trees from the set to decorate the office surroundings, framing a wicker bar. Overhead on the ceiling, the art department rigged a bamboo structure filled with a mass of green foliage and palms. So in many ways, it all evoked the look of a set in itself and felt more like a tropical desert island paradise oasis, rather than an executive office suite.

And it was indeed an island in many ways. Where Ray could take refuge from his hectic lifestyle in peace and tranquility to focus on all the many tasks he had to carry out each day.

The office suite was nestled deep within and protected by outer offices, occupied by his assistant and her team who vigorously ensured that Ray was not disturbed if he did not want to be. Unless it was due to any matter which might need his urgent attention.

Very often he would take some time out and simply be unavailable when he was writing or composing. Or even taking a half hour nap - as he was prone to do on occasion - in his hammock in an attempt to re-energize and refresh if his chakras were out of alignment.

Many of the crew could see where the characteristics and philosophies of Tai San probably originated. And in later series of 'The Tribe', due to Ray's obsessions with germs, even the character Ram.

Ray was pleased with the rushes when he viewed them. Mostly from footage in the main mall set which looked good. He rewound the tape to take a second look and reflected that the Phoenix shopping mall may end up to be one of the most famous in the world if the series was a success. And yet no-one would ever visit it, apart form the cast and crew.

It was a huge set located in Studio A. Built within a solid steel beam structure to accommodate the two levels of the store and shop sets, which had been constructed by hundreds of builders and craftsmen who worked around the clock to have it completed in time for the commencement of principal photography.

From the rushes, Ray could also see that the cast were still settling in well. He was encouraged by all the performances and that they were finding their characters.

He always referred to the cast on any production by their character, rather than their real names. So it was difficult at first to think of Amber as being Amber, rather than Princess Vara, which he had become so used to on 'The Legend of William Tell'. From which he had also been able to cast Jack, another talented actor who made his Cloud 9 debut in the same series.

'A Twist In The Tale' was the prime source for other lead roles. Such as Bray and Zandra - who starred in Jessica's diary, Salene and Ryan - from the Duelists, Trudy - from A Crack in Time, and a gifted young actress from The Magician who Ray just knew would be perfect as Patsy. Amber had also impressed yet again in a recent performance of the episode, the Green Dress.

Lex, Ebony, Paul, Tai San, KC and Chloe, along with most of the subsidiary cast required for the first block of production, had come through agents and auditions.

Ray had already found his perfect Zoot. The charismatic actor had first come to Ray's attention on the very first Cloud 9 production 'The Enid Blyton Adventure Series' when he was short listed for a role.

But in the end it went to yet another actor who would feature later in 'The Tribe' - Sacha. In addition, the two Blyton titles had also starred another future Tribe regular, Ellie.

The young man on the short list of the very first Cloud 9 production had not been forgotten, however. He was cast to star in the follow-up 'Enid Blyton Secret Series'. And Ray just knew that he would also be absolutely perfect to play the part of Zoot in 'The Tribe'.

He, along with the rest of the cast, possessed a unique screen presence, something extra special described by many in the industry as the elusive 'X factor'. But Ray was also impressed with all their qualities as human beings. As well as being gifted artists they were really lovely individuals, and that was all important.

Casting was always a difficult process. Ray hated having to disappoint those not finally chosen, realizing that it might cause so much disappointment, perhaps even feelings of rejection. Most actors and actresses were sensitive by nature. An essential and a natural resource which fueled the need to express themselves through acting in the first place. And a by product of that quality produced a vulnerability.

Outside the industry, so many think that actors and actresses must all be confident to be able to get up on stage or to go in front of a camera to perform.

Yet so often the opposite applies. Many are shy. From famous marquee 'A' list names, to young cast just starting out making their screen debut, Ray had always observed that they possessed not only a sensitivity, but a fragility, a streak of self doubt which he always found to be extremely endearing, stirring within him a feeling of a need to reassure, champion and protect.

Perhaps they were kindred spirits and he simply recognized in all a mirror image of himself. The same longing to self express creatively from the roots of the very essence. But the trade off was that the same emotions used could also leave one open to great heartache and disappointment. That was the ying and yang. But not always in equal measure.

And part of the reason why Ray rarely read reviews. A positive one could lead to feelings of elation. While a negative one could bring about great despair.

The tenants of the power of positive thinking have long been embraced as being a potent force. But equally, the negative can so outweigh the positive.

Ray found when he first started out in the industry that he would fixate on one bad review. And ignore one hundred good ones. A series might regularly achieve a high rating with 15 million viewers enjoying an episode, as had occurred on 'Howard's Way', and yet one newspaper critic could undermine that with a cynical or negative article about the series.

There was something in the human condition which made him aware that if someone was not careful, they - along with himself - could easily be drawn to focus more on the negative rather than the positive. As with him dwelling on the one critic who seemed to hate a series, rather than the 15 million viewers who loved it.

Ray could never fathom why anyone would ever wish to be a critic. And to make a living out of it. Never able to understand the kind of people they were, how they could somehow manage to obtain some kind of job satisfaction or sense of personal achievement by spending each day criticizing the efforts of others.

It took no talent to point a finger and criticize. Anyone could do that. Ray felt a degree of sympathy for them in many ways, if they had become so negative that they were immune to the positive endeavors of others, gaining some bizarre, vicarious pleasure in being overly critical of anyone out there trying to do their very best.

So he decided never to pay much attention to either the positive or the negative press where his creative aspirations were concerned. But just to follow his instincts and to remain truthful to them - as well as himself - in the hope that the majority would respond favorably.

Over the years, Ray also developed an intolerance for anyone in life who is overly critical and this was not confined to the so called professional cynics. He never has a problem with anyone expressing an honest opinion and champions freedom of speech, believing it to be an essential human right. And the cliche of someone seeing life half empty rather than half full, didn't even apply.

The root cause was that Ray had observed that there are just some people - and thankfully in the minority - who seem to whinge for the sake of it and can never be pleased. The type that if there was a competition offering one prize, then they would complain why two prizes were not made available. Or if they won a million in a lottery, would be disappointed not to win two million. Or moan about paying a 30% reduction off goods in a sale, feeling hard done by that it wasn't enough. It should have been 50%.

Perhaps in the end Ray had simply come to realize that for those afflicted with negativity or envy or bitterness, it erodes even the ability to applaud, let alone poisoning the very soul. Resulting in the 'I'll believe it when I see it' outlook, rather than believing it - which Ray was convinced to be the first vital step to - seeing it. And reaching any goal.

Ray gets a lot of letters from young people asking for advice on how to get into the industry. Apart from patience and persistence being the two main virtues, in Ray's view 'attitude' is all important. From acting to writing, make up to wardrobe, editing to even being a runner, which is the first entry role on the actual production side. Attitude is noticed and noted almost as quickly as talent. And often is the deciding factor in someone being hired.

Part of the reason Ray never forgot about Zoot was that along with the young man's talent and charisma - he noticed that the actor picked up a piece of litter from the floor when leaving the audition room. That told Ray a lot. He wasn't the negative type to think, why should he pick it up if he didn't drop it. He just did it. He fit the profile of being a team player. Which is so important in any industry.

Ray was invited once to give some motivational thoughts to members of the All Blacks who were playing for their teams in the NPC league. For each game Ray chose a theme. And for the Championship final suggested to his friend, who was also the Captain, to focus the players on the notion that someone negative will alway see and attract the negative. Someone positive - the positive.

The team were not perceived to be favorites to win the Championship title. And were the underdogs. If they viewed themselves that way, Ray felt it might evolve into a self fulfilling prophesy.

He recommended that all bear in mind that skill was not the only element of importance. Heart and desire were probably the more potent forces. As it is in whatever one does in so called normal life off the rugby field.

Ray's mantra was that if someone falls, pick them up rather than walk over them. Never criticize but encourage. Never pay attention to those who doubt. Equally, ignore those who label anyone or anything as being the best. But strive always to do one's best.

And to remember that no-one needs to be the best to achieve a desired result. Ray, more than anyone, was a good example of that. Achievement only manifests FROM desire. And that desire, once discovered and channeled, can fuel triumph over all adversity. Dreams are made for those who really try. In whatever form. Even if it is picking up a piece of litter to try and maintain a clean floor.

The team won the Championship title against all expectations. And Ray shares the medal with the captain who has become a dear friend.

Ray attributes their success to the fact that all the team started to view themselves as champions, rather than underdogs. Not in an arrogant way. They remained focused in the present. Not worrying about the future. Or regretting the past.

And above all, tried to see things not as the way they ARE. But as the way THEY are. And in so doing, the pressure evaporated. They celebrated the Championship. But also the realization of a vital life skill.

Knowing that they could never lose if they try and do their best. Even if they did lose the match, they would have won in any event. But if they did not give of their best and had won, in reality - in their essence - they would have lost. And let themselves, along with their team mates, down.

The same team spirit and attitude is important on any production. Along with a high degree of care and attention to detail through any phase. So during any casting, Ray was careful not to discourage anyone from chasing their dreams and championed those who had given their best and really tried.

He had an empathy for anyone who was put up for a part but did not get chosen. Hoping that it did not fuel feelings of rejection. Often the choice was not simply due to talent but also came down to matching looks or heights or personality types.

Other times within the industry, those with the most natural talent were not thought to be ideal if they were perceived to be temperamental or difficult to work with and that a studio might be not be large enough to accommodate an ego. Or, yes - were just negative people at the core, who would drain all the positive aspirations of those around them and therefore be incompatible to the goal which was set out to be achieved.

Fortunately Ray and the Cloud 9 team had been lucky not to suffer or experience this type of problem. On all the productions, the cast and crew were not only talented individuals but possessed great attributes and qualities as human beings as well. All down to earth, well balanced, level headed people. Team players. Never stars.

The cast and crew of 'The Tribe' were no exception. Ray recognized in them a creative passion and integrity. And knew they would be committed to working shoulder to shoulder to bring into existence programing that wasn't just commercially successful - but special, too. Which all concerned would be proud to have their name on, knowing that they all played a part in ensuring that it emotionally connected to its intended audience in a profound way.

The only member of the cast oblivious to this was Bob the Dog. But he was also so unique that maybe he wasn't quite as ignorant of the aspiration as anyone might have thought.

Bob was Ray's pet dog and had also appeared in the Matter Of Time episode of the 'Twist in the Tale' series. Ray felt that he would be ideal to play 'The Tribe' pet and mascot, though the animal trainers felt that the golden retriever would struggle a bit with the screen name which had been given in the scripts - Sherbert.

So to make it easy on everyone, most of all his special canine friend, Ray decided that the name should be changed. And Sherbert became Bob the Dog, which was his usual name, whether or not he was starring in front of the camera or doing what he did away from the studio - simply being a pet dog.

But Bob the Dog was more. An enigma. Rumor has it that he was found by the animal trainers walking along a railway track. Like a hobo. And seemingly had no home. He certainly had no tags, looked to be about two years old, but the trainers did not know for sure. And there was great mystery surrounding just exactly where he came from and what he was doing on the track.

Concerned for his safety, the trainers took the dog in and christened him Bob. After a period of time with no-one claiming him or reporting him missing, Bob became a regular fixture. He got on well with all the other animals with whom the trainers were working - cats, pigs, chickens, cows, sheep, birds, other dogs, horses - every conceivable species made available for production, including even insects and spiders.

He seemed to love and excel at the training regime, so that by the time he joined Ray as the household pet, Bob the Dog was capable of doing all manner of tricks and stunts. From leaping off of roofs to playing dead, opening doors, windows, and finding his mark in front of the cameras. He could - and very often did - even pry open the door of a refrigerator to go on an unauthorized midnight raid if he was hungry.

It was difficult to know if he was acting or full of remorse when he got into mischief. He could melt anyone's heart if they tried to scold him. All he had to do was put on his hang dog expression, which seemed to punctuate his huge sad eyes, and he was forgiven in no time at all.

Ray smiled as he watched Bob in the rushes. He certainly had a screen charisma. And seemed to know it. He could turn it on when needed. All HE needed was to see a camera and he would adopt a pose. Ray swore the dog even knew which was his most photogenic profile.

But as well as being an accomplished canine actor (he might think a star) Bob epitomized the saying of a dog being someone's best friend, exuding loyalty, unconditional love, and such an empathy of understudying as if to say that I might not be able to talk but I know exactly who you are and what you're going through. And you can rest assured, my friend, that I'm your special friend and will always be there for you, do my best no matter what. Until the very end.

When Bob wasn't on set, he would laze around Ray's office or take himself for a walk around the other offices to get some attention or scraps of food from the studio commissary, Take 9. And everyone on the team adored him as much as he did them.

Most department heads in New Zealand worked to the Executive in charge of Production, who reported to Ray, along with the Director of Production Finance. The Managing Director of Cloud 9 in London oversaw all other aspects of legal and business affairs, as well as most administrative matters. He, along with the Head of Marketing and Sales, also worked to Ray, as did Harry as Head of Development.

Harry was based in London - and later Spain - and was in almost daily liaison with Ray directly on all script matters either by telephone or email.

But apart from those who reported directly to Ray, the flow of communication for all staff was through department heads, structured to ensure a strict protocol which was important so that Ray could focus on his creative tasks as Executive Producer, and had been implemented by the management of Ray's joint venture partner.

He would speak to all on the team, of course. But having all the range of activities across all departments delegated, meant that Ray was able to maintain an overview without getting bogged down in any unnecessary minutia or irrelevant detail, so he would rarely be disturbed or distracted with minor problems. Or good news. Only if there was a major problem. And in production - problems occurred each and every day.

It could be something to do with story lines for the next block of scripts being impossible to facilitate logistically and which would mean they would have be rewritten. Or inadequate coverage being available, which would cause difficulties for editors finding themselves unable to cut the footage together.

No two days were ever the same. But as sure as the sun sets and rises again, each day would herald some kind of unexpected problem to contend with, requiring Ray to make decisions so the Cloud 9 ship could alter direction and yet still somehow remain on course.

The definition of insanity, according to Albert Einstein, was to do something the same way and yet expect an alternative conclusion. He should have been a producer, Ray always thought. As in life, when one is in production, the only way to solve a problem is to define what the problem is and then alter the way of operating to bring about a solution which manifested after examining all the options. And then doing something different would bring about a different result.

'The Tribe' production was running really smoothly for almost two weeks after Ray arrived back from Cannes. He thought it was unusual - and was thankful - not to have any major problem as such to contend with, apart from a bit of slippage in minutes being filmed each day to keep the production on schedule. But that kind of thing was normal.

It wasn't serious enough to cause Ray or his team any major concern as a second unit could pick up the material needed. But the situation always needed to be monitored to make sure they didn't get too far behind, otherwise it could cause a real problem to be caught in a trend of having to play catch up.

And then out of no-where, Ray was called into an urgent meeting with his production team.

CHAPTER TWELVE

JOURNAL: NOVEMBER 1998

'We don't think Paul is very happy,' the Executive in charge of Production informed Ray.

'Has something happened?' Ray asked. But deep down he knew what the difficulties would be and these were confirmed by the team. They had alerted him weeks earlier in Cannes that Paul was struggling with homesickness. But there were more serious issues to address.

To many outside the business, the film and television world is a glamorous one. But behind the red carpet and spotlight it is a long and arduous process for all concerned bringing motion pictures or television series to the screen.

The cast and crew work on average a twelve hour day. That could extend to fourteen on occasion, which is draining enough over a six month production schedule for adults - but exhausting for a young cast. With very early wake up calls needed to make sure they are ready to go into make up and wardrobe prior to going on set. On location they might be required to get up even earlier to allow for travel time.

Between filming scenes the cast would rehearse what is to be shot, or spend time with a dialogue coach, or do school work in the Cloud 9 classroom which was located within the studio. On location this activity would be carried out on the cast buses or trailers.

The Lunch break on both location and in the studio is normally 45 minutes, but beyond that there are no formal breaks. Due to the nature of filming, it can require a lot of seemingly just hanging around waiting while the crew prepare to set up between takes. Either to light a scene or lay camera tracks for a new angle to be shot, which means a change of direction is needed, with backgrounds being cleared or re-set.

The constant waiting and stop - start - stop - go - routine is draining in itself for a cast member trying to retain concentration and remain in character. But this can be further diluted if several takes are shot. Very often the very first or second take is the best as it is fresh. Which might not work due to a technical problem, such as a camera losing focus.

The next take might work technically but not artistically. An attempt to get a better performance can then be counter productive since delivering lines convincingly might evaporate if too many takes are shot, resulting in ever decreasing circles whereby attempts of obtaining something better, both artistically and technically, might produce the opposite effect - something worse.

Perfection does not exist. But those with a creative or artistic streak pursue it on any and every production, hour after hour, day after day, week by week.

An infrastructure of support was always placed around the cast. For the younger cast members - chaperones, house parents, tutors, dietitians, even psychologists were retained to monitor how each cast member was coping being away from home and to ensure that the post apocalyptic story lines, let alone the character interplay, was having no negative effects.

The themes were hard hitting. From attempted date rape, to teenage pregnancy and post natal depression, the attempt to bring about social justice in an anarchic and lawless society, to facing the prospect of mortality, with the dangers ever present of becoming infected with the deadly virus.

And the impact could have a traumatic effect for any younger person watching it all at home, just as much as the cast involved off screen.

Ray thought that on screen it was important for Amber and Salene to provide elements of comfort and nurture to the younger characters as a surrogate mother or a big sister might. Always reassuring.

The introduction of a character like Tai San was vital to inject spirituality and another different dimension. Even the bully, Lex, and his sidekick, Ryan, possessed redeeming qualities to evoke a sense of hope, otherwise there was a danger that it could all become very sombre and dark.

Bray and Amber were essential as forces of good. But they were also tortured by inner turmoil. So Jack provided elements of humor and ingenuity to counterbalance all the hardship in the quest to survive and build a better world.

Fictional romances simmered with very attractive people acting out sexually charged story lines. And it was important to ensure that did not overspill away from the set. Any adolescent infatuation could easily disappear as quickly as it surfaced, making it difficult to maintain a professional approach if a personal relationship soured, which could precipitate conflict and jeopardize morale within a group of young people not only working together - but living closely with each other as well.

The group dynamic was forever monitored. Off and on screen. Matters of care and welfare were always paramount for any member of team, whatever the age on any production.

But extra attention to every detail across all areas was made in an attempt to ensure that the time spent filming the series was a rewarding and fulfilling experience for all the young cast, rather than a frustrating and unhappy ordeal.

The crew themselves became very protective and supportive. And very quickly all on the team bonded and looked out for each other as a family might - or even a Tribe - united in adversity and working closely together to achieve a common goal.

But for the cast it was like a cross between joining the army and attending a boarding school. Very structured. Very disciplined. And it didn't suit everyone.

Issues of homesickness would always surface. The schedule allowed for occasional trips to visit family, and social functions like barbecues or outings to bowling clubs were regularly arranged.

Most weekends or any spare time though, would be spent learning and memorizing lines from the scripts. Or doing homework. Or dealing with interviews for press releases. And if a series became a success, the workload would only increase with promotional trips and footage which might need to be shot, along with answering fan mail.

So Ray knew full well - and could sympathize with - any of the innumerable difficulties that a young member of cast might experience. Not just on any production but in the industry overall. It was highly competitive. And as in sport, required a dedication to stay on top and perform to the highest professional level. The workload was forever relentless.

For anyone who chose to pursue a career in the creative arts, as a form of artistic self expression, meant that they really needed to love it if they wished to survive in a professional arena. Doing it as a hobby was different.

But no-one could - or should - ever go through all the emotional hurdles and the overwhelming effort that is required by simply liking the industry or the creative process. They had to love it. And rather than simply wanting to do it, have a need to do it. Above all else, a need to do it almost as if it was a calling, which fuels the determination to continue on and chart one's way through all the myriad of complex vulnerabilities and difficulties.

Paul had given a great performance and was certainly an asset to the series but there was no point in trying to enforce any contractual obligations by insisting that someone, let alone a younger member of the cast, stay and do what they are not happy doing. That would be counter productive to not only the well being of the project but the welfare of the young lad himself. Who was hearing impaired, as was his character.

The surreal part was that Paul enjoyed some of it. And didn't want to leave, as such. But overall it had been noted that it was a struggle for him, and with the grueling schedule ahead it would not get any better, only worse.

'The issue is probably down to the fact that's it's all not turning out to be what Paul expected and he's missing his friends and family and routine. So let's get him back home. We'll just have to work around it,' Ray advised his production team.

He admired the fact that Paul had really tried to make a go of it and did not want him to feel distressed or disillusioned in any way. He had, after all, committed to playing a part in a television series. It wasn't a prison sentence. But it wasn't all fun and games either.

It did leave a question though of how to explain any sudden disappearance in story terms. So Ray spent a few days considering the options.

Scripts were written in blocks, which meant that if 12 Episodes had been written in one block, parts had already been filmed and it would be very confusing to write Paul out and explain why he disappeared, only to have him appear in another location. Or if his sister was concerned that he had gone missing in some scenes, but apparently not in others. So there was a huge continuity problem.

Production is also in blocks. Footage is not shot in story sequence but how best the block might work economically and logistically to maximize the most productive shooting time. This might mean that all or most material in one particular set or locations could be lumped together and scheduled over a few days in one place, rather than zig zagging back and forth to other sets and or locations.

Scenes in a rail yard would be grouped together and filmed at the same time, even though some scenes might not feature until much later in the block. So new scenes to reveal any disappearance could result in the character appearing again, having gone missing due to material which had already been shot.

In the end Ray inserted a few lines to imply that Paul was sick and tired of the bully, Lex, being mean and had taken off - basically editing around the continuity problem both in scripting terms and in post production of the block, deciding that it would be better to just have the character disappear, rather than definitively explain what had happened.

It was possible that Paul could have even been re-introduced in another series. So it was felt that it would make sense to leave the story line doors open, rather than slamming them shut through a fictional death. Zoot's demise would be traumatic enough.

Where Paul's sister Patsy was concerned, Ray felt that it was necessary for her to refer to missing her brother, but again it was entirely plausible that she and the rest of the Tribe would not dwell on the fact that Paul had gone out one day never to return.

This punctuated the changing attitudes of the characters and that they had become sensitized to what occurred in this fictional new world they inhabited, being so different to the real world.

Strays roamed the streets and lands and could be captured and sold at any time as slaves. With the death of the adults and the clock also ticking for those advancing in age where they might be vulnerable to catching the virus, the sanctity of life as well as routine, would take on an entirely different meaning.

Survival in a post apocalyptic world would generate a different imperative, point of view and set of reference points from how one might react in the real world. Besides, there was no other option other than for Paul to simply disappear and for his sister and fellow Tribal members to continue on, confronting all the struggles and challenges they faced to get through another day.

Although the continuity of a missing Paul seemed to have been resolved, another problem surfaced a few weeks later when the editors delivered a first rough cut of the first few episodes of filming.

Ray had been reviewing the music which was delivered by the composer and really liked all the cues, including the title track 'The Dream Must Stay Alive', which evoked exactly the right kind of sentiment he had in mind for 'The Tribe'.

He was keen to get on to spotting where the music would go in the early episodes so that they could get locked off. Which required a fine cut, which is the process following the rough cut when his notes had been implemented by the editors.

Notes were thoughts and suggestions given by Ray to the editor. He might feel that an episode could benefit by tightening or a restructure to pace it all up, for instance. Or that a bridging scene might be required. Or perhaps even that a scene would play better by inserting reaction shots. Often the drama could be more potent by cutting away to observe how a character might be reacting to whatever another character might be saying.

But the problem he was having was that he instinctively felt that something just didn't work in the first few episodes. And that it would require more remedial action than his normal set of notes, which would average one hundred adjustments on a single twenty minute piece of material.

He couldn't work out quite what was wrong. And wondered if his 'beginning phobia'- that he suffered in writing - was now transcending to the screen. The first few scripts had always been strong, with a solid structure.

But now, having seen all the footage assembled, Ray felt it was a little confusing. The geography of the fictional landscape and backdrop was not very clear.

The story started in the city with the young character, Chloe, being saved by Dal and Amber as the menacing locusts Tribe (Locos) and their leader, Zoot, patrolled the city.

Then it cut away to rail yards where Zoot traded goods with Lex, his moll - Zandra, and the body guard - Ryan. A few scenes later, Lex, Zandra and Ryan met up with Amber, Dal and Chloe, who themselves had stumbled upon Patsy and Paul in a playground, being watched over by the wayward Salene and their pet dog, Sherbert, now known as Bob the Dog.

Lex had dialogue that he owned the sector. But then Zoot and the Locos appeared again and gave chase to Lex, Zandra and Ryan. This was seeded so that the other characters could also disperse and discover a shopping mall where the lone figure of Jack, yet another key character, lived. Lex, Zandra and Ryan would arrive at the looted shopping centre later.

The structure in the scripts focussed on how all the characters came together in the disbanded shopping mall (being the core set in the series, where much of the action would take place, revolving around the character interplay) so that an audience could quickly see them all deciding to live together, united as a Tribe. And understand the set up - that the mall would become their home and a fortress citadel to protect against the dangers from the outside world.

The key characters of Bray and Trudy would also arrive at the mall seeking a safe haven because Trudy was pregnant and on the verge of giving birth. But in the structure that did not occur until very much later.

Although there were no so called 'leads' in the series, as it was an ensemble piece, Ray thought it was important to try and get Trudy and Bray in earlier, in the very first episode as if anyone would be perceived to be the hero, it would probably be Bray - who was also an important juxtaposition to Amber being the natural leader, having formed the Tribe.

Bray and Amber were not destined for any romantic liaison until much later but it was important to introduce Bray as soon as possible, in Ray's view, as he was also an essential contrast to the bully, Lex.

Placing all this aside, the biggest concern was the premise. It was not very clear. The theme of a world with no adults and what actually happened would all unfold as the series did, but having seen the rough assembly Ray thought that a few essential elements were missing.

So he wrote several linking scenes to make the geography work better, introducing Trudy and Bray traveling to the city, as well as some material within the city of the other characters traveling to the mall. He believed this would help make the landscape and backdrop a little clearer.

He also thought he could deal with the premise in the main title sequence by arranging for some footage to be shot of a file marked 'Classified' being removed from a cabinet by a mysterious figure in a decontamination suit. Also, of a news anchor on television announcing that authorities were appealing for calm throughout the evacuation process.

Which, in turn, led to the idea that it might also be worthwhile linking the news anchor to a scene in a house announcing that priority would be given to those aged under eighteen years old. And to actually see parents saying goodbye to their child who was to be evacuated.

And if this was to be shot, then it would make sense for the child of the parents to be Trudy, in a flashback scene. That would also mean that she and Bray could be introduced even earlier, in which case they could reveal some essential exposition at the very beginning. They didn't have to explain everything. Just a few vital elements.

Ray then believed that if he inserted shots of a charred newspaper blowing in the city with a headline proclaiming that the pandemic was reaching unprecedented proportions, it would imply that something had happened. Which, along with the title sequence, would make the basic premise easier to comprehend. And if they had a unit shooting this material, then another new scene might as well be filmed to help illustrate the world the characters inhabited.

Which is what led to the very first scene appearing in 'The Tribe' of an ominous official vehicle with darkened windows, so the occupants were obscured, patrolling suburbia with a voice blaring through loudspeakers urging people to stay inside, due to code 9, isolation now being in effect.

Shooting the additional material might have solved one problem but Ray realized it could also create others if episodes were not locked off with the Christmas break fast approaching. The team were due to stand down for three weeks. Ray did not want to get into a position if any delay meant post production had further down time waiting for the new material to be shot.

An option was to bring forward later episodes and hope they could be post produced if the second block became the first, which could offset the wait for further footage.

But that could endanger the transmission delivery flow path for the first few episodes, which was already tight, and there was no way Channel 5 in the UK could shunt back the dates when the series was due to be aired.

Filming additional scenes could also endanger the actual production schedule which was multi episodic, being shot out of sequence in blocks. If the team stopped and lost a few days to shoot the new material, then it would mean that the footage needed to keep the overall schedule running smoothly would be knocked out of kilt.

There was already a second unit obtaining parallel material which really had to remain intact to obtain the required daily amount of footage, which was on average twelve minutes a day. Or one hour per week. To end up with 52 half hours in the six month shooting schedule.

It was all a huge logistical maze. There were fiscal matters to be aware of as well, regarding the budget needed to source additional sound, lighting and camera equipment. Let alone another director and crew to shoot the extra material.

The team could utilize the existing make up and wardrobe at the studios but the other cast and crew would need to be transported to the new locations and be fed and watered. Which meant finding a location manager to arrange it all, which was a complex enough task at the best of times. And time was not on anyone's side to identify the specific locations required to obtain the necessary permissions and insurance.

After several hours re-examining options, Ray decided that the only way was to run a small unit during the time the title sequence was due to be filmed, which would take away the pressure and concern that the core production schedule might be impacted. This team could feed off the main unit if Ray himself directed, shooting the new material at his home and surrounding areas.

So the very first opening shot of 'The Tribe' in episode one, Series One, of the official vehicle driving through suburbia - is actually on the road leading to the house Ray owned in New Zealand.

The flashback scene when Trudy and Bray are introduced was filmed in his living room and the traveling shots of Bray and Trudy along the water inlet and taking cover from the Roosters, was within the environs of his property.

The remaining material of all the other traveling and linking shots was picked up with the applicable cast being whisked between the studios, and from one location to another, in one day in the city.

The figure in the decontamination suit and news anchor were tagged on as extra scenes in a corner of a studio at the end of the second day, with the traffic leaving the city obtained by a small second unit during the time the Mall Rat Tribe were strolling along the beach in the front title sequences.

Ray worked with the editors to insert the new material into the early episodes. The problems he identified had been rectified. The structure was more coherent, as was the geography. And the premise of the series easier to comprehend plus the added bonus of introducing Bray and Trudy earlier.

He really enjoyed the post production process. Ray often thought of it as polishing up a brand new car before delivery. Or decorating a house prior to it being sold. A time when all the important touches are added. Such as music and sound effects, which are then all mixed together to enter into the last phase, being color grading, followed by final technical quality control and check, culminating into delivery to broadcasters.

In motion pictures, a director would normally work with editors to lock off a fine cut. Studio executives might then ask for changes, holding the ultimate editorial control. That is why the public are intrigued to view a director's cut, which is shown after a movie, as it can differ from the version initially released which accommodated all the notes from studio executives or distributors.

At Cloud 9 Ray was in an unusual position of having total editorial control over the final cut. Which was important to him to ensure that the branding on what he had envisaged remained intact. The post production phase, though challenging, was a special time when he could see the final results of often years of work, come together.

He always had high hopes for 'The Tribe' and was encouraged as the post production continued and the last block of raw material footage came in from the studio floor.

It was all working very well. And no other major changes were made. Apart from Ray deciding to interweave a satellite circling the earth, revealing an adult voice giving a message to the Tribe who had travelled to the mysterious Eagle Mountain Observatory base, advising that whoever picked up the transmission held the fading hopes, crucial to the survival of the entire human race.

Ray was convinced that it would be a tremendous cliffhanger. And he had many ideas on how it would all unfold if series two came into existence. A lot depended upon how the viewers would react when the series premiered in the UK on Channel 5. Along with the reaction at the market place in the industry, and if other broadcasters purchased the series at the MIP television festival.

During the wrap party for the end of filming, although there was still a period of post production to complete, the cast and crew celebrated the completion of principal photography.

Ray gave a speech to thank everyone for their commitment and supreme efforts. All cheered when he stated that he thought 'The Tribe' was special and would become a landmark series.

With the drinks flowing for the adult contingents, and encouraged by the exuberant atmosphere from all dancing and partying the night away, Ray took to the stage to jam with Lex, who proved to be an accomplished musician.

It was approaching the end of February, 1999.

As Ray played the guitar and sang along with other members of the cast and crew who whooped it up and joined in, he could feel a unique bond had formed amongst all present. On every production the team arrived almost as strangers but always left as friends.

But it was as if this team had also become more like a family. Like a Tribe - within a Tribe, replicating the theme of a group of people drawn together to become united on a long and arduous journey, overcoming obstacles and adversity along the way, determined to reach the summit of a common goal.

It seemed like no time at all since the welcome party. Now all present were celebrating the end of filming.

Ray wondered what lay in store ahead. Sensing that rather than the end, an exciting new journey for all would soon begin.

TRIVIA - THE TRIBE - SERIES ONE

With an average of 5 drafts per script and each script containing around 90 pages, this equates to about 23,400 pages being used to tell the story of Series One of 'The Tribe'!

Each of these scripts contained approximately 9540 words. 106 words per page. Or 496,080 for the whole 52 episodes. That's a lot of talking!!!

If someone read all the scripts out loud (at a rate of about 3 or 4 words per second) it would take around 25 hours non-stop! And that's without allowing time to pause for breath!

There were approximately 500 people involved in the making of 'The Tribe' Series One. Including writers, the cast, art and set designers, costume designers, make-up, lighting, camera, directors, production crew, editors, music supervisors, sound effects, chaperones, teachers, catering crew, dialogue coaches, photographers, background artists, drivers, nurses, cleaners, security and safety personnel, and administrative staff!

Series One represents a total of 1352 minutes of screen time. Or about 13/14 motion pictures. But another equivalent of 2/3 movies ended up on the cutting room floor with an approximate ratio of 15% of footage shot not making the final cut.

Each minute of screen time took the equivalent of 11,094 minutes to complete in people hours – that's 185 people hours per minute of screen time - and a lot of hard work!

250,000 people hours - is enough time to watch 576,923 half-hour episodes of 'The Tribe'!!

If one person produced 'The Tribe' by themselves and worked 10 hours a day for 5 days per week, with the number of people hours required, it would take one person over 96 YEARS to make Series One. Imagine the wait to know what would have happened in Series Two!

There were 85,000 liters of fuel purchased for the vehicles used to transport equipment and people.

Someone could drive 970,000 kilometers on that amount of gasoline, which would be enough to get to the moon and back.

This liquid equates to about 220,000 cans of soft drink. 220,000 cans piled one on top of the other would be 92,000 feet high (28km high).

This is almost three times the size of Mt Everest. To put this in pints of milk terms, this would give someone 130,000 bottles. Or 1.3 million tubes of toothpaste. And if that someone went through a tube a month, that amount of toothpaste would last 108,000 years.

Inside the studio and interior based scenes (but also used on exterior locations) large lighting rigs enabled the required quality of light for the cameras to record scenes on film.

The lighting rigs have a capacity each of about 12,000 watts of electric output. That's the equivalent of over 200 light bulbs per lighting rig or 1,500 sets of Christmas tree lights!

In addition, powerful electrical generators were used by the production crew on location to power the lights, cameras, sound, video playback, catering and communication equipment.

These generators emit over 65,000 watts of electric power. Enough electricity for 800 television sets!

If anyone felt they got hit by a thunderbolt watching the Series - then they were right. More power was regularly used in the making of the Series.

The computers used in post-production (for editing and music/sound effects) are also very powerful – they each have memories about 1.5 million times more than the memory a typical computer at home had 25 years ago (anyone want one for Christmas!).

There were so many nails used in the Phoenix Mall set that it would form a line of nails 75 miles long!

520m of gaffer tape was used in a typical week around the office and studio. This equals about 13,520 meters of tape per series. 45,000 feet!!!!

The animal trainer could line up in a row 3000 elephants to cover 45,000 feet.

45,000 feet is as long as 90,000 hotdogs. (The catering manager would require a huge BBQ).

Cloud 9 received on average 4000 phone calls per month. This is a total of 24,000 calls for the production aspect alone (placing aside the other elements).

If the average duration of the call was one minute, then 24,000 minutes of talking or 400 hours were taken in Series One to answer the phone. That would take nearly three weeks to talk non stop.

24,000 minutes is as long as 200 Shakespearean plays. In 24,000 minutes you could say the word TRIBE 1.6 million times.

In the time it took to film the first series of 'The Tribe', over 230,000 cups of coffee and tea were consumed by everyone involved in making the series.

That's the equivalent of 2,500 jars of coffee (with 40 cups) and 2,500 packets of tea bags (with 40 bags).

That's enough coffee and tea to last a single person drinking 4 cups per day - for almost 158 years!

For production stills alone, in an average week the stills photographer used on average 10 rolls of film, that's 260 rolls to accommodate 9,000 photos taken throughout Series One.

If someone actually laid out all of these photos in a square, it would cover 1.3 miles sq.

The other type of film used (for continuity) was polaroid. On average about 600 still photos per month. That's 3600 polaroid shots for the Series.

About 900 feet of film was used for every half hour episode of 'The Tribe'. That equates to about 47,000 feet of film over the 52 episodes.

Or 8 miles of film – and that's as long as a traffic jam with over 2,200 cars in a row!

The series was filmed on both 4×3 and 16×9 aspect ratio formats – which means that fans around the world can enjoy the series on both the television screens used today, along with the new widescreen television screens of tomorrow.

The master tapes can be adapted for High Definition transmission.

Throughout the six month production period 30,000 meals were served to the cast and crew. Imagine all the washing up!

Those 30,000 meals weighed about 30,000 pounds – or 13.6 tonnes!

That's as heavy as four hippopotamuses!

The Cloud 9 production offices used 5000 paper clips in the six month filming period.

If anyone joined all the paper clips together, this would form a line about 416 feet long – that's as long as 28 family-sized cars, or as long as over 60 people.

It would take about 6 hours non-stop to join all 5,000 paper clips into one long chain (assuming 4 seconds per one paper clip)!

If someone climbed to the top of the famous Pyramid of Giza in Egypt (about 450 feet tall) and dangled the chain of paper clips, then it would almost reach the ground!

The 416 foot long giant paper clips would also be longer than 6 Diplodocus dinosaurs or 12 giant boa constrictor snakes!

The make up department used 164 cans of hairspray, 75 containers of gel, 160 tubes of hair color and almost 40,000 cotton buds.

The music department featured on average 15 minutes of music each half hour episode. Or 780 minutes on average of music for the Series, which equates to 13.9 hrs.

It took about 5 days to spot and edit music to picture per episode, a long and time-consuming process to match each cue to each frame.

Over all, 250 different pieces of music were used.

From the time of starting to work on the last incarnation of the premise and format, it took approximately 3 years for

Cloud 9 to develop the title, prior to even the commencement of principal photography on 'The Tribe' Series One.

As far as Ray is concerned, it took him about 38 years to bring 'The Tribe' Series One to the screen (From the time of having the basic idea - not the actual premise.)

That is a LONG time for a writer to have been in development hell.

Or to start writing the first page of a story!

'The Tribe' is often referred to as being an overnight success.

No-one has ever mentioned this to Ray.

For all who know him, it would take 1 second to realize that if they DID mention it - they would have little hope of getting out of his office alive.

Saying that 'The Tribe' was an overnight success is a way of making Ray angry.

Giving him a pair of blue socks is one sure way of being forgiven.

Watching 'The Tribe' - and Keeping Your Dream Alive - is the easiest way to make Ray happy.

Other than telling him that he looks young for his age.

CHAPTER THIRTEEN

JOURNAL: APRIL 1999

It was difficult to gauge the reaction at the official launch for Series One of 'The Tribe' at the MIP television festival in Cannes.

Key broadcasters, as well as the press, had been invited. Ray was initially encouraged by the interest as he mingled and informally discussed his latest production during the cocktail reception prior to showing the trailer which had been cut together. After which he would take the stand to answer any questions.

Amidst an air of nervous and excited anticipation, the lights dimmed and the trailer began. And Ray could just tell from the expressions of all who were watching that this series wasn't quite what was expected.

He hoped that perhaps he was just tired and misreading the reaction, feeling really jet lagged, having just arrived in the south of France earlier that morning.

As always, it had been a long journey from New Zealand to Cannes. But an even longer one to produce the series. The last of the 52 episodes were nearing the completion of post production. And Ray had many late nights during the lead up to his departure, working with the team to get the trailer ready in time for the festival.

He hadn't had much of an opportunity to discuss with the Cumulus team how the trailer had been received on the distribution stand. He missed the first few days of the festival, unable to attend for the full duration, since he needed to spend as much time as he could while he was in the northern hemisphere for meetings with his board in London. Also, to have a story conference with Harry about a new series Ray had created - 'Atlantis High'. Plus discussing a potential second series of 'The Tribe'. But a lot depended on how the first series was received and he was determined to be present at MIP to attend the official launch.

The lights in the elegant hotel banqueting suite were switched back on when the trailer finished. And it received a round of polite applause from all present. But it was hardly enthusiastic.

Ray felt a bit like the Zero Mostel and Gene Wilder characters in the original Producers film. The story concerned two producers who devised an elaborate financial scheme to purposely make the worst Broadway musical. Ever. Guaranteed to lose money. So that they could achieve a tax and insurance refund.

Both were thrilled by the audience staring open-mouthed, in pure disbelief at the stage, stunned to see a chorus of Nazis singing and dancing to the song 'Spring time for Hitler and Germany. Autumn for Poland and France'. It was so full of bad taste. Outrageous. And guaranteed to fail. Which would bring about success for the two main characters.

Ray had some sympathy for anyone in Germany who viewed the film. He hoped that they would see - and even enjoy - the subtle black humor. He was sure it was never intended to insult a nation who had also suffered from a dark and devastating time in the world's history.

The film was written and directed by the comic genius, Mel Brooks. With a brilliant twist. Despite trying to sabotage the musical production, the audience and critics eventually erupted into wild applause, hailing the production as so different it was pure genius. So the perpetrators succeeded. And through that success - failed.

The problem for Ray though was that the sparse applause after 'The Tribe' trailer had been shown didn't expand. But quickly faded. And as Ray took questions from the floor, he knew immediately that he was in trouble.

There was a subtext within the questions when he was asked why he ever wanted to make the series. As if they were really saying - are you crazy? Others probed what made him think that viewers would respond to such a wild look of make up and wardrobe design. Just from the tone, Ray instinctively knew that the people asking the questions were not enthralled. As were those who referred to the post apocalyptic thematic, which seemed to be very grim and dark.

It was as if they thought that like the film 'The Producers', Ray had also devised a sure way of losing money for anyone who had invested. But rather than failing because they succeeded - Ray's production was bound to fail.

He was not given an opportunity for any meaningful exchange about character or plot and why he thought the series would emotionally connect with an audience.

Or why he believed that the theme of building a new world order out of the devastation and heartache of the old one was positive and aspirational. Few seemed to be that interested.

Preferring to discuss past productions. Along with what the next production might be for Cloud 9.

Ray gave a basic overview of 'Atlantis High'. He would never go into any great detail on any series until an official launch, let alone one which hadn't even been developed yet. So was determined to keep it all under wraps and tried to steer any conversations back to 'The Tribe'. Announcing, to the surprise of everyone present - including Ray himself - that he was planning on producing a further 52 episodes. Before a single episode of the first series had even been aired.

'Do you think that is wise, Ray?' the Chairman of Ray's joint venture partner asked at the board meeting in the Cloud 9 head office in London.

'No, if you want to know the truth,' Ray replied. 'I don't think it's wise at all. Anyone would have to be out of their minds to do what I'm suggesting.'

Ray could see that the board were more than a bit confused by what he was saying, as well as concerned. Though some on the board couldn't help but smile at the contradiction in terms as he continued.

'But that hasn't stopped us before. It was a huge risk to do the Classic Collection. And to produce even 52 episodes of 'The Tribe' in the first place. That was like jumping from the fifty second floor. All I'm recommending we do is climb a few more storeys.'

'And?' the board enquired.

'If we fall from the fifty second floor or the hundred and fourth, it won't make that much difference. We're still going to get hurt. If it doesn't work out, we're commercially vulnerable either way. But I believe that it will work out. Passionately. I'm convinced of it. And if it does and we don't have a follow up series ready to go, then we'll regret it and would hit the ground - hard - when we didn't need to. It would be tantamount to pushing ourselves over the edge.'

Ray wasn't being cavalier. Or glib. To him, it was certainly unprecedented to produce product without it being tried and tested. But rather than do a pilot, they had taken the risk on the first 52 episodes. To do another 52 was a calculated risk and one that they simply had to take. There was no option, in Ray's view. And he was unable to understand why anyone else did not understand. It seemed so obvious.

They couldn't just strike the main mall set. They would have to leave it standing. Empty. Which entailed costs for security and insurances purposes.

It would make no sense to strike the set. Only to rebuild it again. Building costs had already been incurred and expended on the set in the first series so they could amortize that into the second series.

Likewise with all the costumes and props and post production equipment which had been capitalized. There was a huge overhead in having the studio base which they would have to pay for whether or not they were in production. A fleet of cars to maintain. Houses which had been leased. They had options on all the cast and other members of the crew. And if they were not taken up in the defined time, then some may not be available.

And if they wanted to secure the availability, then they would have to pay salaries to core members of the team, so they might as well be in production anyway.

Cloud 9 could always undertake another production so that the infrastructure which had been put in place would not be in dry dock, so to speak. But there was a risk of that not being successful in the market place. Just as with a second series of 'The Tribe'. It carried no greater risk. Ray wasn't put off by the luke warm reception at MIP to the launch. Broadcasters were not the true consumers. Only viewers were.

'The Tribe' was different. Broadcasters preferred to follow a safe trend. He knew all about that from his time at the BBC.

If the viewers responded favorably to the first series, as Ray was convinced they would, other broadcasters would come on board.

Operating outside the system as an independent, he felt that it was commercially dangerous and even complacent for Cloud 9 to rely on following a trend, believing the minute anyone in the industry does it - then they would lose. Derivative product rarely spelt anything other than mediocrity. Ray's aspiration was to set a trend. Never to try and follow.

He wasn't arrogantly saying 'The Tribe' was the greatest series which had ever been produced. The team did their very best within the budget and time constraints. But it was in no way derivative. Or sanitized. Or soft.

He had set out to accurately portray the world young people inhabit, examining all manner of themes which were relevant. Including the dream of building a better world. And dreams, Ray believed, were important. Not only to him. But viewers. He was convinced that it would connect. An audience could always tell whatever the constraints of any budget and time frame, if product had been make with conviction and integrity. And Series One of 'The Tribe' certainly had. Along with every other title produced by the company to date.

Above all, Ray just had an instinct that it was vital to fuel the momentum of the first series with a second one being readily available, otherwise any protracted delay might undermine the audience awareness of the brand he wanted to build.

'Can I ask everyone sitting around this table just one question before I rest my case?' Ray asked the board.

'Of course you can,' replied the Chairman.

'Risk investment carries a return and can be viewed as making a contribution to any budget. Or a commitment. So do you consider yourselves to be pigs? Or chickens?

All on the board deadpanned. One said, shaking his head in bewilderment, 'I'm not sure I entirely understand, Ray. And even if I did - why on earth is that relevant?'

'What has 'The Tribe' got to do with breakfast?' replied Ray.

All shrugged in mounting confusion, wondering where all this was going.

'Think of bacon and eggs. The chicken makes a contribution. But the pig makes a commitment. For me, this series is in no way a chicken. 'The Tribe' - along with myself - is a pig. And I'm committed to it. I just hope you all are, too'

'Well, we can always rely on you for a different way of looking at things,' the Chairman smiled, as did all on the board.

And Ray knew that there was no need for anyone to say anything further. He had their full support. 'The Tribe' Series Two was officially green-lit.

'The Tribe' Series One made its debut in the UK on April 24th. The ratings for the opening first episode were respectable, rather than overwhelming. Ray was back in New Zealand by then in pre-production, planning the next series, and was disappointed with the initial result, wondering once again if he had scored a spectacular own goal.

But 'The Tribe' had caught the attention of the consumer press, who viewed it as a landmark series and one to watch. Ray didn't pay attention to any reviews and what any critics had to say in the trade press. It was important though that entertainment and television magazines and newspapers had taken notice, recommending the series as a pick of the day and even the week in several major publications. Which might encourage an audience to tune in and decide for themselves whether or not they liked the series.

The Cumulus team were also having enquiries from broadcasters who wanted to see episodes. Given the reception at MIP, it was difficult to know if it was due to a genuine interest. Or as a segment of the population, who slow down when driving to see a car accident, stemmed from a similar vicarious need to view what they might perceive as being a multi million dollar disaster. An absolute wreck.

But positive word of mouth spread in the UK over the ensuing weeks and the viewing figures increased. Along with growing interest from foreign broadcasters, who were monitoring the performance on Channel 5. Before long, the series was sold to Finland. Then Norway. With more requests for viewing cassettes coming into Cumulus distribution every day. The world it seemed was slowly going Tribal.

CHAPTER FOURTEEN

JOURNAL: SEPTEMBER 1999

By the time Episode 8 of the first series had been transmitted in the UK, Ray felt more confident that the trend was showing that 'The Tribe' was finding an audience. Viewer research illustrated that although they were a little taken aback by the gritty story lines, they were also enticed by them, along with the overall series thematic.

Almost all were particularly surprised however by the death of Zoot. Ray knew Zoot had the potential to become an icon within 'The Tribe' mythology and that many would think it was a great mistake, let alone really odd to kill the character off so early, if at all.

But he instinctively believed it was essential. He had a story framework in mind to resurrect the character way down the line. And for the next few series the story of Zoot had been designed to fuel a range of character interplay and conflict.

During his time as Head of Development at the BBC, Ray discovered that so many producers and writers thought in part, rather than totality, as indeed he had also done on occasion. But being on the other side of the table brought about a different awareness.

A producer or a writer might make a pitch for instance, convinced that their idea or format could become a long running series, knowing that is exactly what most broadcasters are always searching for. Yet when Ray asked what happens in future series, it usually drew a blank and they were sent away to rethink so that they could outline how it would all unfold.

The first rule that writers are taught, or very often discover when they start filling the blank pages, is that a single story in whatever form is structured in basically three acts. Or parts. The beginning. The middle. And the end.

Each part is essential to the other. In almost equal measure. To provide conflict for the characters through a story evolution. So that an audience shares in the journey of a narrative, unfolding with twists and turns in a non predictable and contrived manner. Culminating in a plot resolution or revelation - and hopefully an realization - that a character is different in the end than it was in the middle or beginning.

Not in personality or trait. But from gaining an understanding. Something which has been learned or achieved on the journey. Central to the thematic. What a story might be about. Which is not the same as what actually happens in the narrative. And that also needs to be structured. Ideally in three acts. Whether it's a single episode. Or a series.

If a story is about happiness - for someone to be happy, they have to be sad. If they are always happy, they might not know that they are happy without being sad. They have nothing by which they can define it or compare it. It seems so obvious. But not always so. Within the three act structure, one would concern happiness, two - unhappiness, three - happiness again. But a different realization in the resolution, now knowing that for someone to be happy, they have to be sad. However simplistic, it is a good illustration that points of view ideally need to evolve.

There can never be any drama without conflict, heroism without adversity, good without evil, redemption without understanding, emotion without motion. Themes and stories require opposite and contrasting forces in order for them to unfold.

Take a story about organized crime. And imagine a writer having to portray a mafia figure as being heroic. The mafia don't do that for a living. They are never perceived to be the so called 'good guys'. And a mainstream audience always needs a hero to cheer. Or a villain to boo at the root of a story. Otherwise, they cannot emotionally connect. So it is only possible to portray someone intrinsically 'bad' as 'good', by introducing someone else who is 'REALLY BAD' in a comparative context, which is what occurred in the motion picture 'The Godfather'.

Redeeming aspects of the main protagonist were portrayed in such a way that an audience, although not approving of the mafia in any way, had a sympathetic understanding from an awareness of something worse and more dangerous with which to compare the endeavors of the central characters.

And they actually found themselves caring and cheering for the stereotypical 'bad guy' in any normal story, but who now is heroic and somehow 'good'.

For all the flaws and evils of contract killing and extortion and placing a severed head of a horse in a bed, if comparison exists within the framework narrative structure, even the mafia can be heroic.

When Ray first started out in television, he was astounded to be told by many a producer that the dialogue in a first draft script felt weak. Or that there needed to be more dimension to the characters. And the story felt a bit flawed, as well. Leaving Ray to think it was a total right off. With nothing at all left to build upon in a second draft. Only to be told that the selection of elements was solid and that he should build upon those. Confused? Ray was.

But then he began to realize that the selection of elements fueled all the key areas. Not confined to what happens - but more what a story might be about.

So that in a police series the story of a missing child in act one might be gripping enough. But by introducing another comparative dimension within the structure in act two, of the discovery that the child had actually run away, the story of an apparently abducted child could take a compelling about turn. And end up thematically in act three as being about child abuse, when introducing elements of why the child had run away in the first place.

A broadcaster who read the initial scripts of 'The Tribe' asked if it would be possible to have Zoot live. Sure that the character would become a cult, anti hero. And yes, that was possible. But it would have been a different series to the one Ray envisioned and planned. Zoot dying was an essential catalyst in the first act to fuel all that Ray had in mind for ensuing series.

It certainly could have been possible to have Zoot traveling around in his modified, graffiti-covered police car leading his Loco Tribe, intent on dominating through his anarchic ideology of Power and Chaos. But Ray thought that might run out of steam and end up as being repetitive, if not in the first series, certainly in the second. With the absence of a fresh comparative element.

He could have even seen the light and become a force of good. But there were already enough characters carrying that mantle in the Mall Rats. Which meant that if he couldn't evolve, he would have to remain bad.

Which would have been difficult within the structure, as redemption had been planned to interweave another dimension when he gently held his baby in his arms and pondered what future would lay in store for his child.

Which in itself seeded another element which was to be introduced through flashback scenes to show how Martin became Zoot, to shed light on why he chose his path of darkness.

Ray was always fascinated how both brothers might have become estranged - and so different, having had the same influences of both parents. And had considered that perhaps they shared the same mother but a different father, which he was always keen to explore. But there would be no time in the series and that would have to wait for a novel.

Zoot, as Bray's wayward brother, helped personify man's eternal battle through the aeons between the contrasting forces of good and evil. But Zoot, as he had been planned to unfold, was more of a young man who lost his way.

Within the framework of the elements selected, Ray had felt that Zoot's death would fuel not only some essential story lines and themes - but also various, interesting dimensions of conflict within the character interplay.

Even in the first series. Lex gloated at the prospect of his reputation being enhanced as the one who took out the legendary Zoot - but then felt unease at the price he would have on his head on the streets, with the Locos intent on retribution - which placed him, as well as the Mall Rats, in a vulnerable position. Ebony rose to take over leadership of the Locos, which helped her character evolve. There was inner conflict for Bray after his brother died, along with Trudy. And overall, so much rich and dramatic material which could not have been explored had Zoot lived.

Zoot was also central to punctuating the underlying thematic of young people building a new world order in their own image - whatever that image might be. And that in itself was fueled by an intriguing subtext - does consciousness determine existence? Or does existence determine consciousness?

And it wasn't only confined to the characters in the series. But an audience empathy as well. Some might relate to the Mall Rats. Others, the Locos. Others, even both. Or a different Tribe. Or whatever character with whom they might connect and identify. But new situations needed to be introduced to keep it all fresh, with long form drama having a ravenous story line appetite.

In Series Two, Zoot's death made provision for the introduction of the fanatical Guardian. And for Trudy to be the Supreme Mother and her baby the chosen one. And again, had Zoot lived, it could have not happened otherwise.

Ray cast an exciting actor with a tremendous range and knew he would be perfect for the part. The Guardian, and his tribe of the Chosen, followed the word of Zoot with an obsessive, zealot conviction, intent that Zoot's ideology live on and that his death would be avenged. So they would replace the Locos as the prime threat.

It was also an ideal metaphor to explore themes of worship, religion and dictatorship. How a cult can be enticing and perceived to be liberating for those wishing to belong. But can also become dangerous under the manipulation of anyone driven by an obsessive, manic conviction born out of misplaced idealism.

Principal photography of Series Two of 'The Tribe' commenced on the 9th August, 1999.

Ray was pleased to have also cast the talented young actress, with whom he had worked on the Blyton titles, in another new role of Ellie, convinced that her quirky romance with Jack would inject an endearing element.

And Ellie's elder sister, Alice, was played by a gifted young performer whom Ray believed would bring about a humorous and special quality to the character interplay. And having noticed another newcomer to the Cloud 9 fold in a subsidiary corporate production, 'Choice', which had been produced by Little White Cloud, Ray knew he had his perfect May, and that she would be another welcome new character.

The introduction of Alice and Ellie would help open the series up through exploring the backdrop of farming so that key areas of self sufficiency and growing crops could be featured. And another dimension of life on the dangerous streets would be viewed through May.

And with Amber needing to be written out to facilitate educational matters, Ray was sure that the feisty and determined new character of Danni would bring an interesting element with her quest for social reform through the introduction of a bill of rights.

The search to shed light on the mysteries of the virus, along with a possible antidote and cure, was also vital to drive the narrative and several story threads. And overall, Ray was convinced that Series Two had a sufficient framework of elements in place to fuel a diverse range of compelling human drama.

All the new characters looked as if they fit exactly into place during the 'show and tell' - a time when all cast were paraded prior to filming in full make up and wardrobe before Ray and his producer and executive in charge of production.

This was a forum to make any adjustments on any element of costume design, which was important to Ray so that he could ensure the branding and continuity remained intact. Wardrobe and makeup needed to remain within the style guide which had been devised. With every tribal marking, of every character, being thought out and having a different meaning.

Bray's wardrobe, along with his single hair extension plaited by vine, punctuated, for instance, that he was in tune with the natural world and Shintoism. Ebony's red makeup across her forehead signified a flame, which had been seeded to reflect a character which would be introduced much later. And the tattoo of Abe Messiah on her arm would also be featured in future storylines. Ryan's matchstick man logo on the sleeve of one of his hockey shirts represented the symbol of a Saint and had been actually been derived from the popular series of the same name which Ray watched back in England in his youth in the sixties.

Not all elements of make up and wardrobe had a particular significance. But there was a branding continuity Ray wanted to preserve within all the grungy fashion. From the metallic and futuristic look of the Demon Dogs, to even the twisted metal hair extensions worn by a Loco who might use a welding helmet or ice hockey mask - to illustrate that any item scavenged from society was adapted and worn as a fashion statement. And to portray an attitude.

Make up and wardrobe is always an essential aspect of any production. Even in real life, people dress as if in a uniform. There are exceptions to every rule, of course, but generally an accountant looks like an accountant, just as a biker looks like a biker.

For some reason a writer looks like a writer, just as a teacher usually looks like a teacher. Something would jar on screen, just as it would in real life, to walk into a bank and meet the manager with long hair, denims and leathers discussing a loan. Just as it would to see someone in a pin-striped suit, collar and tie riding around on a Harley Davidson.

An aging rocker still dresses as one and seems to possess the same attitude even though he might also be a grandfather. But sitting by the fireside with slippers and a cardigan is a different brand and image, in contrast to Sir Mick Jagger, still strutting his stuff on stage after all these years. Even though he's a grandfather, he doesn't seem like one. From his uniform and attitude, he looks more like he really is. A Rolling Stone.

So Ray was always pedantic with wardrobe and design, realizing the importance of it in all his productions. And 'The Tribe' was no exception. All characters had to look as if they truly belonged and utilized fashion as a method of self expression, living in a post apocalyptic world.

Elements of the very first show and tell for Series One were filmed to be shown to broadcasters and the footage contains works in progress make up and wardrobe. The material is planned to be released in a future limited edition dvd, considered to be a vital collectors item for fans interested in 'The Tribe' heritage. The footage was filmed in the same studio where the sequel of 'Worzel Gummidge' was produced back in 1987 which starred Jon Pertwee in the title role - who also occupied a place in 'Doctor Who' folklore, having played the third generation of the character.

Ray missed Zoot at the parade for the Series Two show and tell. He was very fond of the actor, as well as the character itself. And with an increasing workload, decided that he needed to recruit another member of the team in the inner circle of his executive office. So Zoot was retained as Ray's personal runner throughout Series Two.

Runners are contracted in all departments, from the art department to production, in the motion picture and television industries. The role is a great entry for someone wishing to get a foot in the door and gain experience. A runner literally runs errands, which involves every aspect of tasks carried out by the applicable department.

In the case of Ray, that meant that a runner could get an insight into all departments, as well as other areas in which the executive producer and chief executive were involved.

On one occasion, a previous runner to Zoot had a busy day with tasks which Ray's assistant outlined. The young lady was just keen to get a start in the industry and was really pleased to have obtained the role.

That day the runner's duties included purchasing some new socks, since Ray was in writing mode. Then she had to collect his car which had gone in for a service, which was to be followed by taking some notes he would dictate to her in the mixing suite when he viewed a playback. Later in the afternoon she had to go into the city to collect a visa from the passport office regarding a trip Ray was planning to Japan in the coming months.

And the runner would also need to deliver a video trailer.

'To where?' she asked, marking all her duties in a notepad.

'Cannes,' replied Ray's assistant

'Cannes? Where's that?' enquired the runner.   She was not from Wellington and didn't know the surrounding areas that well. But this run had nothing to do with the suburban environs.

'The south of France. And you'll need to leave tonight.'

'Are you serious!?'

'I've booked you out of Auckland, through Los Angeles and London, to connect with a flight to Nice. You'll be met by one of the drivers and can stay overnight. But for the return, I've only managed to get you out of London, through Singapore, Christchurch and Wellington.'

'Hey - not a problem,' said the runner, stunned and overcome with excitement.   She had never traveled much. 'Think I'm going to really love the film and television industry!'

Ray was late locking off a MIP trailer and could not endanger any delay with it being couriered. He was not due to leave for a few days himself and wanted the trailer to arrive in advance so that it would be checked and tested on the stand before the beginning of the festival. And the only way of knowing that it would arrive on time and safely was for the runner to personally deliver it.

Just over thirty hours later the runner not only found herself unexpectedly in the south of France - but her return trip had been rescheduled for a few days later. She was helping out on the Cumulus distribution stand.

Ray was pleased with the results of the rushes and rough assembly cuts as the footage for Series Two came in. The additional cast injected a fresh dimension. But they were not the only new members of the Cloud 9 team. Others had been hired to look after Internet services.

The 'Tribeworld.com' name for the website had been registered the previous October. Within a year, actually, of Google also being registered and coming into existence. Now fans were starting to use the website to interact. Which was expanded later in the year to provide more features, which in turn required more staff with the technical capability to service the growing demand, with so many aspects of Tribeworld being upgraded.

Nevertheless, the bulletin board on the website often crashed, which brought no end of frustration to the fans and especially Ray, since he liked to visit occasionally to monitor feedback.

He had little time available in his hectic schedule however with overseeing production, let alone Cumulus and Cloud 9, and needed to steal any available hour to sketch thoughts on the 'Atlantis High' series he was developing. In addition, the record producer, John Williams, and his team were in New Zealand recording a Tribe album - so the workload was increasing.

Ray welcomed the opportunity to have a few weeks break to wind down in the tranquility of the South Island in a secluded resort outside of Queenstown during the Christmas and New Year production stand down. But found himself pulling a cracker and writing a page. Deadlines never made provision or allowances for holidays.

Queenstown is a popular destination all year round. Tourists flock to the area to enjoy adventure sports, such as white water rafting, bungee jumping or jet boating. In winter the small picturesque town is busy with the alpine region attracting a host of skiers and snowboarders. In summer there is a good selection of golf courses, tracks for horse trekking or hiking and really good fishing available.

With the new millennium approaching, Ray had nothing special planned. He arranged to enjoy a quiet dinner with friends, then went back to his hotel suite deciding to at least see in the New Year. Being raised in Scotland and never one to ignore tradition, he liked to celebrate Hogmanay but wanted to have an early night.

As the clock struck midnight, he made a toast with a glass of malt whiskey in one hand. But spilled the mug of hot chocolate he was holding in his other hand, which had been ordered from room service. All over the deep pile white carpet, now stained brown, and a total mess.

The first few seconds of 2000 were spent with Ray covered in scalding hot chocolate, hopping around to relieve the pain.

And he wondered, with this auspicious start, what the next year might bring. Let alone a new millennium.

ATLANTIS HIGH FORMAT

'OUT-THERE' OUT-TAKES

Giles Gordon, a teenage student nerd, moves into Sunset Cove with his eccentric mother, Dorothy, and wacky Grandpa.

Sunset Cove appears perfect in every way - it is an idyllic coastal town where the beach is always around the corner, the sun forever blazes onto endless golden sands, the surf is up and never down.

And the people of the town are beautiful. All of them. Every single one. After all, this is a world of sunshine soaps where everything is perfect in tone - but as Giles soon discovers when he starts his new school, Atlantis High, there is more to Sunset Cove than meets the eye.

The students at his new school seem to be - weird. Really weird. Along with the teachers. Could the school - reputedly built on the lost city of Atlantis - have anything to do with this?

Giles soon falls in love with classmate, Octavia Vermont, who is beautiful and amazingly intelligent. However, Giles has a rival for Octavia's affections in the form of Josh Montana, the wealthy and handsome bad boy of Atlantis High.

Little does Giles know that Octavia is really a secret agent. And Josh Montana himself masquerades as a crime-fighting superhero at night.

And that's not all. Giles also makes friends with Beanie, a kid with very large, pointy ears and a fascination with flying saucers. Beanie doesn't know his origins - could he really be an alien?

Giles also becomes friends with Jet Marigold - a feisty, blue-haired chick with attitude - and a strong belief in wild conspiracy theories. Might some of her bizarre theories actually be true?

The science teacher at Atlantis High, Mr Dorsey, has a strange accent and a fondness for rodents. He has also developed an appetite for mice.

Or at least, Giles was sure that is what he saw when the tip of a tail disappeared into Mr Dorsey's mouth - a mouse had also vanished from the classroom cage that day.

Mr Dorsey also looks up to the stars and speaks into a flower. Is he just eccentric - or an alien on a secret mission?

Jet feels that is the case. And Giles, Octavia and Beanie set out to try and assist her in unravelling the mystery.

Along with a few more.

What is the secret of Giles' mother? Is there something lurking from her past - and who does she work for? Really?

Why does Giles' Grandpa always seems to have something to hide?

The military, under Commander Vermont, certainly seems as if it does, a constant sight around Atlantis High and Sunset Cove - but what are they searching for?

Whatever they discover, one thing is for sure. Giles, along with his friends, will all find themselves in for more than just a few unexpected adventures and surprises.

From a trip around the wonders of the world in a bus, to encountering ninjas and secret agents, a toy rabbit with a mind of its own, to making friends with a trio of intrepid alien travelers.

Oh, and there is a poltergeist or two, super-villains and superheroes and melodrama which may affect the world - and universe - forever.

This really is a series that has to be seen to be believed. And will entertain the entire family. Check it out. If you dare.

CHAPTER FIFTEEN

JOURNAL: 2000-2001

Ray sat on the Cumulus stand and was preoccupied, half listening to what the buyers were saying in each of the meetings.

He was more interested in their vocal inflections. And just couldn't stop himself from also glancing away on occasion to observe people in the crowds passing by. Or more precisely, their footsteps.

This was a habit he picked up in his early years when he was fully in music mode and became fascinated by the rhythm of how people walked or how they talked. Ray believed rightly or wrongly that it could show a lot about the person. Like a musical equivalent of body language.

Not just concerning personality type. But also their emotional state. He had discovered that someone well balanced and contented seemed to walk or speak in regular 4/4 time, for example. Others might have a different time signature or rhythm. Like 3/4, if they were stressed or going through a difficult time.

Since placing music on hold in favor of focussing on his writing and producing career, the habit disappeared. He still had a great love of music and was involved with it, of course, spotting cues for the soundtracks with the editors. And he enjoyed playing his guitar or the piano to relax. But he had no desire as such to compose, due to his workload and time pressures. Though Ray always wanted to come back to it someday. Music was his real first love.

Sitting with a broadcaster from Germany, Ray heard what the man was saying but it seemed to be in the background. In a different dimension. At the forefront was just the inflection and the rhythm of the voice.

'We're very interested in 'The Tribe'. For Germany. Would we be able to have free access to the masters for a dub?'

Ray gazed absently at the broadcaster. Having worked on the format of 'Atlantis High', as well as with John Williams on the Tribe album, Ray was in a different mode. And one which was unfamiliar. A sort of music - meets alien.

What struck Ray now and intrigued him was that the broadcaster was speaking in the same time signature as a waltz.

'Are you happy?' asked Ray, examining the man's face, searching for contentment in the eyes. Then he suddenly glanced away again at the footsteps of someone he noticed walking past in Latin American time. Like a salsa. That's different.

She seemed to be a very outgoing type. Or perhaps the rhythm was to mask how she really felt beneath a social veneer. He couldn't detect if there was an element of latent aggression. Or if it was more down to someone being a little insecure beneath the overly confident surface. Maybe it had nothing to do with this at all. And she was an alien. From a different planet.

Ray glanced back at the broadcaster, noticing him looking at him, a little off put and confused.

'You mean happy to obtain the series for Germany?'

'Of course,' replied Ray. 'That is exactly what I meant. Yes. Exactly. It had nothing to do with aliens whatsoever. Or music. But in a way it does.'

He managed to cover up and explain that he was referring to a new series he would be producing, 'Atlantis High', and also the Tribe's album which had been recorded. He was really keen to know how the broadcaster felt about 'The Tribe' and would have a member of the Cumulus team follow up.

Ray made a mental note to try and concentrate more in all the meetings, not let his mind drift. Above all, not to speak his thoughts out loud. But he just couldn't help check out how the German broadcaster walked when he left.

And it was as Ray expected. One. Two. Three. Like a Strauss waltz. A slow type of shuffle, like the broadcaster was skating. Nice and relaxed. No rush. Totally laid back.

In an encounter at festivals, such as MIP, everyone is polite and friendly. But this man's warmth was genuine. And Ray was sure that he was content within and well balanced, happy in all aspects of his life. And he hoped negotiations would resolve for 'The Tribe'. Ray liked the broadcaster and would enjoy working with him.

This would be the last television festival which Ray would attend for a long while and he would miss having the opportunity to chat with buyers and soak up the all market feedback.

But there was no option. His board agreed that extra staff would need to be recruited at Cumulus with an expanding catalogue of programming coming on line for distribution, and that Ray needed to be free to focus on the priority tasks, which were in all the creative areas.

More and more broadcasters were acquiring Series One and now also Two, of 'The Tribe'. Other titles in the company's back catalogue were also performing so well that Series Three of 'The Tribe' was green-lit and due to commence principal photography on July 4th.

This was slightly earlier than normal and would mean that the first blocks would be filming throughout the winter in New Zealand, which was not ideal but was essential in forward planning terms. And the scripts had been written to allow for a lot of adverse weather cover, so there were contingencies in place.

'Atlantis High' was scheduled to begin pre production in September, with filming commencing three months later, in January of 2001.

By then most of the work on Series Three of 'The Tribe' would have been completed. But post production would still be underway by the time the new series was filming. Logistically it was much more achievable, rather than taking a chance on trying to produce two entirely different series at the same time.

Producing one project was difficult enough. But two in parallel would invite problems, with the limited infrastructure and facilities Cloud 9 had in place.

The company was viewed by some to be a large operation. And in relative terms, for an independent company, it certainly was - with its range of subsidiaries handling distribution and ancillary rights. But although Cloud 9 also had its own production center, it was in no way the size of a Hollywood studio, many of which were more multi national conglomerates.

On the long flight back to New Zealand from the MIP festival, just the thought of the workload ahead was exhausting and difficult for Ray to comprehend, without referring to the schedule.

Series Three of 'The Tribe' would entail another 52 half hour episodes. With the 26 episodes of 'Atlantis High', that would bring a total of 78 scripts to oversee.

Plus, some cast members of 'The Tribe' were going on the road. Ray really enjoyed working with John Williams and the cast on all the recording sessions. And now promotional tours were being arranged for both Series One and Two, along with the debut album, which would add to all the tasks. Time was stretched, to say the least.

Ray knew the cast would be great ambassadors for 'The Tribe', Cloud 9 and New Zealand. All were unassuming and would handle themselves really well and enjoy meeting the general public, as much as the fans would enjoy seeing their favorite members of the cast.

The tour would involve press interviews, radio and television guest spots. But also some live personal appearances, so there was a lot to arrange. From rehearsing dance routines to security being in place, itineraries to briefing the cast on how to deal with different situations.

If they arrived at an airport to be met by screaming fans, all the cast were so unaffected by celebrity that they would probably look behind, wondering who else must be in the terminal to warrant such a reaction. They would never consider themselves as being famous or as stars.

But now that their faces were in peoples' living rooms on television screens and no doubt on posters on bedroom walls in so many countries, Ray wanted to make sure that they were adequately coached to cope with every eventuality which can come from being thrust into the public eye.

During a flight from Nice to London, Ray once noticed a familiar face in the seat in front of him. It was Ringo Starr, traveling with his actress wife, Barbara Bach.

'I can't believe it,' said a younger member of Ray's family. 'I know who that man is.'

'So do I,' replied Ray, in an undertone. 'But don't stare. Let him travel in peace.'

'Wonder what Thomas the Tank Engine's doing on our flight?'

Ray did a double take at the youngster and reflected on the meaning of any theory of relativity. And no. Not because he was in transit with a family member! To the child, Ringo Starr was rightly the voice of Thomas The Tank - whereas to Ray, he was the drummer of the iconic Beatles.

In the terminal Ray stood beside Ringo as both men retrieved their luggage from the belt. And was astounded when Ringo nodded and exchanged a long glance as if he recognized Ray somehow. Rather than the other way around. It was a strange and off putting feeling.

Perhaps he had read an article and seen a photograph of Ray in one of the MIPCOM trade papers, since he was probably in attendance. Ray certainly knew where he had seen the face of Ringo. He had almost hero worshipped the Beatles since the first time he heard them on record.

But now he did not even want to speak in case Ringo was not the same as Ray thought he might be in so called real life. He had an overwhelming fear that he might be disappointed if the easy going and fun member of the legendary fab four Ray had idolized since he was a young teenager turned out to be in reality a grouchy temperamental super star.

He was heartened however and felt a little sorry for Ringo, who was hounded by fellow travelers in the airport, taking photographs and asking him to sign autographs. Ringo was very generous and did this, but was experienced enough to know when to draw the line, otherwise it would have been never ending and he would have been there all day.

The first lesson for 'The Tribe' would be to always be there for the fans who are there for 'The Tribe'. And to never disappoint any who might ask for an autograph. That could be so devastating. The cast were not the sort of people not to do this anyway and were very warm human beings by nature. But when on tour - they also needed to learn when to draw the line and move on, otherwise they would never be able to do all they had to do with their hectic schedule.

Scripts were being written with the tours in mind and also to allow for some of the other characters to have time away to fulfill their educational commitments. And there also needed to be room in the Tribe production to make provision for 'Atlantis High'.

It was going to be a very quirky series. So quirky that by the time Ray briefed a composer with all the complex musical themes and elements to punctuate each scene, he thought it would make more sense for him to work on the music himself since he knew exactly what he wanted.

Otherwise, if the tone and flavor did not match what Ray had in mind, there was no window to put it right. Some who had read the format thought it to be quite bizarre. It was certainly different. And it might take forever to try and describe what it was all about in the first place, let alone attempt to brief a composer who might get lost, unable to grasp and assimilate all the nuances in such an offbeat premise.

Halfway across the Pacific, on the return flight from Cannes, Ray worked on the lyrics for the title track and even had a tune in mind.

He also sketched out some thoughts for 'The Tribe' Series Three which was shaping up well. New characters like Luke, Ned, Tally and Andy would help bring an interesting dimension to the story lines.

And especially with the reintroduction of Amber. Or resurrection, more like. The character had seemingly died previously - so Ray knew the audience would be in for a surprise.

The writing team were more than surprised during the earlier story conference when Ray explained what was being planned. Some felt it was stretching credibility to suggest that Amber had, in reality, survived the explosion at Eagle

Mountain. Ray believed how he envisioned it could all be played was very plausible.

Even in real life people had faked death for a number of reasons. The exposition could easily be revealed in flashback, showing that being entangled in a complex love triangle, never mind a power struggle, Ebony was more than motivated to want Bray and anyone else to think that Amber had died.

Ray never liked to pull rank and force a story line on writers. He had a great respect for all involved in the craft and was always open to any idea or suggestion. But on an assignment like 'The Tribe', all had to follow the brief and direction Ray decided. He had an overview of the brand and where it was all going fixed very firmly in his mind. For better. Or worse.

If a writer was working on an original piece of work, or even an adaptation of source material like a novel, it was possible to have more input. But in a long form series or serial it was normal for any writer to be confined within a very tight brief, otherwise characterizations would be inconsistent and not portrayed correctly. Or story lines could veer off into an entirely different direction. And everything written had to fit within a logistical or budget capability.

To be a jobbing writer in television required talent and a unique skill to be able to make a creative contribution within a team structure which was collaborative. But primarily to operate within whatever brief and framework applied. It was no easy task.

There are branding issues even on an anthology series. To obtain a commission, a writer would need to submit a story of the week. And if that was accepted, he or she would be retained to work on a treatment, which is basically a scene by scene breakdown.

Then they would be given approximately two weeks to outline the structure. If that worked, that is the stage when they would be commissioned to write a first draft. For a one hour episode they might be given one month to deliver. For a half hour episode, two weeks.

If the first draft was accepted, the normal practice is for the producer or editor or script consultant to give a series of notes and revisions required, which would form the basis of a second draft.

If either the first or second draft was not accepted, the script would be written off. Or if there were elements which worked in part, an editor on occasion might rewrite the parts which did not work to bring it all in line with the continuity of the series.

Where 'The Tribe' was concerned, given that it was not an anthology, writers were not required to submit a story of the week but were given the story outline and narrative which would occur in the episode. And would go though the same process of doing a scene by scene breakdown to outline the proposed structure on which the narrative would hang.

Harry, being Script Consultant, might rewrite on occasion to accommodate his own notes and certainly any notes and thoughts Ray would have. And Ray himself would revise if a script did not work for whatever reason, be it logistically or creatively, as he had overall accountability and editorial control with the direction of the series fixed firmly in his mind.

Amber was an important character. And Ray was really looking forward to introducing her into the Eco Tribe, having been long interested in ancient Greek mythology and the Titan, Gaia, personifying earth.

Also the ecological theory of Gaia, which purports that all components of all life forms - including human, animal and plant - are interconnected and evolve so that they adapt to the ever changing environment of the planet.

The hypothesis was not new though and purely scientific. Indigenous cultures, such as the Native American Indian which had always intrigued Ray, had been spiritually in tune with all aspects of our Mother Earth. Probably since time began. And Ray had always been fascinated by and felt connected with the elemental, and thought that an audience would respond to themes of the natural world in all aspects and another culture being explored.

The Eco Tribe would give the opportunity to interweave nature and the environment and also pay homage to the principles of Shintoism.

The tree houses and camp from Swiss Family Robinson would be utilized and enable the Tribe milieu to have another dimension by providing a different backdrop, away from - and contrasting with - the urban landscape.

Ray was especially pleased to finally have a character to take the name he had wanted to use since he first had the idea for the series. Pride.

CHAPTER SIXTEEN

JOURNAL: 2001

At one point Bray was to be given the name of Pride. But Ray felt it was better for the Mall Rats to retain normal names. They were the hero tribe after all, representing a more conventional and stable outlook - in an unstable world.

There would be conflict within the tribe, just as there would in any family or group of people living and working together. But they formed the nucleus around which all else revolved and one in which an audience would be most likely to identify.

Many would have met a bully like Lex in whatever incarnation. Likewise, all the other characters within the Mall Rats. Some might even represent the friend they wished they had or even have.

That is not to say that no one would be drawn to - or have an affinity with - other tribes and ideologies. But the Chosen or the Locos, even the Ecos, portrayed an unfamiliar everyday ethos.

With a dystopian and lawless canvas, Ray felt it was important to have a familiar and stable framework to counterbalance all that would occur in the post apocalyptic backdrop. Above all, to reflect a fairly recognizable emotional dynamic. From the ideals and values expressed, to the loves and fears, dreams and desires encountered. And it was vital that humor always played a large part.

So mostly normal names were also a part of what was required within the Mall Rats to portray a point of view which one might expect within a group of young people in a civil and caring society aspiring to build a better world.

Consequently, Ray never felt comfortable with Bray being named Pride. And once he became fixated on matters like this, he could drive everyone around him, including himself, totally mad. Pursuing an almost obsessive, pedantic quest to make sense of something by examining every microscopic detail.

Would 'Pride' have been the given birth name in the old world? And if so, why would the parents choose such an odd and unusual name? Not impossible, but it would be stretching it. They could have been proud to have a son and named him Pride. But were they not proud to have another son? Why wasn't he named Pride? Or were they prone to flashes of florid language? Naming one Pride and the other Martin.

Bray could have been the one to change his name to Pride in the new world. Just as his brother Martin changed his name to his alter ego, Zoot, when he unharnessed all the simmering anger which fueled him to rebel and unleash Power and Chaos.

But if Bray changed his name, why would he and not the other members of the Mall Rats? And if they did, that could get complicated and lead to the unfamiliar.

What would Bray have been proud of? Or what did he feel pride in? It couldn't be the world he now inhabited. That was a mess. Or even himself. He hadn't really achieved anything. It couldn't really be pride in something he had created. Because he hadn't really created anything. At least not yet.

He might have been proud that he was a 'nice guy', which the character certainly was, but that would have seemed a bit self centered to walk around introducing himself as Pride. He might as well have called himself Hero. In Ray's view, at least.

Pride, being the leader of the Eco Tribe, or co-leader when Amber would return as Eagle - just seemed to be such a natural name. And to fit. There was no question at all in Ray's mind. It felt right. Just as the actor he cast seemed so right to play the role. From the first time he saw him, he knew that he would be perfect.

Ray could imagine that with the quiet self assurance of this gentle and attractive young man, living with his Tribe and being connected to nature and all that entails, would bring about a large degree of inner contentment. And Pride.

There would be a lot to be proud of in his Tribe. There was respect for one another. Even themselves. Along with the environment. And the subsidiary characters, such as Moon and Hawk, exuded a special quality.

Being at one with the natural world, and aware of both the power and yet the wonder and beauty of our Mother Earth, would no doubt bring about an endearing dignity and a sense of being at peace within. And at ease. Through every sunrise. And sunset.

When Ray saw the rushes of Amber living as Eagle with the Eco Tribe and interacting with Pride, he knew his instinct was right. And he was just as pleased with the results of all the other footage. Series Three was shaping up well.

A few weeks after the Series had commenced principal photography, Cloud 9 held a studio open day which was attended by over 20,000 people, eager for a behind the scenes look at the studio,

It all originated at a lavish, black tie formal event. And an important one in the New Zealand social and business calendar. The Wellington Gold Awards celebrated achievement across every aspect of industry. Cloud 9 had often been nominated and had won awards on two separate occasions within the creative sector.

Ray was thrilled to be presented with another award for Cloud 9, recognizing innovation. But toward the conclusion of the evening, when the envelope was dramatically opened to announce the recipient of the prestigious and highly sought after Supreme Gold Award, he was stunned when Cloud 9 was announced as being the overall winner.

He took to the stage amidst much fanfare and great applause and felt humbled that the achievement of the company he founded was not only distinguishing itself in the creative sector but was now even being championed for displaying the highest standards of excellence in the commercial arena.

'On behalf of the Cloud 9 team, it's an immense honor for us all to have won this award,' said Ray, blinking from the glare of so many camera flashes illuminating the podium. 'For me personally, New Zealand has opened its doors to welcome Cloud 9 so warmly, and it means a great deal to have all our dreams and endeavors acknowledged in such a way. So ... it might be time for Cloud 9 to also open its doors.'

Ray thought that maybe 1000 people at the most would turn up for the opening day, which would have a Tribal theme. And that the event could raise some funds for his charity, the Cloud 9 Children's Foundation, with auctions planned, costume parades and graffiti competitions, as well as tours of the studios.

The cast were also due to make a surprise appearance. Ray felt it would be an interesting showcase for their live act and dance routine which would be used on the impending

European tours. And to see if in practice, it connected and was accepted by members of the general public.

Ray had arranged for the cast to work with a talented choreographer, who also performed with a local vocal group. Ray was so impressed that he especially wrote them into some episodes and they featured as the sinister, all-girl singing troupe, Smile.

As details of the open day were either leaked or picked up by the national press, Ray knew there was a strong chance that attendance could grow quiet substantially.

So the event itself started to evolve a bit like a snowball and take on a life of its own, especially when some of Ray's friends from the rugby world wanted to attend. Along with dignitaries and politicians, as well as a range of celebrities from Cloud 9's other shows, eager to show support.

Ray thought that it would be appropriate to hold an official opening, where a tree of hope would be planted for children. And to welcome the high profile guests with a powhiri, a traditional greeting ceremony within the Maori culture whereby guests are called on to the land.

He was heavily involved with the Maori, supporting in any way the aspirations to maintain the culture, language and heritage which was steeped in wonderful folklore, music and dance.

Ray had actually received a feather cloak which was presented to him at the local Marae in a traditional ceremony. It was a great honor and one not regularly given, the equivalent of a knighthood within the Maori culture.

Ancestors are acknowledged, as well as all present in the ceremony. So that homage and respect of generations of those who have gone before, are almost invited to participate.

And if anyone has ever been fortunate to have witnessed a live Haka preceding any All Black rugby game, it would take little to imagine the energy and rousing atmosphere which seemed to give all present at the ceremony goosebumps. Long before the wind was whipped up, which occurred as the cloak was placed around Ray's shoulders in exactly the same manner in which even the great explorer James Cook, had been honored in history.

There was a spirituality which Ray could especially detect. Just as he could within any indigenous culture. And he found it easier to relate to it all in many ways, perhaps due to the DNA of his own Romany Gypsy ancestry. The cloak, and honor it symbolized, would became one of the greatest treasures of his entire life.

Ray was now able to visit the Marae as any other member of the tribe and felt it was an appropriate gesture to invite the elders and have them by his side to call on and welcome guests to his own Marae, the Cloud 9 Studios.

To further show his support and acknowledge how much the cloak and friendship meant from all within the Marae, in the welcome ceremony on the opening day Ray spoke both in English and Maori. He stumbled mostly with the words alien to his mother tongue but the gesture was appreciated and applauded.

Crowds swarmed to the studio, with press and television news crews also present. The police even had to close the roads during the event. It was total gridlock, to such an extent that many were convinced the attendance was far in excess of the 20,000 expected. But it was difficult to record how many exactly since there was no ticket price which might help quantify numbers. It was free entry.

A substantial amount was raised for charity, as well as goodwill exhibited by all. This was important for Ray. He always maintained a social conscience, as well as a commercial one, and viewed the day as one whereby he could give something back to the community.

With the scripts of 'Atlantis High' and 'The Tribe' Series Three coming in, along with Ray sketching out in overview terms what might happen in ensuing years so the production team could get a heads up for early planning purposes, the workload was becoming a little overwhelming, to say the least. And given that Ray was also composing and recording music, his assistant now needed her own assistants to help keep her on track - so that she could keep Ray on track of all the tasks which needed to be carried out.

Series in the back catalogue were also coming up for re-license in various parts of the world, which meant they were brand new titles to the press who requested interviews.

Ray found it odd after a long day at the studio to return home and speak on the telephone to so many reporters, from so many countries, about past titles as if they were new.

One might ask about 'The Enid Blyton Adventure Series' due to premiere somewhere in the world. Again. Others might ask questions about the other series, from 'Swiss Family Robinson' to 'William Tell', 'Return To Treasure Island' to 'A Twist In The Tale'. And very often, where 'The Tribe' was concerned, Ray would refer to what was happening in Series Three, when Series One or Two - or vice versa - was actually being transmitted.

Other trade papers were eager to discuss what was coming next, which meant that within a few seconds Ray had to switch from one call discussing the Tribe's impending tour - to the new series 'Atlantis High'. Then on another call, it would be back again to what it was like working with William Shatner.

Then questions about fashion could get confused, with Ray thinking it was a reference to 'The Tribe' when it was to do with the research he undertook to produce costume drama. Some of his earlier shows at the BBC invariably came up for discussion, as well as his feeling about education and schools.

Tribeworld.com was starting to become such a popular website to visit that schools were referencing 'The Tribe' to study relevant social issues. So when Ray might reply that he wasn't happy at school, a reporter actually wanted to know if he would be starting an educational division.

Somewhere in Ray's mind, he recalled about the head office in London being approached to check if it would be possible to devise a learning module to trial 'The Tribe' in 7000 UK schools.

Some interviews were more about Ray returning to his music roots, knowing that he was working on some soundtracks, as well as finishing an abandoned symphony which he started to compose in his youth.

Others were to do with an association with the global children's charity UNICEF, with whom Cloud 9 was planning a link. And there was always an interest and many questions regarding Asperger's Syndrome, which Ray's own charity supported.

It all coalesced and became a blur. Ray felt like he was a sink, with the tap constantly running and everything was overflowing. And with all that was being planned, it would only get worse.

He welcomed the opportunity to get out of the office and studio to direct the first three episodes of 'Atlantis High' to set the tone. It was a tight schedule but considering all else that was going on in his hectic lifestyle, it felt like a total break to be out on set and location. As if he was taking it easy just working 12 hour days. Like his foot was off the accelerator.

After one take, Ray blurted out in helpless laugher. It was a fun series and the performances and situations in the story lines put a smile on everyone's face most days. But this day, Ray just couldn't stop laughing. Which made the cast and crew laugh. Take after take was interrupted. Ray thought the series must either be hilarious, or due to the work load, he was actually losing his mind.

He really enjoyed working so closely with his cast and crew. And to be reunited with some of the cast from past productions. Cloud 9 was like a repertory theatre company in many ways and it never ceased to impress Ray that no matter what part he cast an actor or actress in, they always delivered in whatever role they had been offered.

It was a revelation to see some of the members from 'The Tribe' whom Ray had cast in 'Atlantis High' exhibiting such a flair and range. Jack played Giles Gordon, May - Jet Marigold, Salene -the peculiar dual roles of Anthony/Antonia. And some of the subsidiary characters from 'The Tribe' also made an appearance, such as Moz playing Vita, Spike as Josh Montana, Top Hat as an alien, and even the Joker as Beanie.

Without exception, all excelled and Ray had high hopes for the radical new series which would premiere next year.

After his directing tasks had been completed, he was eager to get back to all of his other duties and especially the post production of Series Three of 'The Tribe'.

The last day of filming was in a top secret location. The Ohakea air force base. With a skeleton small crew who had signed confidential clauses.

There was no cast at all present. Just senior members of the Royal New Zealand Air Force.

And a Special Forces unit who would be dropped from military aircraft in the sky.

An invasion force from a foreign land would feature in Series Four of 'The Tribe'. The adults were about to return.

Or were they?

CHAPTER SEVENTEEN

JOURNAL: 2001

The decision about whether or not to introduce adults into 'The Tribe' kept Ray awake most nights. It was all he needed. The workload was exhausting enough as it was and he needed to get some sleep without being tortured by a story line.

He had spent an entire week tossing and turning before getting up in the middle of the night to go into his study to map out various options and scenarios continually swirling around in his head. Well until the early hours.

By then there was no point trying to get back to sleep. So he utilized the time with more work on the soundtracks, some of which had been adapted from his symphony, which at least had finally been completed.

The base melodic structures in two of the movements had come into existence when he was a young boy. Now all these years later, he finally stamped the end on the music which he had baptized as 'The Spirit Symphony'. It was due to premiere at the Michael Fowler Centre in Wellington with a performance by the New Zealand Symphony Orchestra and Orpheus Choir on the 13th of April, 2001.

Production was still underway on 'Atlantis High'. Series One, Two and Three of 'The Tribe' were being transmitted in several countries, along with other titles in the company portfolio.

And yet another new series Ray was planning was about to enter development - 'Revelations'. But production was not due to commence until the next year, around February, 2002.

This would keep the production centre active while some key cast members of 'The Tribe' undertook more tours. The series was showing in several countries and more and more fans were discovering what it is to be tribal. Or a tribee, as the fans had christened themselves - those who had already become fanatical devotees and were regularly visiting the Tribeworld website or had joined the fan club.

Cast chats had proven to be popular on the bulletin board and all seemed to really enjoy interacting with friends around the world, united through the cultural divide by 'The Tribe'. A team of twelve had been recruited to administer and oversee it all.

Plans were also underway for a German language version of the website. With the technology available at the time, Tribeworld was struggling to accommodate the huge traffic increasing each and every week, so it was thought that another site for the vast German market would help ease the strain.

Many fans throughout the world, inspired by the make up or wardrobe design in the series, used similar fashion as a way to express themselves. Others were utilizing the themes explored in the series for study. And Cloud 9 had an educational division in London. A Tribe learning module was being tested in schools.

Series Four was due to begin pre-production in May, and Ray had to make a decision on which way it would all go.

The first few blocks of scripts had been written in January. They would still feature the Technos. But now it was March. If Ray wanted to reveal that the supreme leaders of the new Tribe were actually adults to whom the Techno leader Ram reported back in the homeland, then he would have to act now to steer the story lines accordingly.

What tortured him was that he was concerned that by introducing adults, it would betray the integrity of the theme of a world without adults and young people left alone to rebuild a new world order.

But Ray was aware that with the cast aging each year, in reality they would soon become perceived as adults. If not by the audience, certainly by the broadcasters. And there was a danger that 'The Tribe' could fall between the adult and traditional youth transmission schedule, which could pose a problem. So he thought it might be an idea to address it now while he could and try and get the Cumulus team to recommend to broadcasters that they introduce 'The Tribe' into a different broadcasting slot. That would ensure longevity.

Besides, Ray was desperate to pay off the message from the mysterious voice coming via the satellite in the last episode of Series One.

At one point many years ago, long before 'The Tribe' had ever come into existence in its present incarnation, in one of the first ever drafts of the format the children of the world had been evacuated by adults to a new planet. To survive. There was more of a sci-fi element to the story way back then.

But it evolved. Ray dismissed any notion of adults and felt the series to be better suited to a contemporary setting, although a quasi sci-fi element still remained.

There were many theories from all the fans around the world about what had actually happened and where the virus had come from, throughout the first three series of transmission. And as with Amber being resurrected after the explosion on

Eagle Mountain, Ray had some surprising twists which he had wanted to interweave and reveal.

He had the entire Tribe mythology planned out in overview terms. It was just a question of when and how to introduce all the elements. But a series like 'The Tribe' was also organic and he wanted it to breathe and grow and expand in a natural way.

So in the end, Ray decided to let the Technos remain as is without introducing too many new elements, such as adults into the mix, which could complicate matters. He could always come back to what he had in mind in later series, if needs be, or even stories through novels.

There was more than enough material with the Technos to fuel story lines for Series Four. And it would probably overspill into Series Five.

Ray was considering a Wild West type of backdrop which would involve a feisty saloon owner and a bounty hunter who would arrive in town. At one point he was even thinking of bringing this element forward since there was a town already in place on the studio backlot which could easily be adapted to fit the location.

But logistically he needed to be careful. He would also need to use the backlot town in the new 'Revelations' series. So it would be much better to complete production on 'Revelations' first. Then change it all to fit the town he had in mind for 'The Tribe' and bring all that in on Series Five.

The invasion force would make provision for themes of technology to be examined. Ray was never really technologically inclined and struggled to change a light bulb, let alone understand all that could be accomplished by the micro chip.

He first became intrigued with software and the computer age after seeing the Stanley Kubrick motion picture classic '2001, A Space Odyssey', in which H.A.L. takes on a life form of its own.

But Ray still resisted using a computer himself for several years until, when in the days at the BBC, his assistant persuaded him that he might find word processing more beneficial than his old Underwood typewriter when writing.

Being obsessed with tradition, Ray was reluctant to replace his beloved Underwood which had kept him company through many a long and lonely night while he struggled to fill blank pages. He had become accustomed to the rat tat rhythm as he two-finger typed. It somehow gave him comfort.

But he knew that to deliver in the professional world he needed to keep up with technology and make his life as easy as possible. After all, someone must have decided at some point to replace ink and a quill with a typewriter.

So he obtained a computer. An Amstrad. And had a tutorial on basic word processing. He was impressed that it could spell check and stick and paste and thought it would be wonderful if the contraption could also write. But no such luck. He would still have to live with that struggle, but could see how word processing could make the entire process easier. Especially as he could delete.

He really like that word. He didn't know why. Delete. It sounded ominous. Threatening. Frightening.

But also comforting. As Ray was to discover on the first project he wrote when he decided to give the computer a go. And it was to become an experience which can only best be described as being totally surreal. Having strived to create, Ray found technology - and delete - as a way in which he could self destruct. The Amstrad computer would probably have replaced in the spell check of its memory the word 'delete' with ... E-A-S-Y.

He was commissioned by BBC Scotland, through a co-production with a French broadcaster, to develop a series set against the wine industry. After spending weeks researching in Bordeaux, Ray went into his study, switched the computer on and stared at the blank screen. For days. He just couldn't get started. And when he finally did, drove his assistant crazy, constantly questioning what button to press to save or spell check.

The producer was very established and Ray was in awe, sure he had perhaps mistaken him for another writer. But his agent reassured Ray that no, there had been no mistake. As much as this was flattering, it all brought a degree of pressure. Ray hoped he could deliver. And that the producer wouldn't regret commissioning him.

Four months later, Ray completed three scripts and went from feeling pleased with what he had written, to really disappointed. But he was already way past his deadline and had to deliver the material. There was no time for any revisions. After one final read through, a new term flashed up on the screen: Run disc data manager.

Ray didn't have a clue what that meant. So he phoned a writer friend who was very computer literate and was also about to head off to bed, having achieved his page quota for the day. Which had overspilled into the night.

'Just make sure you save everything. And whatever you do - don't press F5,' Ray was told. 'Or you could delete everything.'

'What? You mean by pressing F5 I'd delete, as in 'lose' everything? As in E-V-E-R-Y-T-H-I-N-G?'

His writer friend confirmed that to be the case, unaware that on the other end of the line Ray was staring wide eyed at his finger - which was moving slowly to F5.

Ray couldn't believe it. He dropped the receiver in mounting panic so that his hand was free to grab the other hand to try and yank it back.

But it was no good. The other hand seemed to have a mind of its own and more strength. And no matter how hard the other hand tried, the other hand yanked itself away.

And Ray watched in absolute horror as his finger continued to move forward to the key, almost in slow motion.

'Noooooooo!!!!!. Not F5!!!!!!!!" he yelled.

'What's going on?!' his writer friend screamed, on the other end of the line.

But it was too late. The seemingly disembodied finger pressed F5. Then Ray lifted the phone again, 'It's going! Page after page! All of it! The scripts. Everything seems to be disappearing!'

After the initial panic in his voice, there was resignation. And relief. Huge relief.

Ray poured himself a glass of wine, sat back in his chair, put his feet up on the desk and watched the computer screen. All the scripts were vanishing, page by page, before his eyes.

'That F5. It's something else, isn't it?' Ray said, feeling so much more relaxed. Like a huge weight had suddenly been lifted from his shoulders. 'Four months of work. Going. Now the producer will never know how great it was. I really pushed the boundaries on this one, I'm telling you. It was my best to date. A real shame. What a waste. Ah, well. It happens, I guess.'

His writer friend was so anguished he couldn't imagine how Ray must be feeling, unaware that when the last page disappeared, a smile of utter contentment spread across Ray's face.

For all that he said to his friend that he was devastated, which he was in a way, he was also more peculiarly - and unknown to his friend - in reality at total peace. Loving it. All of his hard work had gone. Thanks to - delete.

Ray offered to repay his entire fee, feeling that it would be in the best interest of the project for another writer to be retained. But was persuaded to keep going.

He finally delivered the scripts. But the project got lost in development hell. Leaving Ray sure that his instinct had been right to self destruct all he had written. As it probably wasn't that good anyway.

F5 would become a term Ray used and a trusted ally in later years. A way to measure whether or not to abandon or progress anything. Not solely confined to his writing. But other aspects of his life.

Where bringing the adults back in 'The Tribe' was concerned, the notion was placed in pending. But was leaning more toward the F5 file. To delete.

After viewing the rushes when the series commenced principal photography, Ray was encouraged. The introduction of the Technos - with Ram, Java, Siva, Jay and Ved - injected a refreshing dimension, as did the new characters of Patch, Mouse and Sammy. Ray was really pleased with the actresses and actors cast, all of whom possessed a special quality and screen presence.

The use and responsibility of technology would be an interesting theme. With characters literate in the computer world, and the capability of introducing virtual reality. Which could be dangerous in the wrong hands.

And Paradise Net was an interesting vehicle to safely explore addiction without having to get into drugs and all that entails, which could prove to be difficult for broadcasters, given the child/teen slot in which 'The Tribe' was being transmitted.

The series was already pushing the boundaries with edgy story lines and Ray didn't want to push it further. Which could precipitate issues of compliance, a term within broadcasting codes for classification purposes.

At its core, Ray aspired to maintain a balance and never wished for 'The Tribe' to become too dark. But equally was adamant that it shouldn't be squeaky clean either.

'The Tribe' transcended all of that anyway with its own ethos and karma. Hope would always triumph in the end. On screen and off. And the introduction of Dee was a good example of this. Ray was especially relieved that Dee was settling into her role so well. After the way Dee had obtained the part, which was unusual to say the least.

Ray received a lot of mail. With the best will in the world he could never hope to respond to all the letters due to the volume but always ensured there was space each week to write a reply to some of the fans. Feeling that if they had gone to the trouble to contact him, then he should really do the same. At least to as many as he could.

A package which had been delivered was brought to Ray's attention by his assistant during the production of the previous series. It contained a tape. From a fan.

Ray listened and was really impressed by the girl's voice but more by what she had written, which he found endearing. She was a fanatical follower of the series from the UK. So Ray thought it would be great to give her a call. And offer her a part.

'You're really something,' his assistant said, never knowing what the day would bring, working with Ray.

Nothing really surprised her anymore. Her first task of that morning had been inching the furniture a little bit this or that way under Ray's supervision. The night cleaners must have knocked a few chairs and he was worried that they were not pointing in the right direction. And with this being a musical day, everything had to be exact. He was planning on adapting more elements of his symphony for 'The Tribe' soundtrack.

The correct positions were already marked with tape. And didn't look to be out of place. But Ray was sure they were, so his assistant went round all the furniture to make sure it was set just right. Even if it meant an adjustment of a few centimeters.

Ray was listening to the audition tape while watching intently to make sure the realignment of all the furniture was conducted correctly - and was also obsessively wiping his piano over and over. His assistant had been reading some of the scripts about the new Techno Tribe which would feature in Series Four and could see where the character of Ram's germ hang-up must have come from.

Ray kept an endless supply of wet wipes. Which he would constantly use to wipe surfaces or to clean his hands, as he had a phobia of germs. It was always there but seemed to manifest more when he was overly tired.

After the direction of the furniture had been triple-checked and all the surfaces had been wiped down, his assistant was a little uneasy having to phone the young lady who submitted the tape and put her through to Ray.

Who found himself speaking with the father, who suspected the call was some kind of cruel joke. And hung up.

Ray's assistant wasn't entirely surprised by the reaction. But Ray was. Unable to comprehend why anyone would think he was joking. So he called back and reassured the father that he was serious. He wanted to fly the family down to New Zealand to discuss appearing in the series of which she was such a fan.

In the end, the mother accompanied Dee, having never flown anywhere before, and was reassured that all was in order.

Dee was thrilled. She couldn't really believe that one day she was gazing at posters of her favorite characters from her favorite television series on her bedroom wall, and out of nowhere she would meet and befriend them and be in the show herself.

Less than a few months later, that is what happened.

Ray was probably more thrilled than Dee. And delighted that she had settled in and was happy and giving such an excellent performance. The karma of it all just felt so right.

Ray became aware of just how much 'The Tribe' meant to fans around the globe when so many emailed the office and interacted on Tribeworld, afraid and confused by what had tragically occurred in New York on 9/11. The 12th of September in New Zealand.

The website team, cast and crew at Cloud 9 were as equally shocked. It was a defining moment for so many. A time to reflect on the state of the world. And it was touching that across the vast oceans, fans exchanged their views and fears amidst all the anguish and despair, hopes and prayers for a better new world. And future for all.

Series Four of 'The Tribe' completed principal photography in December and post production continued while the new Cloud 9 series, 'Revelations', began filming in February, 2002.

It would also prove to be another defining and life-changing moment for Ray.

CHAPTER EIGHTEEN

JOURNAL: 2001-2002

Ray spoke regularly with his family by phone in the UK and really missed seeing them. But there was no time within the workload which would allow travel for quite a while.

After 'Revelations' was completed, Series Five of 'The Tribe' was due to commence later in the year, in October, and Ray felt as if he was drowning in a sea of scripts for both series.

There were more Tribe tours being arranged, press interviews, and he had also been approached by senior Government ministers to comment on working papers about the state of the film and television industry in New Zealand.

In addition, he was required to do more soundtracks and was discussing expanding into animation.

And as with his Charity, where Ray wanted to give back to the community, he was intent on giving something back to the industry. So he accepted an Adjunct Professorship to lecture and mentor post graduate students in the creative arts faculty at Queensland University of Technology, Australia.

'There just doesn't seem to be enough hours in the day. Or night,' Ray said to his younger brother on the phone. 'I've got a lot on. But with a bit of luck, I might be able to fit in a trip to the UK later in the year. It would be so great to catch up.'

'I hope so. It's been a while,' replied his younger brother. Then he added, concerned for Ray's welfare, 'You make sure you take good care of yourself. With the amount of hours you seem to be working - you've got to watch your health. You're no spring chicken anymore.'

Less than three days later, Ray was back in England giving comfort to his father, sisters and his brother's wife and children.

His brother had died unexpectedly. Within only hours of speaking with Ray by phone. A blood clot caused a cerebral hemorrhage. He left a wife and three young children. Ray and all the family were heartbroken.

Ray stayed in the UK for as long as he could. And felt the need to also go to Disneyland, Paris, where his brother and his family had accompanied him a few years previously. And it brought back many memories. Mostly happy times. His brother was a huge Disney fan. And loved Eeyore.

The theme park also gave Ray a degree of comfort as well, knowing that this was where he was when his mother had taken her final breath. And he was searching in the aftermath of his brother's death, almost to get in tune with her. Feeling there was no better place. Which had also brought such joy to his brother.

As the parade made its way down Main Street, Ray sat alone on a bench near the entrance of the park. Sadly watching helium balloons of Eeyore which he had purchased and released and were now climbing higher and higher into the sky.

Back in New Zealand, it was a struggle to come to terms with his brother's passing. Ray felt numbed and a great need to be with his family back in the UK. Especially his father, who was torn apart, as any parent would be when outliving a child. But all insisted that Ray had to do what he had to do.

It would be impossible for him to take time out. His creative endeavors had evolved into a vast and complex commercial merry go round. He was responsible for a 150 million dollar production portfolio.

The livelihood of so many were at stake. Not just within Cloud 9. He had responsibilities to his joint venture partner. The company was in production and contractually obliged to deliver more titles, musical tours, merchandising, all manner of activities.

Success had come at a high price. Ray, as key man, was legally bound to banks, insurance companies, bond agencies, broadcasters, distributors and publishers. It was such a highly pressurized world. But no longer confined to filling a blank page. Ray was entangled in a world governed by a fiscal bottom line.

He had often heard of the cliche about there being no sentiment in business. Now, beyond a week on compassionate grounds, he knew that with the whirlwind of growth of the company he had founded, there was no clause in any contract or room in any schedule for even bereavement.

And it was something he intended dealing with. As always, when he could find the time. But it was essential. He was driven, trying to keep everyone's dream alive, but needed to ensure that he kept his own dream - along with himself - alive as well.

Ray found a lot of comfort in the spirituality and themes of the 'Revelations' series. And admired the performances from the very first time the footage came in. Several members of 'The Tribe' appeared, along with Cloud 9's talented stable of actresses and actors. And as always, they displayed a tremendous range and brought a lot to all the parts they played.

He had cast Ram in the leading role of Jesse, and was impressed by the versatility of the young actor who was able to inject a sensitive and vulnerable quality, a longing as the narrator traveling through history from the beginning of time in search of the meaning of life and existence.

It was a question Ray had often asked himself. And concluded that it was to give love. And to receive it. It could be the love of a man, woman, child, music, anything. But without experiencing the purity of it, in whatever form, it would bring about dysfunction and imbalance to the heart, spirit and soul.

Although some stories had been loosely adapted from the parables, 'Revelations' was not a religious series as such. But it was certainly inspirational in tone. A celebration of the human condition. And Ray was very proud of it. Of all the ideals and values the stories explored.

Later, when the series was broadcast, some viewers thought that it was reminiscent in many ways to the iconic title 'Touched By An Angel'. That was an accolade which meant a lot to Ray. Ironically it had been one of his late brother's favorite television series.

Ray revised the Spirit Symphony and dedicated the album, which was recorded during another performance by the New Zealand Symphony orchestra, to the memory of his mother and late brother. The inlay sheet also contains lyrics which he had written the night he found out that his brother had died.

It was overwhelming for Ray to listen to the Symphony performed live. By an orchestra with almost 100 players and a full choir. But difficult as well. When it was premiered, there were many political figures and dignitaries in the sell out audience and Ray tried so hard to stay for the duration.

But half way through movement one, he had to leave, having become sensitized. Not by the occasion. But the music. It was as if it was living, flowing like blood through his veins. He could feel every subtle nuance from each instrument in the very pores of his skin, which tingled, and seemed to send shock waves through his entire body and essence.

It was bitter sweet. Bringing a sense of utter joy. Yet also an agonizing pain that he had never experienced. Perhaps due to the music being loved by his late brother, who found it comforting to listen to when thinking of his mother's passing years before.

It was as peculiarly distressing, as it was moving for Ray. And only occurred when performed live. In real time. Never when he heard the music after it had been recorded. So he just had to get away, only returning to the auditorium where the symphony was being performed when the last movement had concluded.

Derivative themes of 'Spirit' were used in the soundtrack of 'The Tribe'. In Pride's requiem, which in itself had sadly become a requiem for Ray's brother. Other themes featured in some of the incidental music which Ray composed for 'Revelations'.

At the conclusion of filming Series Four and 'Revelations', some cast members of 'The Tribe' embarked upon another European tour. And Ram collected an award on Ray's behalf on the American leg at the Dragon Com festival in Atlanta.

It was an honor for Ray to have been recognized by the festival and a real thrill for the cast to participate in the parade though the city of Atlanta, along with having the opportunity to perform for the American fans.

During the preparations for 'The Tribe' Series Five in October of the same year, Ray was astounded to discover that he was to be presented with another award.

His assistant handed him an official looking envelope marked personal which he handed back, asking her to deal with it, suspecting that it should be forwarded to his accountants, sure that it was to do with tax or other business matters.

'I've just opened this,' his assistant said, re-entering Ray's office a few minutes later and handing him back the envelope. 'I haven't read any of the details. But I don't think it's for the accountants. It's private and confidential. From Elizabeth R.'

Ray's assistant left and he read the letter, slightly confused at first. He didn't know any Elizabeth R. Except, of course, that it was also the name of the Queen.

Then he realized. The letter was indeed from the highest authority, advising Ray that Her Majesty would like to have him feature in the 2003 New Year's Honor List for services to television, and the investiture would occur the following April.

Until it was formally announced, Ray would be unable to mention it and had to keep matters confidential. But he had to notify the Governor General if he would accept the honor. It took a few seconds for Ray to say yes.

Although he couldn't really assimilate or understand what he had really done to deserve such recognition. He genuinely never considered himself to have any particular talent as such. And having a special need, had always struggled. But he always tried. And did his best. To keep his dream alive.

The year had brought about a series of profound highs. And yet heartbreaking lows. He would have given anything, all he had to have his brother and mother present. Even for one minute. And to share it all with them, along with the rest of the family. But he knew. That his brother and mother knew. And that they would have been proud, as was Ray's father and sisters, and all members of the clan.

Series Five of 'The Tribe' commenced principal photography around the time he had received notification of the honor in October. And would conclude production in April, when Ray was elected to the New Zealand Order Of Merit.

He was touched by all the support he received from all over the world, including letters of congratulations from the Prime Minister, to other dignitaries. But Ray was especially moved by the surprise celebrations which had been arranged by his Cloud 9 team.

The production centre was certainly expanding with the addition of Slade, Ruby, Gel, Daryl, and Lottie to the cast. As always, Ray was very pleased to have been able to recruit gifted performers, as well as very special human beings with qualities which were an enormous benefit to the series and team.

Now that 'Revelations' had completed filming, the backlot was re-dressed to become the small town of Liberty, which really helped open up the series, offering another photogenic backdrop.

Ram and the enigmatic bounty hunter, Slade, more than met their match when confronted by the feisty saloon owner, Ruby, who controlled her domain with a rod of iron.

And the Techno Tribe continued to fuel an interesting dimension of material within the Mall Rats through all the story threads. Siva, Java and Ebony were reunited as real sisters in the recording studio and Ray was impressed by their extended version of 'Tribe Spirit', the closing title track.

Mouse, Sammy and Lottie provided endearing elements of a younger generation, with the other characters getting older and assuming the mantle of elders of the Mall Rat Tribe, setting the example and charting the way to build a better and sustainable future.

Zoot, who had been working in the art department after being Ray's personal runner, had also returned through the technical wonders of virtual reality, replacing Daryl's very capable impersonation of the legendary Loco leader.

The presence of the character had remained as a sinister undertone and source of conflict since his death way back in Series One.

Now the real Zoot was back. But had never really been away. And once again through his new incarnation was fueling an ominous threat.

The theme of the responsibility of technology was taking on an 'F5' nihilistic dimension. For all the wonders of the computer age - in the wrong hands it could also bring about an element of self destruction.

It was a touching moment for Ray to see the rushes when Slade confronted his brother, Mega, who died. It might have been a work of fiction, but the emotion it evoked was very real.

As the Mall Rats embarked into the boat to flee the disintegrating city at the conclusion of the last episode and post production continued on Series Five, Ray decided to also get away for a few days and convened a story conference in Queenstown in the South Island.

It was time to plan Tribe Series Six. But more unexpected surprises were to lay in store along the way.

SERIES SIX OUT-TAKES

EXT. MOUNTAINS. DAY.

TRAVELING over a photogenic mountainous region to reveal FLAME, the charismatic leader of the Privileged.

On the VERY top of a snow-capped peak. Overlooking a breathtaking panorama.

The ultimate guitar hero. Long blond hair blowing in the wind as he head bangs, trance-like. Playing amidst deafening, whistling feedback the most awesome, wailing electric guitar licks anyone has ever heard, reverberating seemingly around all the lands. Even the heavens.

FLAME is high maintenance, temperamental, forever petulant, even bitchy - and we could be forgiven for asking if he is really male? Or female? He sure is striking looking. Even beautiful. A rock star god.

EXT. FIELDS. PINE FOREST. MOUNTAINS. DAY.

The DISCARDS, the peasant slaves of the Privileged, work the land. Still the music and feedback reverberate around and around.

In the far distance FLAME is visible, rays of sun protruding over the crest of the mountain top behind him, enshrining him in a way, and he almost now LOOKS like a god.

The DISCARDS are all in chains. Planting. Tending crops. And unlike their masters and mistresses - all are noticeably overweight, unattractive, with bar codes tattooed on their arms.

BACK ON THE MOUNTAIN.

Flame's deputy, HARMONY, along with her SECURITY, watch FLAME continuing to head bang as if in a trance, his fingers bleeding as he moves across the frets and bends the strings, WAILING more amazing rifts.

HARMONY is absolutely gorgeous, long braided hair, a lightning bolt tattooed across one cheek. But she is also insidious, scheming, calculating, the real power behind the throne.

Right now she indicates FLAME to the towering bodyguard, OX.

>   HARMONY
>   Seems a bit off his head. Kava again?
>   (OX nods) Better get him down. He's
>   had more than enough time.

FEATURING FLAME

noticing OX and the SECURITY approach. Then he suddenly turns, runs - and leaps from the mountain. And could it be that he is ACTUALLY FLYING?

THE PEASANT DISCARDS

gaze up at FLAME in free fall in the distance, twisting and turning upside down - and all the while still clutching his guitar and trying to play.

FLAME

is suddenly yanked by the vine/rope around one leg (as per a bungee jump) and whoops it up and starts to laugh manically amidst all the FEEDBACK as he is catapulted, hurled back up - and he loses grip of

THE GUITAR

... which twists, falls through the air, landing near

AN ASTONISHED DISCARD SLAVE GIRL

who crosses to the guitar, lifts it, overwhelmed - and gives the instrument a huge ecstatic hug.

REVEAL

ALICE and KC in chains working nearby, exchanging disdainful glances at the reaction of their fellow slave. They will never worship Flame. He is more reminiscent of the devil. And all enslaved and oppressed by his twisted ideology are living in pure hell.

INT. FLAME'S INNER SANCTUM. PRIVILEGED RESORT. NIGHT.

The DISCARD GIRL seen in the slave fields is now naked and having sex with the guitar she retrieved.

The room is dark, illuminated by flaming torches, casting looming shadows as she sensuously runs her tongue across the curves of the wood, caressing the instrument, before opening her legs and thrusting it between them.

She is watched impassively by FLAME, HARMONY and OX, surrounded by SERVANTS who look to be asexual, like the lady boys in the Pacific Islands. Beautiful, androgynous creatures.

One thing we can't help but notice. The PRIVILEGED are all so good looking, indulged, decadent, the ultimate of what all young people suffer from as a result of peer pressure. Don't even think about not being hip, cool, attractive.

The DISCARD GIRL finally cries out in orgasmic pleasure.

                    FLAME
     Nice one! 54 Hohner. Pure Ivory
     frets. High tension neck action.
     Sexy time!

                    HARMONY
     You want her?

                    FLAME
     H-e-l-l-o ...

As erotic as it all was – the DISCARD
GIRL doesn't do anything for FLAME and he
scoffs, almost offended.

                    FLAME
     I'm talking about the guitar – not
     'her', Harmony. She's not worthy.
     I mean, just look at her.   Please!
     Can you imagine?

                    HARMONY
     Well, you heard the god, Flame,
     himself, sister. Lose a bit of
     weight, one day you might be a
     candidate to be Privileged.   Right
     now you're still a Discard. Back to
     the slave fields for you, girl. (to
     Flame) Any reward? For retrieving
     the guitar?

                    FLAME
     Give her to Ox. A gift for the night.
     From me.   Even if it is a bit on
     the big size – lots for you, Ox, to
     get your teeth into.

OX grins, nods to a sneering FLAME in
gratitude, licks his lips. He likes the
sound of that.

Even if the humiliated DISCARD GIRL is
clearly not as taken with the notion.

CHAPTER NINETEEN

JOURNAL: 2003-2004

Ray looked out of the small window of the aircraft and could really imagine the opening shot he had in mind in his works in progress script to introduce Flame.

The flight from Wellington was on its landing approach and weaving between the snow covered mountains for its descent into Queenstown.

He had filmed in the area on several occasions. And had achieved incredible footage. Especially on the production of 'The Legend Of William Tell.' The mountains, forests and lakes provided a breathtaking photogenic backdrop and would be ideal to portray the type of aesthetic he wanted for Series Six of 'The Tribe'.

The prime base for the production would still be out of the Cloud 9 studios but Ray was planning on interweaving footage shot in the South Island, which offered such a wide range of desolate and evocative locations.

It was snowing heavily by the time he travelled from the airport to the hotel and he hoped the writers invited to the story conference made it alright. Some of the English contingent would be feeling the effects of jet lag after such a long journey. With this weather, flights might be delayed. Or worse still, the airport could be closed.

The alpine snow-covered setting provided such a festive atmosphere, Ray had trouble believing that it was August. It felt more like December. Having been raised in the Northern hemisphere, he always found it difficult celebrating Christmas in the summer. And those in the Southern hemisphere would no doubt feel the same if they spent the festive holidays in the cold, rather than being outdoors in the sun, enjoying turkey with all the trimmings on a barbecue.

Thankfully, all the team of writers and the deputy story consultant had arrived safely. Over the next few days, Ray outlined his ideas. He thought it would be good to get away and for all of the team to see and gain an understanding of the type of locations available, but more importantly the backdrop and milieu Ray had in mind for Series Six.

Harry was unable to attend, due to another assignment. He was busy developing a title which Ray was considering as another vehicle for William Shatner. But Ray and Harry were always in regular contact, so Harry had been fully briefed.

Amidst all the story discussions, Ray took the team to Arrowtown, which enjoyed a degree of notoriety during the days of the gold rush at the turn of the century, when the population soared. But now it was only a small community on the banks of a peaceful river, surrounded by a range of majestic mountains.

The picturesque town was a popular tourist destination. And nestled within an area offering a variety of adventure sports, from snow boarding to rafting. Ray introduced the team to the famed Shotover jet boat. All were exhilarated by the experience as the boat sped along the river, twisting and turning between the narrow banks of cliffs.

Some of the writers even bungy jumped. But that was a little too extreme for Ray. He couldn't understand how people would leap from such a huge height secured by only a rope tied to one leg, to hurl upside down with their face splashing into the surface of the water in the lake below. And were then left dangling before being retrieved. Not only that - they actually paid to do it.

The writers were pleased by the break and to get out of the conference room at the hotel. Going over story line threads, themes and possibly character interplay was always so draining.

All were intrigued though by what Ray was planning. And could see that the surviving Mall Rats would certainly be challenged if they were washed ashore after a storm at sea to encounter a new and mysterious land. Inhabited by new Tribes.

Ray wanted to reintroduce some of the missing characters from previous series. Such as Bray. And it all tied in very well if it was revealed that they had been traded as slaves by the Technos and now were Discards, serving the Privileged.

The Mall Rats would become reunited with fellow members of their Tribe, which would fuel more story threads in all the relationships and finally have Amber and Bray pick up on the deep love they held for one another.

And a diverse and interesting framework would be in place to fuel all manner of conflict, along with the machinations of Lex and Ebony to power broke and gain control, with Lex becoming enamored by the charms of Harmony.

But the overall arc concerned the Mall Rats becoming instrumental as a rebel force to mobilize other new Tribes which would be introduced to overthrow the Privileged. Prior to considering a return to their own homeland when an informant presented surprising evidence about the true origins of the virus, which would require another visit to the mysterious Eagle Mountain military base.

Ray believed that the Privileged would be more menacing than any of the Tribes featured in past series. The fanatical ideology of their unstable leader, Flame, to create perfection through a master race, was certainly an ominous and dangerous notion.

Yet he had the potential, as with Zoot, to become an enormous cult figure. A true anti hero. Brooding and volatile, an unpredictable rebel with a cause.

For all his manic intemperance and twisted ways to dominate and rule his devoted followers, the great manipulator was himself in reality being manipulated by his lover and deputy, Harmony, who was scheming and devious. But would meet her match in Lex and Ebony. Though Lex would eventually fall victim to Harmony's sensual spell.

Following the story conference in the South Island, Ray spent some time at his holiday home in Queensland. But as always, with the way the company was expanding, he had no time at all in the schedule for any holiday.

He needed to meet Australian broadcasters who had shown an interest in acquiring the past five series of 'The Tribe' and were considering participating in the sixth.

In addition, Ray wanted to progress discussions with his animation joint venture partner, which would trade as Dreamcloud, and might even produce an animated version of 'The Tribe'. Also, while in Australia, he would be able to give some lectures and mentor students under his Adjunct Professor role.

Ray really enjoyed working with the students but wondered how many of the post graduates studying creative writing knew that their professor had no idea where to place a comma, let alone how to spell.

The curriculum seemed to focus more on the theoretical, rather than the practical. So Ray tried to give all of his students an insight into the industry. It was all well and good studying the works of Francois Truffaut or Ingmar Bergman, but that wouldn't really prepare them for the outside world.

Writers were really not being taught the basic disciplines, in his view, of what it really takes to embark upon a professional career in motion pictures or television. And to survive. Which required a need to be aware of a range of areas - from logistics to how to find an agent, how to read the small print in a contract to understanding branding and an audience demographic.

Talent was not enough to make it in the industry. Ray had often hired very talented writers but would never again if they could not live within a brief and given set of budgetary and logistical exigencies. And primarily how to structure.

Where original projects were concerned, to select the elements and be aware of not just what happens but what the story is about. To punctuate the thematic and ensure it all evolves.

In his lectures, he tried to make writers understand the director's requirements. As well as the producer's. And the end users, from distributors to publishers, along with broadcasters.

And above all, to remember that within the three various disciplines of writing, although there are elements which overlap across each category - theater is what people say, novels are about what they think, and in film and television - what they do. And why they do it.

In addition to his lectures, Ray gave so called master classes to a select group of students but felt uncomfortable at such a lofty title, considering himself hardly a master and more than still capable of scoring an own goal. And no-one in the industry ever stops learning.

Ray cared about the students and wanted to give them the benefit of any experience so that they might benefit from the mistakes that he had made. And especially that they were armed with adequate knowledge about what it really takes to survive in the industry so that they could pursue and achieve their dreams.

The theoretical study might provide an awareness of split infinitives in the English language, but in the mainstream, the industry was not governed by the constraints of academia and the overuse of the cliche. Audiences never want characters in a love story to live unhappily ever after. Or for a hero not to come out on top.

In 'Rocky 1', before even seeing the movie or reading the screenplay, everyone probably knew he would go the distance. But the story arc in getting from A to B was what made it all work. Even if no-one enjoyed the motion picture, they couldn't deny that it had been written and produced with great skill, with a creative integrity within the genre and confines of what is required to feed the Hollywood machine. And satisfy the appetite of a mainstream audience.

Ray certainly believed in the importance of studying the esoteric. After all, he had been inspired by the legendary Akira Kurosowa. But investors and distributors, broadcasters and film studios are governed by different tenants.

Where a director is concerned, a great tracking shot in an underground film classic may well be impressive, but a broadcaster would be more likely to hire a candidate with the capability and understanding of multi camera methodologies used in filming a soap opera or fast turnaround situation comedy.

The top and tail of the impressive tracking shot would probably be cut anyway to drive a story forward in the edit room. And a hand held camera may well have been more time and cost effective, rather than a crew standing around waiting for tracks to be laid.

Fast turn around television and even motion picture production was all about getting the required minutes of footage in the can. Not about if a director crossed the line in a shot - a theory on camera placement. So many 'A' list directors in motion pictures and certainly in television crossed the line as a matter of routine, knowing how the structure of a shot would cut together in the edit.

The business was, after all, a business. So for anyone entering the freelance market place and hoping to be hired, they needed to think of themselves as small business men or women, and above all have an understanding of how the business worked.

Such as becoming literate in how to raise production finance, or understanding all the vagaries of intellectual property, even of how to schedule a production and draw up a budget. If a producer didn't know how, then how would he or she know that the production manager hired had gotten it all right? End users would certainly know and would ask some pertinent questions on why a producer thought a six week schedule was feasible, when it might require eight.

So Ray introduced a wide range of topics into his lectures and classes in the hope that his students would gain a better understanding of the industry - from the restrictions in obtaining completion bonds, to what the difference is between gross and net box office receipts, the impact of prints and advertising in any distribution costs, to examining what may or may not constitute a well structured script and all that entails.

After dealing with the Australian broadcasters and government regularity body for children's programing, Ray made a note to include this element in a future lecture.

The broadcaster was very keen to acquire 'The Tribe'. But Ray discovered that the series failed the required classification, due to the gritty story lines which the government body felt pushed the boundaries of what may be acceptable, to the extreme.

275

The rules and regulations did not apply to the State broadcaster. Only commercial networks. And it was frustrating that, although the broadcaster wanted to take the series - it couldn't due to the fact that it needed a 'C' classification. Which 'The Tribe' would not be granted.

Ray had never experienced any problems in this area before in other countries where similar official governments regulated programming.

'The Tribe' might have examined controversial and hard hitting issues. But Ray believed there was nothing derogatory in any of the story lines which had a negative effect on people, whatever their age.

On the contrary, the series had been applauded for the way it handled the themes. And so many welcomed it. 'The Tribe' seemed to even help young people understand - and many of them cope with, in some instances - the world they inhabited.

The series did not sanitize matters. That was the intention. To accurately explore a range of issues which people encountered every day of their lives, from peer pressure to bullying.

There was nothing in any of the themes that any member of the audience might not observe or experience within social interplay, even at school. And the overall theme of building a better world was positive and aspirational.

'The Tribe' had also distinguished itself as a series which attracted people of all ages. From the audience research, parents seemed to be tuning in to enjoy the episodes with their children. The fan club confirmed the wide age group demographic of the people who followed 'The Tribe'. The youngest member was five. The oldest, over eighty.

This was heartening on one hand but posed to be also problematic on the other. Which Ray had identified when he was considering introducing adults into Series Five. And his instincts and reasoning were now proving to be right.

'The Tribe' was straying outside of conventional children's programming.

The Controller of Channel 5 in the UK was always a great supporter of the series, along with all of Cloud 9's portfolio of product, but was becoming concerned how long the premise of a world without adults would work in a series perceived to be targeted at young people and now attracting a wide audience.

Ray couldn't deny that the characters would only get older with each passing year and explained that he fully realized the dilemma and had thought about it himself. He was intending that in line with the theme, the characters would simply continue with the struggle as they got older, along with their own children, to rebuild society.

And that there was enough material associated with that to fuel story lines for over a thousand years.

He could see that it might require moving 'The Tribe' out of a conventional children's slot so as not to confuse or alienate advertisers. And that he would need to persuade broadcasters to think about a different time to transmit the series in their schedules. But that would mean dealing with a totally different set of buyers who acquire product.

Channel 5 were very keen on acquiring a sequel that Ray had been developing which would mean at least that if the characters were younger, it could retain the current slot and solve the problem the broadcaster might have with advertisers and sponsors looking for product, so called age-related, that targeted a specific demographic.

Ray was sure that Tribe fans would really enjoy a sequel and witness how descendants of all the characters coped and what situations they would encounter in the new world.

He had in mind, within the Tribe mythology, that it would be a surprising twist to structure a series initially thought to be a sequel but which in actual fact was a prequel.

So rather than paying homage to the ancestors, the descendants of Bray and Amber, for instance, would in reality be the forefathers of the characters. And that primitive markings found in Series Six of 'The Tribe' in caves in a new land would actually herald a prophesy of a frightening world of darkness controlled by machines.

But when it is revealed that the sequel was actually the prequel of the Mall Rats' ancestors being portrayed when they were young, it would provide an interesting dimension of story line material to shed light on what exactly happened to bring about a world of no adults.

And that rather than a human virus, it evolved from computers and that something more sinister had occurred due to the advanced world of technology.

Given all the circumstances, Ray decided that it made sense to rest 'The Tribe' and place Series Six on hold. This would give him an opportunity of meeting key buyers to seek a better time slot.

In the meantime, he would produce 'The Tribe' sequel (or prequel) to which he had given the working title 'The New Tomorrow' and this would satisfy the commitments which were made to Channel 5, as well as an Australian broadcaster, for the company to deliver a series.

Also, rather than the production center being in downtime, it would remain active. Which was essential with overhead and other costs running at a quarter of a million dollars a week when a new series was filmed.

All involved at Cloud 9 agreed. Channel 5 were happy with the development of 'The New Tomorrow'. As was the Australian broadcaster. The problem had been resolved.

Wrong.

The government regularity body, alas, would require revisions to the proposed story lines of 'The New Tomorrow' if Ray wished to have the required classification which, like 'The

Tribe', was vital - otherwise, the Australian broadcaster would be unable to transmit the series.

Ray respected the reasoning for the revisions which had been requested, which was to simply comply with what had been set out in the legislation.

No-one was being difficult or unreasonable but had to ensure that all of the boxes in the guideline were ticked so that the series could be approved and would obtain the classification.

And Ray made another note to mention to his students in a future lecture that although the creative integrity of any project should never be compromised, a writer or producer also needed to keep an open mind on the realities of what might occur in the marketplace. And at times a pragmatic, rather than an intransigent, approach was wise.

If that didn't work, then perhaps the students should consider going into therapy, as Ray was beginning to feel. So that they might cope with a self-inflicted nervous breakdown which they might experience, given the frustrations they could encounter in the industry.

And that has nothing to do with the esoteric. Or the academic. Or even any creative elements.

It was more to do with digging endless holes - and constantly filling them in.

CHAPTER TWENTY

JOURNAL: 2005

By the time pre-production began in January, 2005, most of the story lines had changed quite substantially from what Ray had originally planned for the sequel in order to accommodate the revisions required to obtain the classification certificate for the Australian broadcaster.

Preparations for filming ran smoothly, though it was difficult to find a way to portray the machines which would feature in the Forbidden Zone.

In the end, prior to the commencement of principal photography, Ray took a small team to his vineyard to shoot second unit footage. With the ingenuity of Kiwi number eight wire exhibited by the production designer and the art department, the mammoth heavy duty viticultural equipment was redressed and disguised to serve as the menacing machines on patrol, evoking an image of being from almost another planet. Certainly not from this world.

Ray was pleased with the rushes and assembled footage as it came in. And was particularly impressed with the performances of all the cast.

He saw Lex in the studio Take 9 cafe, taking a break from working on the post production foley. 'The cast are terrific. And seem so young.' Ray agreed and smiled to himself. Lex was hardly ancient himself.

The cast of 'The New Tomorrow' did indeed bring mature and well observed dimensions to their characters for children of such an age.

Ray mentioned how pleased he was with the results to all concerned and gave particular credit to another member of 'The Tribe' team involved in the production. Alice was working with the cast as dialogue coach and doing an outstanding job.

It was a strange feeling working with a younger cast and to see Flame and Harmony in a different incarnation to the one Ray had ever envisioned. But the actor and actress possessed an incredible screen presence, as did Sky and all the cast.

Ray tried to explain the back story and how it linked to 'The Tribe' to assist them in their interpretation of the scripts.

Having worked on most of the series of 'The Tribe', the crew were engrossed by it all, as might any fan viewing at home, continually asking questions and drawing their own conclusions.

The character, Sky, must be a descendant. But equally - maybe the series was set in the past and not the future?

Were the markings Sky discovered in the caves, referring to the two babies being born, a prophesy? Or did something occur before? In a dark age? And if so, what?

Other markings in the caves seemed to point to a boat leaving a great city which had been destroyed. And what about the compound which had once been home to a Tribe known as the Mall Rats? Sky said that from stories he had been told, it was a special and spiritual place. But did it really exist? Or was it merely down to myth and legend?

The crew knew, of course, that the Mall Rats existed. They had been working closely with them all for the past five years in the huge Mall set. But they were still enthralled by the mythology, and second-guessing what had - or would - happen in all of the story threads.

The series was well received when it was premiered, drawing a new and younger audience, most of whom were unaware of 'The Tribe'.

But it is fair to say that some Tribe fans were disappointed, feeling that the sequel was not exactly what they had expected. Other aficionados though, were as intrigued as ever, recognizing the nuances and elements which still remained intact after the story lines had evolved to accommodate the classification.

Many Tribe fans in later years seemed to enjoy 'The New Tomorrow' more when it was repeated. And having re-watched it a second time around, they saw so much more in all the layers.

The audience of 'The New Tomorrow' even became fascinated to discover more. Ray received so many letters enquiring about the references to the great ancestors, Bray and Zoot. He asked his assistant to reply, recommending that the new fans try and watch 'The Tribe'. Then they would gain a better understanding of 'The New Tomorrow'.

Ray hadn't attended any festival for a few years but was determined to be present for the official launch of the new series. For all of the difficulty in obtaining the classification and that it had changed so much from the series he had originally imagined - he was still, nevertheless, really proud of it and the endeavor displayed by all the cast and crew to bring it to the screen.

Rather than fly to Europe to attend MIP, Ray decided that he would sail back on the leg of a world cruise. His father was visiting New Zealand and Ray thought it would provide an ideal opportunity to spend quality time with his Dad.

If they caught up with the ship in Singapore, then they would have about six weeks together. Ray had just about enough of a window in the schedule as the ship was due to dock in Southampton a few days prior to MIP. He would then connect to Cannes with a flight from London Heathrow.

Ray was always close to his father. He regretted that with his work load and lifestyle, he hadn't been able to spend more time with him, along with other members of his family. Ray had seen them all regularly, of course, but it was always in passing. A fleeting visit for a day. Or even for only for a few hours before having to rush away to catch a flight and travel somewhere.

In reality, he probably saw his family as much as anyone would their own relatives or friends. But there was a feeling of isolation being on the other side of the world, rather than down the street or in a town nearby. Even if they did speak a few times each week by phone.

Ray had flown his Dad out to New Zealand and Australia on several occasions, but again they only had limited time to spend together, with Ray being at the studio all day and most nights having to deal with business telephone calls across all the time zones.

When one country closed, another opened. Being based in New Zealand meant that the nights were reserved for the overseas calls, or writing or composing. With the days being full with tasks associated with being in production. Ray's schedule meant that he either worked. Or slept. There didn't seem to be room for anything else. Not these days.

Ray enjoyed visiting all the interesting ports the ship visited on the voyage between Singapore and Southampton. Such as Mumbai in India and Durban in South Africa, where he and his father visited a Zulu village.

Cape Verdi Island was especially moving as this was a port used in the days of trading slaves. Ray and his Dad enjoyed hearing a children's choir sing folk songs which had been handed down through so many generations.

Ray had heard the legendary Harlem Gospel Choir live in New York City once - but the genesis of gospel and the blues had originated elsewhere and the children's choir gave a good example of all of their musical heritage.

It meant a lot to Ray to have some time with his father, which he really treasured. Sadly, even that was interrupted most days due to business calls which came to the ship by satellite phone. Mostly from the Cumulus distribution team to do with the impending festival. But also from Ray's advisors and his joint venture partner, alerting that a bid had been received, which meant that Ray's corporate partner was subject to a takeover.

It was hardly surprising, given that the company had expanded so much over the past years and was now a major multi media giant with many 'A' list clients in the music divisions. But in business, there is always a bigger giant targeting opportunities, like a commercial shark.

Being a public company meant that the shares of Ray's joint venture partner were traded on the stock exchange, and multi national conglomerates are forever looking to acquire so-called units to expand their own vast empires.

Ray did not have that problem since he held the shares he owned privately in Cloud 9. But he would probably have a new joint venture partner if the takeover went ahead. The bid wasn't a hostile one. And had been accepted in principle by a majority shareholder vote. So negotiations had entered into a phase known as due diligence. The voyage gave him much needed time to assess all the implications.

'The New Tomorrow' was well received at MIP, but Ray was struck by how much the industry had changed in the few years since he had last attended the festival. With the advent of new technology, so many more platforms were being planned to carry programming, from the Internet to even mobile phones.

And with more cable and satellite outlets, terrestrial broadcasters' market share had been diluted. The industry referred to it as convergence.

The digital domain was revolutionizing the entire landscape of the multi media business.

Retail book stores were beginning to struggle as consumers could purchase online. Following the trend in the music industry which was also suffering, with fewer people purchasing CDs through retail outlets now that music was made available to download.

Many in the business were also becoming victims of cyber theft, which was a serious crime and subject to criminal conviction. And it would pose a problem for Cloud 9 in later years, with piracy diluting potential returns for investors, resulting in a reluctance to risk further funds.

This was exacerbated with the advent of YouTube. And people innocently uploading material, resulting in consumers viewing product online rather than through conventional outlets. Hardly surprisingly that there was a rapid decline in the DVD market.

Ray never had a problem with clips being used on YouTube. In fact, he was impressed by how some fans had re-edited material, which he thought was highly imaginative, and he loved to see fans expressing themselves in such a creative way through clips of 'The Tribe'.

But he could never accept why some people - and thankfully only a minority - uploaded entire episodes. And in some cases even the whole five series, misrepresenting - within the terms outlined by YouTube on any upload - that they owned the copyright or had permission to do it.

It was understandable how people would be drawn to view any material if it was there. And Ray was sure he would have probably also watched his favorite shows, unless he knew all of the implications.

To upload entire episodes and series was tantamount to opening a department store and allowing consumers to help themselves and just take whatever they wanted.

It was difficult enough as it was to bring about a new production in the economic climate, without having to devote time to warrant that adequate systems were in place to offset illegal or pirate activity.

And Ray was weary of it. But had to make sure he took steps to protect the interests of a range of people with whom he was involved, from banks to broadcasters, investors to distributors. Along with the consumers who would ultimately suffer if, as a result of the illegal activity, their favorite series were no longer produced and were unavailable.

He was sure most who uploaded the entire series and episodes just didn't think. And didn't mean any harm by it. Ray believed that the market would self regulate. And that if the consumers were educated in all of the implications, then the inherent decency and honesty of the vast majority would stamp out all the problematic areas once they fully understood.

Back at the MIP festival, he also became aware that slots for live action drama were in decline, to pave the way for a new form of programing. Reality television was coming into fashion. It was a new art form evolving from the conventional documentary approach, interweaving a light entertainment aspect.

Audiences seemed to love it. As did the broadcasters. But perhaps not solely due to the content. They were able to acquire shows which achieved high ratings, and being fast turn around production, meant that it was all available at very low costs.

The Cumulus team was constantly approached by so many broadcasters enquiring if Cloud 9 would be diversifying into reality. Especially as it was expanding into animation.

Ray enjoyed many of the reality shows himself and admired the skill and craftsmanship which went into producing them. But his interest was confined to being a viewer on a personal level. Professionally, it wasn't really what he wanted to do.

But what did he want to do? It was a question he couldn't really answer at this stage of his career, as he reflected upon which path he might take in the future.

He was sitting on the same bench near the entrance of Disneyland Paris where he had released the balloons after his brother had died, having decided to take some members of the family away for a few days' treat before he returned to New Zealand.

They were having fun in the Magic Kingdom and had left Ray for an hour, knowing he wanted to take some time out alone to think of his mother, as well as his late brother.

Ray noticed a cleaner nearby and watched, fascinated, as the man went about his work. He was fastidious, sweeping every bit of litter he could find into the small container he held stylishly with his other hand. It was as if he was dancing. He seemed so debonaire. Like Gene Kelly or Fred Astaire.

If they were giving an Academy Award for the best cleaner, then this man would win. He was clearly dedicated to his profession. Ray was in awe. And full of admiration. Thinking that it was such a great example of 'It's not what you do but the way that you do it.'

The cleaner displayed such a passion and conscientiousness that Ray was on the point of offering him a job. But no doubt the cleaner would refuse. He was clearly already doing what he wanted to do.

Ray never considered that he had ever worked a day in his life. Because he was not only doing what he wanted to do, but what he loved and needed to do.

But now he couldn't put his finger on what it was that was troubling him as he thought about where he had come from, where he was now, and more importantly where he was going in his life.

So much had occurred since he founded his company and the past 12 years had sped by in a blur. Ray felt like he was in a time warp. As if he had gone into a room in 1994 and had come out but now it was 2006.

He had been constantly in production, delivering almost 600 episodes of programming. One completed episode each and every week. Solidly. Over the twelve years. Which was the equivalent of 145-150 motion pictures. In screen minute terms, at least. Or twelve every year. One a month. It was an extraordinary output. But crazy. And amazing that he had not killed himself in the process.

Ray certainly felt worn out. And wondered if he had simply burnt himself out. It wasn't so much the creative elements which had drained him. But all the business aspects. Which he never really enjoyed.

He had set out to be a composer and a writer/producer, which had been achieved. But he never wanted a business the size of which he now had. He had no dynastic aspirations and no heir apparent to build a corporate empire. The corporate world never held any interest in that way.

Now he was facing the prospects of an unknown joint venture partner, and advisors believing that Ray himself should consider floating his company. He could probably earn a small fortune.

But again, it held no appeal whatsoever. He was more interested in people and ideas and dreams than matters fiscal.

And as with the principles of risk to return, had been fortunate with all that he had initially risked to earn more than he could ever spend. He was a multi millionaire in asset terms but there was no cash under a mattress or in a bulging bank account, so to speak. He had reinvested every dollar and cent back into his company and in so doing, himself. And his beloved portfolio of programming.

And if he ever wanted to sell or trade his creative endeavors on the stock market, how would he ever value it? How much was the sky or earth worth? Or having a dream? It was all priceless. Just the same as if nothing had ever been produced, no music ever released, no story ever published, Ray still could not have placed a value on it. He would have done it every day, even if he was the only person who ever read the story he had written or listened to the music he had composed.

Ray had been able to earn a living doing what he really loved. If someone paid one dollar for the work, then that was no different to someone paying one million. It was the same piece of work. Ray would have created it for nothing. Which is how it all begins anyway. No-one creative sets out to write an expensive car or a house with a swimming pool or a stock market float. It's all a passion and not a process like manufacturing nuts or bolts.

So rather than trade his shares, Ray walked away from a substantial sum of money and asked his advisors how much it would cost to acquire the shares unencumbered, which had been held by his original joint venture partner.

It would never be the same without them around. And rather than selling out - he was in the market to buy. Not just to acquire the remaining shares in his company - but the entire intellectual property associated with all the underlying rights which were held.

He didn't like the notion of anyone owning a part of his dream. Unless they formed part of that dream, as his original joint venture partner once did. But with the takeover and the commercial world being what it is, Ray preferred freedom. To continue to do as he wanted. And that freedom was more important to Ray than any sum of money.

He was determined to keep his dream alive. And that his dreams would never be for sale.

CHAPTER TWENTY ONE

JOURNAL: 2006-2011

Shortly after arriving back in New Zealand, Ray decided that what he probably needed most, was a sabbatical. To take an extended period of time out. So that he could creatively recharge and refresh while negotiations took place to acquire all the shares in Cloud 9.

But he found himself busier than ever during a protracted visit to his vineyard. He really enjoyed the opportunity to experience all the wonders of the natural world. There had never been room in his busy schedule before.

And found himself getting to 'know' each vine. Which was also a living entity. With a cardio vascular though not a nervous system. They were miraculous plants. Tactile. They loved and needed to be touched to flourish. And would communicate through their leaves. If they wanted water, they would change color. Like a blood pressure warning system.

But the vines would seldom be watered, to encourage them to work harder and draw up all the nutrients in the alluvial soil to enrich the grapes they were themselves feeding.

Others - usually the younger inexperienced vines - worked far too hard and really needed to slow down. Not yet learning that they would have to pace themselves if they had any hope of getting through the growing season.

Some of their leaves were plucked so that the grapes would be exposed to the morning sun before being protected by the afternoon shade, which would assist the flavors in developing and becoming sharper, without the need for constant nourishment.

Ray even arranged to have some speakers strategically placed around the vineyard so that the vines could have some soft and gentle music played to them. And they certainly seemed to respond in much the same way as when someone moves a plant, thinking it didn't seem to like a particular place in a house and finds that it flourishes better elsewhere.

Since time began, viticulture has mostly attracted those interested in the geology or science of the natural world, viewing the process of winemaking as an intriguing molecular chemical reaction. Whereas the romantic believes it to be a precious reminder of the miracles of nature. Or an elixir from the ancient gods.

Way back in history, the monks considered wine to be a medicinal property. And many in today's medical profession view the tannins in quality wine as being beneficial for the body, in moderation, to assist the free radicals in the circulation system. Some even believe a glass of red wine a day will help prevent heart disease.

Wine certainly stimulates the parasympathetic nervous system. And when matched correctly with the appropriate food, enhances the dining experience to such an extent that it's almost another essential ingredient to savor and punctuate the flavors of the cuisine.

Robert Louis Stevenson once referred to fine wine as bottled poetry.

Ray agrees with that observation. But views the grapes as a gift from Mother Nature taken at a most precious time in life, being harvest, when the vines give birth. And the very second the grape is snipped - time stops. But when processed, then bottled, time begins again with the wine living and continually evolving over the years, delivering so many dimensions of textural layers. And when consumed, if all the elements have finally come together, it can produce an aftertaste which will seemingly last forever. The memory of it means that it invariably does.

Ray's vineyard maintains traditional hand-crafted viticultural principles and wine making methods which have been used for centuries. And he is forever proud of the entire vineyard team, who are devoted to the pursuit of excellence. Their dedication has resulted in the vineyard winning many awards. Including the prestigious Romeo Bragato trophy for producing champion Pinot Noir.

During his time spent on the vineyard, Ray came to realize that he hadn't fully - and properly - come to terms with his brother's, let alone his mother's passing. And he found a peace and spirituality in living at one with the land.

As he sat on his tractor moving through acres and acres of vines, he felt somehow connected to the natural world. Simply by observing how all the elements are inter-connected. From the insects in the soil, to the hawks who would gather to hunt prey in advance of veraison, which is when the grapes are due to ripen, instinctively knowing that flocks of birds would also soon arrive, attracted by the scent.

He could see how the Native American Indian or any indigenous culture drew so much from an affinity with nature.

Hawks and eagles flew in a circle, made nests in a circle and life itself was in a circle, as indeed were so many elements of Mother Earth.

Ray was always fascinated by nature and the environment. Ever since he was a boy, and his mother pointed out that a dock leaf always grew near a nettle. If he was stung, then he could find relief and be cured by rubbing the juices from the leaf onto the sting, which made the pain subside. So many homeopathic and natural medicines evolved from the land.

He still had to travel on occasion, especially to Australia where the company had opened offices at the Warner Brothers Studio. But after acquiring his shares back, Ray had also decided that he needed to restructure.

And now was the time to do it, with decisions needing to be made on options on studios and crews. So he scaled back his entire business to simplify his life, appointing a distributor to handle the back catalogue and even considered at one point that he might retire. But in reality, that was never an option. He would always need to create.

But at the root, he knew that he could not operate at such a pace as he had, living his life in the fast lane, pulled in so many different directions, with all the pressures of the business and corporate world. If he was not careful, it could have sped out of control. And would have probably also killed him.

It all came to the fore when Ray met a team of doctors on a wine tasting tour who were complaining at having to work 100 hour weeks. He had the utmost respect for all those in the medical profession and felt no-one should ever take advantage of their care and devotion.

But he felt as if he was in a Monty Python sketch, where the participants try and out do each other with tales of hardship.

As he listened to the doctors discussing their hours, Ray was surprised that they thought that 100 hour weeks were excessive. Sheer luxury. Ray would do 100 hours without even batting an eyelid. He was just warming up. It was supposed to be a humorous observation. But it also made Ray reflect, because as well as seeing the funny side - it wasn't actually a joke. He was being serious.

He decided that after the type of schedule he had undertaken for so many years, he needed to re-educate his mind and body and soon began to slow down. To the normal speed of life.

This provided an opportunity to attend to his charity work and especially the activities of his own Foundation, which was important to him. Having a special need himself, Ray was always keen to support and become a flag-bearer to anyone with a disability or facing hardship. He knew all about it. He had been there. And still struggled in so many ways.

But the vineyard provided a welcome refuge throughout his sabbatical and was a sanctuary in many ways. Apart from visits to Australia and to undertake necessary administrative tasks, Ray could regularly be seen on his tractor, or pruning his beloved vines, or helping out at harvest.

Ray briefed the vineyard team that he wanted to be incognito. And to even help out at the Cellar Door. Along with picking up customers on occasion who were due to dine in the vineyard restaurant, as he found it fascinating to meet and talk with everyday people outside the world of Hollywood or so called show business.

They were unaware that Ray had anything to do with the entertainment industry. Being mostly unshaven and wearing his favorite scruffy sweater, customary shorts and running shoes, he looked down at heel. Some probably believed that he was more of a transient casual worker who had fallen on hard times, rather than the actual owner of the vineyard who was also a producer and writer.

Ray recalled when first starting out in the industry that with so many advising the pursuit of an alternative, less risky career, that it was rather like embarking upon a journey. And that he thought no-one would ever discover new horizons without having the courage to lose sight of the shore.

Now, all these years later, age had brought another dimension to that youthful philosophy. Ray was becoming aware of the wisdom that the journey was actually better than the destination. And above all, that it was more important to want what one has in life - rather than to have what one wants.

He had observed this once during his time at the BBC, when he was fortunate enough to take his mother and family on a cruise on the iconic flagship QE2. And his mother was not very happy. She enjoyed all the fancy food at first, but got a little tired of it all after a few days. She longed for beans on toast. So Ray asked the maitre'd to arrange it. Minutes later, a line of white-gloved waiters carrying silver trays, proceeded to serve beans on toast. Along with a chip buttie, which Ray desperately wanted and had ordered.

'Ah, this is more like it,' Ray's mother said, eagerly tucking in. And she started to enjoy the cruise.

Ray often thought about that dining experience, as well as when his mother accompanied him to the headmaster and he advised, as a boy, what he wanted in life. A Bentley and a table. But not in that order.

He now owned some wonderful tables. And had a 'thing' about them. But his very favorite table was the one he purchased in a junk shop when he was broke and just starting out to write, which he still preferred to use, rather than any expensive antique.

Ray was also able to obtain his favorite Bentley, which was now mostly sitting idle in the garage in one of his homes. It was a Park Mulliner, long wheel base, an extraordinary vehicle, sleek and elegant, like driving on a cloud.

And as much as he still loved the elegance and craftsmanship of the vehicle, Ray felt more at home driving the old, rusty ute or the tractor on the vineyard.

Material objects never brought about true happiness. The lack of money and financial pressures could bring about great unhappiness of course. Ray had experienced that, growing up in so much hardship.

But life's experience had taught Ray that it was not possible to find contentment in anyone or anything. To think otherwise would lead to a long and fruitless search. The only place true contentment could be found was within oneself. And the key to finding that was to accept who one really was.

Ray wasn't a businessman. He had learned much about the corporate world and had even excelled in some areas. But again, like the Bentley, it wasn't him. Business wasn't what he had ever set out to do.

The need to compose or write remained paramount, deep within the core of Ray's very essence. So during his sabbatical, Ray decided that he would focus more on his writing, producing and composing.

He still received many enquiries from broadcasters who were keen for Ray to develop new titles for television. And many were interested in obtaining the changed format rights of 'The Tribe'.

But Ray was unsure if it would all work out. The American version of 'The Office' had certainly turned out well, but it was always difficult to replicate source material unless through a franchise, such as Idol or the X-Factor.

And in his heart, Ray questioned if various versions of 'The Tribe', across different countries and cultures, held any merit - or whether, in the end, it would debase the original material.

Fans were forever requesting more product for all the titles in the Cloud 9 portfolio. But Ray couldn't see himself doing sequels of all the series he had produced, otherwise it would be like painting the same picture for not only several more years - but forever.

As any one creative will know, it is never possible to stamp the end of any story. Least it was never that way for Ray.

His imagination was forever wondering what would have happened to all the characters in all the stories he had ever created, written, or produced. But to attempt to bring it all to the screen would be an infinite and perpetual process. As in life, stories are ongoing. If a character rode off into the sunset, the way Ray's mind worked he would be intrigued to consider what happened next in the new dawn.

'The Tribe' was an entirely different proposition. So unlike the other titles Ray had written or produced. And although he loved them all equally, as a parent might every child - there was something about 'The Tribe' which was special. Perhaps because it, too, had a 'special need'. And had struggled to live and breathe and leave the nest, before becoming established.

The series was like a bird with a broken wing - which to everyone's surprise, against all the odds, took off and flew, soaring to unexpected great heights.

This was testament to the endeavors of the entire cast and crew. And it gave Ray so much pride to see them keeping their dream alive and doing so well progressing their careers.

Many went on to work on major feature films such as 'Avatar' and 'Lord Of The Rings'.

Others, such as Jermaine Clement, who played the part of a reality cowboy, found great success in 'Flight Of The Conchords'.

Not all of the cast remained in the business. But keep in touch with Ray. He remains a mentor to all - taking a keen interest in those still in the industry.

But what distinguishes 'The Tribe' and elevates it to hold such affection in Ray's psyche - are the fans. So many have stuck with the series since it was first transmitted around the world. And with the series being repeated, 'The Tribe' is still attracting a new audience.

Ray is forever touched by the dedication and loyalty of all the Tribal brothers and sisters around the globe. Something about the series connected emotionally in such a unique way. And that has been reflected by the affection from all the fans who constantly give back, always there for 'The Tribe'.

He was always open to doing another series of 'The Tribe' and had discussed it with many broadcasters, as well as a possible sequel. And the options still remain.

If it was just a question of doing it, then Ray would. Even if it meant devoting a year or two to developing and producing it. But it wasn't as easy as that. It requires raising substantial investment to underwrite production costs. And the television and motion picture industry is not immune to the economic recession manifesting around the globe.

That doesn't mean to say that product isn't being made. But the marketplace has evolved, with such a range of platforms diluting commercial returns due to convergence. And with so many end users now being owned by Wall Street multi national conglomerates, it would require a different investment methodology.

Following Ray's sabbatical he preferred to remain as a writer/producer, rather than get back into the arena of the commercial world. And to trade as an independent.

One area Ray was eager to pursue was the development of a series of novels of 'The Tribe'. Then he would be able to explore so many areas which he couldn't within the confines of television.

He still had other unfulfilled creative dreams he wanted to achieve as well, which mostly revolved around the development of a motion picture portfolio.

So Ray spent a winter in Australia going back to doing what he really loved, developing an original screenplay, 'The Cowboy and the Dancer'. It is a gentle love story set against the country music industry. And in Hollywood sound bite terms, might best be described as Rocky 1 meets Being There, Sleepless in Seattle meets Forest Gump.

The screenplay attracted a lot of interest within the industry, to such an extent that Ray was signed by a major Hollywood agency who were keen to represent him. They asked what else he would ideally like to do within his motion picture portfolio. Ray advised that he was considering developing 'The Tribe'.

The agency believed that 'The Tribe' had enormous potential as a motion picture franchise and encouraged Ray to progress it. But he didn't need much encouragement. It was something he always wanted to do and agreed to work on a screenplay.

He knew that it could be a long and painful process. And hoped that he wouldn't become trapped in development hell. But he had the faith that whatever was meant to be - would be. And that as he had done all his life, he would keep the dream alive and never give up in the pursuit of what he wanted to achieve.

Shortly after re-reading the treatment he had written and staring at the blank page of the screenplay, his assistant called to suggest that Ray also work on the memoir and inside story of what he had experienced in the industry to date, as well as a behind the scenes journal on bringing 'The Tribe' to the screen.

As always, Ray was anguished just exactly where he would start.

But for the first time ever - was intrigued, wondering exactly where it would all end. Sensing that with the unique support and loyalty of all the fans around the world also keeping the dream alive, there may well be so much more to come in the story of 'The Tribe'. And perhaps there would be no end.

Or if so .... the end may well just be the beginning.

SCREENPLAY TREATMENT ENDING OUT-TAKES

.... In the cave the Mall Rats discuss strategy. AMBER reveals that the time for battle is not of their choice. TRUDY needs to stay with the children, and KC will help protect them.

All the Tribes in this new land have been mobilized. And they have intelligence that the army of the Privileged have already gathered and have started their march. The Mall Rats have no other option but to prepare for war and not only defend themselves, but any fading hope of building a better future ....

HILLS.

A Tribal WARRIOR high on a hill, framed against the rising dawn sun, blowing into a bull HORN - the call to arms.

301

PANNING ACROSS THE CRESTS OF OTHER HILLS.

Pounding war drums. TRIBES, with standard Flags and Banners fluttering in the winds, appearing over the ridge, marching on their way to battle, carrying pikes tagged with feathers, home-made shields.

SEA.

WARRIORS in long, dug out canoes decorated with intimidating designs for war, also on their journey, frenzied chanting, paddling in unison.

FORESTS.

The GAIAN TRIBE marching through forests, some on horses, the faces of the animals also streaked with fierce war paint.

FROM THE AIR.

Descending AERIAL SHOTS of the gathering hero FORCES marching, coming together across open fields, plains - the pine forests and mountains of the lands of the Privileged visible in the far distance.

And it is a breathtaking visual - a mixture of different cultures, colors and designs. Not reminiscent of modern warfare in any way.

The base aesthetic is MORE like the clans at Culloden explored in 'Brave Heart'. But even that is a superficial comparison. This is all so strangely familiar, yet also looks like something we have NEVER seen before.

Most of the TRIBES are marching on foot. But some are on horseback, some even have wild looking dogs, snarling and straining on heavy chain leashes.

WARRIORS (and only a few) are in graffiti-tagged vehicles, trucks - the hoods painted with frightening images, scowling faces, wild eyes, jaws of sharp teeth, all modified, like chariots with blades protruding.

And if we didn't know better, we would swear that some are even sitting on motorized lawn mowers, tagged, streaked with war paint, long pole lances set straight ahead.

Other WARRIORS are riding motorcycles. And there is one bus. Amidst the tagging we are aware of the surreal sight of a red cross sign, on this, the Tribes' medic facility.

Anything and everything scavenged from society is almost used or worn - garbage can tin armor, twisted wires as hair extensions sprouting from welding masks, hockey masks.

Some inspired by the elemental, with feathers and war paint, look like a cross between the Apache and the Zulu. Others, with animal skins and horns almost more like a cross between the Vikings, barbarians, and wild motorcycle gangs.

And we have already seen the GAIANS, who now join the columns of the gathering hero FORCES.

But it is also the sounds that are just so striking, rousing. Beating drums. And pipes. Accompanying the frenzied cacophony of chanting from all the TRIBES.

FEATURING BRAY, AMBER AND THE MALL RATS

leading the assembled ARMY, forming as a united force behind - and just ahead of - the SHADOWS, following the MASTER in his tank. The only Mall Rat vehicle is CLOUD'S dune buggy, on which she is sitting on the hood, another WARRIOR driving.

The RATS look awesome. Faces streaked with war paint, feathers adorning their grungy clothes, hair, banners and flags fluttering in the wind, expressions set, determined, proud.

Now the faint sound of a distant guitar is suddenly audible amidst all the noise of the chanting, the pipes, and beating drums.

Which brings some unease, especially to SALENE, JACK and BRAINS, and they swallow in nervous anticipation.

PINE FOREST - MOUNTAINS.

FLAME, in the mountains, though this time not at the very peak. Head banging, back and forth, back and forth, playing a repetitive wailing note which reverberates all around, the sounds almost deafening, amidst whistling feedback, his long blond hair blowing in the wind, framing the horrific sight of his face - covered entirely in blood.

OUTER FRINGES OF THE PRIVILEGED COMPOUND.

EBONY, on a white stallion, the same lightning bolt tattooed on her face - painted around the eye of the horse, which even has the very same feathers as she does plaited in its beaded mane hair.

She is trotting slowly down the PRIVILEGED front line as they prepare to move on and into battle, though the DISCARDS, featuring HARMONY and OX, are being marshaled well in front, still shackled, chained.

And the PRIVILEGED forces look so intimidating, formidable, threatening - especially the militia, with their tattooed faces. All are streaked with war paint, horns, animal skins, shells, and they seem as if they have been conjured up from hell.

FEATURING FLAME

visible on the Mountain ridge, the rays of sun enshrining him like a god, his repetitive wail of the guitar whipping all into a frenzy and some are head banging as if lost in a manic trance.

And we can hear the distant chanting, pipes, pounding of the drums becoming louder ... LOUDER - as the Tribal armies approach closer ... CLOSER.

EBONY

reigns her mount, yells above it all, addressing the PRIVILEGED forces, reminding them that the Discards will act as human shields. They will fall first. Ebony will lead the charge. And no way she's going down!

The PRIVILEGED forces' chanting evolving into a manic shriek as EBONY whips them, as well as herself, into a frenzy, adding that all should now look at the god, FLAME.

They should note his face is adorned with blood. The blood of all the infesting Rats they could find. And that should remind them that defeat from the MALL RAT forces is not an option if they want to rid the lands of the impure.

The PRIVILEGED forces gaze up at
POV FLAME

head banging on the mountain ridge.

And even more of the PRIVILEGED start head banging themselves. EBONY yelling above it all, to dig deep, Tribal brothers and sisters. Seek courage - and if needs be lay down their lives for the cause. And generations will look back on this day of all days, knowing that this is where it all began, when the ancestors of the pure set about taking over the world, ridding it of any and all Mall Rats ... along with the scum of their vermin forces!

All erupt in even more of a frenzied SHRIEKING, ULULATING and start to march into battle.

BATTLE FIELDS.

The pounding drums, pipes, wailing guitar, chanting — the two ARMIES approaching closer, closer — the divide narrowing.

And now nerves are starting to play a part for other members of the RATs, with even LEX, AMBER and BRAY displaying increasing unease, in addition to JACK, BRAINS and SALENE.

But CLOUD is calming herself on the hood of the dune buggy by adopting a lotus position — and emits her mantra.

FEATURING BRAY

as both ARMIES suddenly slow the pace, gaze across the narrowing distance at each other.

The drums and pipes stop.

But not the distant wailing guitar, the sounds of the wind whipping up the fluttering banners, flags, bringing a sense of peace in the tense silence.

Both ARMIES just seem to stare at each other. Sizing each other up across the divide. BRAY swallows, takes a breath, gazes each side of him, behind, then ahead again, finally nodding — it's on!

THE CHARGE INTO BATTLE.

A deafening ROAR as both ARMIES, featuring the MALL RATS and PRIVILEGED, yell, running flat out towards each other - and into battle.

HUGE WOODED CATAPULT STRUCTURES

are released by the PRIVILEGED back lines, hurling flaming balls of material through the air.

THE APPROACHING HERO FORCES, FEATURING THE MALL RATS

as the fire balls land, slightly disrupting the advance.

AND AS BOTH ARMIES ENGAGE

in mostly hand to hand combat, LEX is wielding a giant club bound by chains, taking anyone in his path out.

THE DISCARDS,

featuring HARMONY and OX still bound, shackled, screaming helplessly, caught in the charge, unable to defend themselves as the ARMY of the hero forces pass, most - featuring BRAY - going round, avoiding them.

EBONY

on her stallion, swinging a pike and
cutting down her enemy.

PRIVILEGED BOWMEN

in the back lines, drawing back their
weapons and unleashing

ARROWS

arcing through the air, the sibilant
sound audible above all the noise of the
pounding drums, pipes, wailing guitar -
and the battle.

THE HERO FORCES

featuring SALENE in a column, doing as they
had trained, crouching in a collective,
raising shields for unified protection as
the arrows fall but do not penetrate.
FEATURING BRAINS AND JACK

in another column in the midst of battle,
as one arrow thwacks into the arm of
JACK.

And BRAINS has lost it. He stands frozen
in fear. Can't seem to do anything.
Fight. Help. Even move. Just stares at
the battle raging around him. At JACK,
gripping his arm as a huge PRIVILEGED

WARRIOR approaches behind, raising a club to strike.

BRAY APPEARS IN FRAME

takes out the WARRIOR with a spectacular martial art move, saving JACK.

FEATURING LEX

swinging his club, backing up to give cover as BRAY rips a bit of cloth, quickly ties a tourniquet, yells at JACK over the NOISE of battle to try and get behind the lines. He's going to need some treatment from the medics! And he draws the arrow from JACK'S arm.

BRAINS

sinks slowly to the ground. No, not by any enemy strike, though he is close to having that happen .... He has fainted!

So different to any war game he has ever played on any computer. So scary, full on. Just too much. Raw.

FLAME

on the ridge, still head banging, trancelike as he plays the same repetitive rift.

AMBER

pushing on harder, harder, shielding
enemy blows, fists, poles, pikes, knives,
engaged in the thick of the hand to hand
combat, suddenly gazes dumbfounded at

CLOUD

in the lotus position on the dune buggy,
as the hero FORCES drive on and on through
the thick of the battle.

And some of the PRIVILEGED enemy steal a
confused glance. Mantra and Zen? Or is
this chick a goddess, invincible - or
just plain whacko?!

But CLOUD uses her sixth sense,
occasionally opens one eye to emit a
lethal karate chop if anyone gets too
close.

FEATURING THE MALL RATS

as the relentless drive of the hero FORCES
is pushing back the PRIVILEGED toward
their compound.

EBONY

reining her mount, yells above the frenzy
of the battle for the Privileged Brothers

and Sisters to try and hold the lines!!
Stand firm!!!

Suddenly EBONY is dragged from her horse.
By AMBER. The horse rearing up in panic
onto its hind legs. And wham. AMBER floors
EBONY with one punch.

AMBER

gazes up at FLAME, then indicates to BRAY
nearby, reminding him that they've GOT to
get to Flame! He's the main one!

FEATURING BRAY

twirling, kicking, in a series of awesome
martial art movements, taking out any
enemy in his path. Then he runs, leaps
onto the hood, roof of a vehicle to
elevate him, then onto the tank and yells
to SHADOW that it's time for phase two!

APPROACHING THE PRIVILEGED COMPOUND

as the tank explodes through barricades,
making way for our hero forces to advance
even further.

BRAY leaps from the tank onto a passing
motocross scrambling bike, knocking off
the RIDER, climbs to his feet, lifts the
bike, mounts, kicks out at Privileged

WARRIORS in his path as he accelerates away.

PINE FOREST

BRAY speeding up a dirt track through the pine forest, ascending toward the mountain ridge.

RIDGE - MOUNTAINS

FLAME still in a trance, head banging back and forth, back and forth, repeating the wailing rift. BRAY approaching from behind, leaps off the bike, rushes to FLAME and - yanks the guitar from him.

BATTLE FIELDS

The PRIVILEGED gaze up, around as the guitar playing abruptly stops. The sounds of the hero Tribal FORCES now dominating - the pounding drums, pipes, war cries of battle.

But still the whistling feedback reverberates around and around as if punctuating the anguish from the PRIVILEGED, slowly realizing that the battle is being lost.

RIDGE - MOUNTAINS

FLAME still head bangs, rocking back and

forth, yells at BRAY to give his guitar back! Bray yells back - no way! Can't FLAME see? It's finished! Over!

FLAME sinks slowly to his knees, asks in that case for BRAY to do him a favor. Drive the guitar right into his head. Over. And over. Yeah. Shatter his skull into millions of little pieces. His brain's gone. Can't take any more. But the guitar will take it. It's a Gibson 66 Les Paul.

BRAY considers FLAME, who breaks into manic laughter and taunts BRAY. What's the problem?! Doesn't he want the gig?! To take out a god?! Thought that would be so cool. Sure as hell would be for FLAME. Then he can go to rock star heaven. In this godforsaken world, only the good die young, man.

FLAME gazes up at BRAY in sudden contempt, then snarls and screams in a petulant tantrum for BRAY to come on! Do it! Now!!! He wants to become immortal!!!

Although BRAY has the opportunity to settle the score on behalf of his brother and is clearly desperate to take it - and for a second we even think he might - he ... denies himself.

FLAME suddenly cries out in sheer terror. Noooooooo!!!!!

BRAY is spinning with all his might and hurls the guitar which twists, turns, falling through the air, amidst deafening feedback, breaking branches of pine trees in the forests below.

And we might want to go into slow motion as the guitar lands, bounces on the ground, then settles. Intact. Least Flame got THAT right.

IN THE PRIVILEGED COMPOUND

peace in the aftermath of battle. Privileged WARRIORS rounded up, Discard SLAVES unshackled, freed.

And we find JACK, crouched by BRAINS, outside the hospital bus.

JACK has one arm in a sling, is holding some smelling salts with the other hand under the nose of BRAINS, slapping his face. Come on. Get a grip. All this fainting is starting to freak JACK out.

BRAINS opens his eyes weakly, tries to focus, but quickly comes around when JACK advises that the Privileged have been defeated. BRAINS enthuses. Awesome! The whole THING was awesome. Much better than any computer game. JACK sighs, no. This is real - and indicates.

FEATURING AMBER CROUCHED BESIDE CLOUD

as BRAY, leading FLAME by a rope behind the bike, dismounts, rushes to their side. LEX also crossing to CLOUD from WARRIORS in the background visible, leading FLAME away with other prisoners, including EBONY.

BRAY asks how she is. AMBER shakes her head, doesn't need to answer. From the blood loss and CLOUD being barely conscious - it's clear it's not good. But CLOUD seems to know of BRAY'S presence, that he is there, reaches out to clutch at, to squeeze his hand - hard. Then her grip fades as fast as her life ebbs away.

And it is heartbreaking for AMBER to see her friend die in the arms of BRAY. Ironic. Leaving AMBER feeling guilty that she ended up having the affection of BRAY which CLOUD had so longed for. And LEX himself might even wipe at a tear.

BACK IN THE MALL

a relief for all the RATS as the Tribal LEADERS sign a peace treaty. Now the Privileged have been disbanded and Discards have been set free, maybe it's time for the Mall Rats to return to the city in their homeland and all the Tribes can build a better world together. Even the thought of it is worth celebrating. Party Time.

ON THE BEACH

a spit roast feast as all celebrate with BRAY and AMBER on an elevated sand dune hill, BRAY raising his new born BABY to an assembly of the TRIBES below (as when Simba was presented in The Lion King).

They are at the beginning of something new here. Not the end. Yes, the baby might have the blood of his brother, Zoot. But he is also a symbol that Zoot might have chosen a new path if it was offered. And as the son of AMBER and BRAY, it only takes one look to see the hope in AMBER'S eyes, indeed in the hope of the eyes of any Mother for her child.

But that hope should be shared by all. As the baby represents a symbol of hope for the future, for the future of ALL the tribes, ALL people – and one day it will be written, just like in the ancient parables and scriptures, that Abbe Messiah on this day, even for one brief shining moment, is a savior heralding a new and fair and just order.

For ALL the tribes building a new world and future. In their own image. Whatever that image might be.

The MALL RATS below, FEATURING LEX, TRUDY, JACK, BRAINS, ALICE, SALENE, KC AND SAMMY, step and chant along with the assembly of TRIBES.

Gazing up at AMBER, the BABY being held aloft by BRAY - in a unison of worship, Abbe Messiah, Abbe Messiah, Abbe Messiah....

                    THE END

        (OR IS IT JUST THE BEGINNING ...)

Keeping The Dream Alive

RAYMOND THOMPSON

CUMULUS PUBLISHING LIMITED

NOW AVAILABLE

The Tribe: A New World

by

A.J. Penn

*The official story continues in this novel,
set immediately after season 5 of The Tribe.*

For more details check

www.tribeworld.com

**'Like'
on**

facebook.com/thetribeofficial